Values and the Soci

Values
and the
Social Sciences

An Introduction

Eric Carlton

Duckworth

First published in 1995 by
Gerald Duckworth & Co. Ltd.
The Old Piano Factory
48 Hoxton Square, London N1 6PB
Tel: 0171 729 5986
Fax: 0171 729 0015

© 1995 by Eric Carlton

A catalogue record for this book is available
from the British Library

ISBN 0 7156 2665 5

Typeset by Ray Davies
Printed in Great Britain by
Redwood Books Ltd, Trowbridge

Contents

In fond memory of my late teacher,
Principal T.H. Spurgeon, the most erudite and
most exasperating man I am ever likely to meet.

Introduction

It is as well to begin an exercise of this kind with a definition of terms. Our primary concern here is with values, and values may be generally defined as objects of need, attitude or desire which may be expressed as behavioural imperatives. A discussion of values must subsume the study of ethics (Greek, *ethikos*) which derives from the term *ethos* (disposition or character), which has come to mean the spirit of a people or community. Ethics as a discipline is roughly synonymous with that of moral philosophy which connotes the idea of moral values and moral behaviour. Both concerns are subdivisions of the all-encompassing generic discipline of philosophy, a term coined by Pythagoras in the 6th century BC. It was an all-embracing expression which denoted a love of wisdom, and for the Greeks, particularly Aristotle (4th century BC), it included not only the study of politics but also the proto-sciences of botany, biology, and particularly mathematics, a word that derives from the Greek *mathetes*, a disciple of the philosopher.

Many people find philosophy, which underlies the social sciences, a difficult and obscure subject. It seems so amorphous and unrelated to anything really tangible, and it hardly helps to be told by philosophers themselves that half of what passes for philosophy is virtually unreadable. But why? Well, to some extent, the obscurity of philosophy lies in the nature of the subject itself. Traditionally, philosophers were concerned with such fundamental issues as the nature of the cosmos and the meaning of existence. Ambitious as this may seem, it is not so far removed from basic biological questions, such as What is life?, or psycho-neurological problems, such as What is mind?, What is consciousness? Feeling themselves unable to cope with such fascinating but unanswerable problems, some philosophers lowered their sights a little and posed fractionally more modest questions about the meaning of history and the nature of human society – still subjects of continuing debate.

So the orientations of philosophers vary. Some still specialise in the more general types of enquiry and seek monistic – even metaphysical – 'solutions' to the perennial problems of the human condition, while others, perhaps most, are happier with more mundane concerns such as the nature of language and the validation of 'truth statements', etc. (see the debate in Gellner, 1959). So why philosophise? Why set out on a journey if you are never going to make it to your destination? The answer of some philosophers, at least, would be that the journey itself can be interesting and instructive (Kaufmann, 1958). The composer Edward Elgar once said that when he listened to Beethoven he felt like a travelling tinker looking at the Forth Bridge. And, similarly, Aristotle once suggested that all philosophy begins in wonder – a persistent curiosity about the nature of things. This is rather reminiscent of the psalmist (Psalm 8) who, overawed by the majesty and magnitude of the cosmos, says: 'When I survey the heavens, the work of thy fingers, what is man that thou art mindful of him ...?' It is as though we are congenitally compelled to ask the questions even if we don't get any satisfactory answers. The late C.E.M. Joad admitted that 'philosophers' answers have no finality ... they are merely the record of the soul's adventure in the cosmos' (Joad, 1960). And one of the great minds of the century, Bertrand Russell, anticipated the question and wrote, 'Why then, you may ask, waste time on insoluble problems?' He went on to reply that this might well be the criticism of a historian or a scientist, but hardly the retort of an individual 'facing the terror of cosmic loneliness' (Russell, 1948).

So whether our interests are theoretical or practical, whether they are highly general or related to the more specific issue of moral problems and their behavioural responses, the main concern is with understanding and explanation, in short, *cognition*. But – an important cautionary word. In trying to arrive at some kind of explanation we must beware of the twin traps of *reductionism* and *heuristicism*. Reductionism is the simple – and simplistic – attempt to reduce the complexities of real situations to a rule or principle. Heuristicism is the companion belief that there is an explanation, a theory, an ideology that can serve as a 'key' – a skeleton key – that will open all the doors to understanding. Reductionist principles which pose as explanatory schemata can be found in both the natural and social sciences. Take, for example, the over-used consensus-conflict dichotomy. There are affinities between this and the astrophysical 'steady state' and 'big bang' theories of the universe. The implication is that a common underlying principle is at work in that both purport to explain something of the 'real' nature of existence. Such views find their origins – or, at least, their early popular forms – in the works of Greek philosophy. Pythagoras maintained that all was *harmonia*; he taught that the universe was characterised by balance and ultimate stability, the 'music of the spheres'. On the other hand, Heraclitus, writing a few years later, insisted that the universe was characterised by constant movement, everything being in a state of flux and change. As he was fond of saying, 'You never step into the same river twice.' It is not difficult to see how such ideas are reflected in the social sciences, where they have found a new life in sociological debate. Talcott Parsons and the so-called consensus theorists are part of the Pythagorean legacy, and Marx and his school, who see class conflict as the 'key' to history are undoubtedly the heirs to Heraclitus. But well-meant as these ideas are, they are no more than simplistic analogues of the nature of reality. People of all ages have striven to find answers – or just more clues – to the perennial problems posed by human existence. Philosophy is simply the intellectualisation of those enquiries, and is therefore concerned with the patterning of explanation and the attempt to adduce the criteria upon which such explanations are based.

The other main reason why people have trouble reading philosophy is often the obscurity of expression adopted by the writers. For example, Joad wrote of Kant, whom some regard as perhaps the greatest of philosophers: 'Volumes have been written by his commentators and critics with the object of determining not whether what he said was true, but what he meant by what he said' (Joad, 1960, pp. 9-10). And Kant is by no means alone in this.

All disciplines have to use their own technical terms. The social sciences are replete with them. This can be particularly confusing for the layperson when common words are adapted for special academic usage. So when a sociologist talks of 'groups', he is not thinking of combinations of gyrating strummers, or when an economist speaks of 'elasticity' he is not alluding to women's underwear. These are purposely trivial illustrations but the matter becomes more complicated when words are juxtaposed in an uncommon sequence as with, say, poetry, especially when it is used with a special, cryptic significance. So, for example, when Louis MacNiece begins one of his poems:

> The sunlight on the garden,
> Hardens, and grows cold ...

he is not talking about sunlight or gardens or temperature. For the layperson or aspiring student, therefore, language can be especially puzzling when it is used in unusual ways. It has been said, for example, that sociology is not so much a discipline as a vocabulary. Certainly one of the most galling things in the social sciences is the theorist who deliberately expresses commonplace things in an unfamiliar manner in order to give an impression of profound erudition by his exceptional way with words. But then it is when knowledge is not particularly original that *style* matters. A scientist's reputation may rest upon noting something new, but the social scientist – and certainly the philosopher – must usually be content simply to integrate his 'findings' with previous knowledge, yet express this with verve and originality. It is rather like performing a particular dive in a competition; where the dive is well-known and familiar, and has been executed umpteen times before, what is to distinguish one dive from another? It is just here that style is everything. So often social scientists are not saying anything really new, but simply putting a semantic gloss on old knowledge. It is a cultivated art because their differentiae often become the stuff of the new reputations.

So in the coming discussion on values we cannot hope to discover anything original, but we can explore the nature of the discourse. We will be concerned with such matters as what is 'good', 'right', 'justifiable', etc., and what is the nature of obligation. And are these independent principles or are they merely contrived for social convenience? Are values simply habits or are they, in some way, integral to human beings? Are they subjective certainties, or are they calculated external constructions – imposed by the state, by legal authorities or social convention? Are values man-made or have they some ultimate validity? Are they subjective or objective? Relative or absolute? Determined or volitional? And what exactly do we mean by these terms anyway? At times the arguments can be tortuous and there will be no final resolution. However, when they are reduced to their essentials, they will often be shown to be not quite so difficult as first supposed. And when they are applied to real situations, these arguments usually gain in clarity and relevance. But they are arguments *not* solutions. We can hardly expect cognitive miracles where greater minds than ours have only been able to bequeath us ethical guidelines to apply to an ever-changing world.

1

What Do We Mean By Values?

The academic legacy I

If we regard the primary goal of all philosophical enquiry as the search for truth, this immediately begs the question, what do we mean by truth? And this, in turn, generates two important supplementary questions: (a) is truth discovered or is it imposed? Does it exist 'out there' awaiting our perception and appreciation of it? Does the physical scientist glean new knowledge simply by observing the natural world? Or do we impose patterns of regularity and order on the ongoing flux of events which do not actually exist in any objective sense? So when, for example, the astronomer speaks of constellations of stars, he is really forming an artificial pattern of stars which do not exist as a group at all. They are not a cosmic phenomenon; the stars that comprise constellations are often hundreds of light-years from one another. They are actually perceptual phenomena which become part of our conceptual life-world. Such mental constructs are cognitively convenient, indeed it is as though we are congenitally constrained to impose order on what we call reality, and pattern our experience so that it makes sense to us. And (b) what about the obvious varieties of 'truth'? Can there possibly be *the* truth, or are there different ways of seeing 'truth'? This, of course, has far-reaching implications for the study of values – particularly moral values.

In tackling these issues we must first take a look at the Idealism versus Empiricism debate. This is a legacy of academic philosophy which is indirectly pertinent to our discussion. Idealism maintains the possibility of certain kinds of *a priori* knowledge – knowledge which is regarded as self-evidently 'true' or valid *in advance* of any kind of factual or experimental verification: claims to religious knowledge, for instance, would come into this category. Idealists therefore hold that the thinking subject establishes the standards of objectivity. It is the individual who possesses the inward principles of organisation which set the boundaries of experience. 'Truth' is thus imposed on the world of things – the mind constructs or orders its own reality. So if, for example, I say 'That girl is wearing a red dress', what has actually happened is that I have made an observation, light waves have been converted into chemical reactions and those chemical reactions into electricity, and the electricity has been experienced as the sensation of 'redness'. But does the sensation correspond to the 'truth'?

Does 'redness' exist in any objective sense, or am I endowing reality with those qualities? Is truth imposed or is it discovered?

In contrast, Empiricism stresses the importance of *a posteriori* reasoning, that is to say, deriving conclusions from the facts. It maintains that knowledge of the world is given not by intuition but by actual sense experience. For Empiricists, reality – whatever that may mean – may never be known because all that we can possibly know are the sense-data that the mind receives. We can only know the world *as it appears to us*, yet this everyday world of the senses is a world which is amenable to observation and experimentation. Thus Empiricist philosophy underpins what we know as the scientific method, even though it is at variance with science insofar as the ultimate truth cannot be known because experience is never complete.

Persuasive as the Empiricist approach is, it does raise certain awkward questions:

(1) Are sense impressions adequate? Or are they, in a strange way, a source of misinformation? If, for example, I run my hands over a table-top, I get two very distinct impressions, of smoothness and hardness. But if I had the right kind of measuring instrument, the table surface would be shown to be rough and uneven, and if I had the necessary cutting edge, I could go through the table like butter. So do the smoothness and hardness exist? Or are they relative to my senses?

(2) Are sense-data accurate? For example, when a person has sustained a serious injury and a limb has to be amputated, it is not uncommon for them to insist that they can still clench their hand or wriggle their toes, even though these limbs no longer exist. We all know how our senses can deceive us in certain sets of circumstances, so can we always be sure of our knowledge of the world? Is it really as we picture it to be?

(3) How do we interpret the facts? Given that we place complete faith in the evidence, we must ask what exactly *is* the evidence? Sceptical people, for instance, will understandably say that they can only believe what they can see. But what do they see? Until Copernicus in the 16th century, it was commonly accepted that we lived in a geocentric universe. The Earth was the centre of all things. But the ancient Greeks – or some of them – knew better. Aristarchus of Samos (4th-3rd century BC) knew the Earth was a sphere because of his interpretation of the phenomenon of the eclipse. And Eratosthenes in the 3rd century BC had calculated the distance of the sun, the length of the year, and that we live in a heliocentric (sun-centred) system. If you ask why such knowledge had been forgotten or ignored for two thousand years, it was because people preferred to believe the 'evidence' of their own eyes (Koestler, 1959).

So how reliable is our knowledge of the world? How can we know what is 'true'? This basic Idealism-Empiricism issue is related to the complementary problem known technically as the Nominalism-Essentialism debate, which is relevant to the whole question of values. Nominalist appreciations of truth maintain that definitions are simply *imputed* properties which are arbitrarily assigned to the phenomenon in question. So if, for example, we were talking of religion, nominalists would argue that the term 'religion' is just a convenient linguistic symbol to denote an agglomeration of rites, beliefs and practices which may have no independent or ontological status. It is obvious that this way of looking at things can be applied equally well to all sorts of institutions and practices from marriage to the monarchy which are themselves expressions of particular values. On this view, morality is simply what you make it. Essentialism, on the other hand, maintains that it is possible to arrive at 'real' appreciations of truth. It implies that truth can be an *inherent* rather than an imputed quality. So for the essentialist, religion is more than the sum total of its behavioural expressions; it has an inner 'essence', a property or mystery which distinguishes it from other philosophies, ideologies and the like. And it may be further held that this 'reality' is differently apprehended, that it can be perceived intuitively or known experientially. It is a property which is not imposed but which has an autonomous existence which is thus 'discoverable'. Similar views may well be entertained about particular values, especially moral values which may be regarded as fixed and immutable. Ethical qualities such as 'goodness' and aesthetic qualities such as 'beauty' may be seen as having some kind of permanent – even eternal – validity. So we arrive at this antithetical position: for the Nominalist, truth is truth-for-us, the elaborated codes that we call values are held to be socially constructed, whereas for the Essentialist some values, at least, will be thought to have an objective quality.

But there is this second issue which complicates our search for truth. Is truth of a singular nature, or are there many varieties of truth? By and large, philosophers have – perhaps sadly – abandoned the quest. They have largely given up the old monistic theories of the past for the more mundane pluralisms of modernity. The certainties of the past have given way to the controlled doubts of the present. As one writer has put it, 'As we have found that we know so much less than we previously supposed, we also found that we knew so much more' – that is, the growth of knowledge through science (Gellner, 1979, pp. 203-4). The writer is here suggesting that the old competing orthodoxies have been found wanting, and have been supplanted by other 'answers' which are also unsatisfactory in many respects, but, at the moment, are the best we have.

Similar sentiments could be expressed about values. Perhaps there are no ultimate values, no final authority for values. Many would argue that there is no such thing as *the* truth about values, there are many kinds of truth which, in specific ways, have their own special kinds of validity. Take, for example, *scientific truth*. Science is the dominant paradigm of our time; it is by means of science that advanced peoples explain the world. Science deals with facts and those things which are susceptible of quantification and measurement, and this is done by science's own pre-determined methods, which give it a credibility and acceptability unequalled by any other discipline.

While not wishing to undermine – as some social scientists do – the obvious achievements and authority of science, we must make three observations. First, it is interesting to ask whether the 'scientific revolution' was occasioned by the needs of industrialisation or whether it really had its beginnings in social organisation, which, in turn, was associated with ritual and ideology, without which nothing else was possible (Carlton, 1977). Once under way, there is little doubt that it was subject to what Thomas Kuhn termed 'paradigm shifts', that is to say, model changes in relation to what the scientific community regards as valid (solvable?) problems (Barnes, 1982). This means that moral issues and religious questions tend to be rejected as legitimate areas of investigation and simply relegated to the vague confines of the metaphysical. Whether this is a function of conceptual limitation, financial constraint or simply attitudinal indifference, is not always easy to discern.

The quest for truth, then, may be by *experimentation* – a method which is necessarily limited in the social sciences, by *introspection*, which has to be suspect, or by *survey*, in which the investigator is inevitably at the mercy of his respondents. The scientific mentality has intruded on the social sciences as a form of neo-positivism which advocates that society can be studied in much the same way as physical phenomena. It is even argued that the social sciences should be a form of problem-solving with practical results – in essence, a kind of social engineering – but this has been criticised at several levels (e.g. Berger & Kellner, 1981):

(1) On *disciplinary* grounds, in that the 'scientisation' of sociology, for example, has led to the vulgarisation of the discipline.

(2) On *plausibility* grounds, in that scientisation has led to an obsession with quantification and to the proliferation of esoteric language.

(3) On *practical* grounds, inasmuch as there may be a temptation to go for quick results and superficial conclusions.

(4) On *moral* grounds, because it calls into question just what kinds of application are legitimate. Is the rationality of science the sole source of our 'salvation'? And can science be morally neutral?

The second observation that must be made is that science may not always be the best agent for deciding its own applications. The much-vaunted neutrality of science is something of a myth, especially when one considers the ways in which so much scientific research is actually funded. One has only to think of the important military and commercial spin-offs that have resulted from the 'independent' NASA space programme to get some idea of what is involved.

Our third observation is that science is not always able to cope with the intangibles which elude its empirical procedures. The verification principle of science may be fine for experiments on sub-atomic particles, but it can hardly be employed to validate or otherwise confirm aesthetic and moral values. Science can hardly reduce value-propositions to non-value terms. Indeed, there are no criteria adduced by science whereby such judgements can be made. Can, say, altruism be reduced to hormonal imbalance, or deviance be explained by certain social conditions, or do the social conditions in which it is expressed give form to deviance? Non-moral factors, biological, psychological, social, etc., may account for particular manifestations of good or evil, but they do not explain them. Trying to reduce values to non-value terms is somewhat like trying to reduce a Beethoven symphony to the ink on the music score; a composition must be more than the sum of its physical constituents.

Any consideration of what constitutes truth must also take account of *subjective truth*. There is little doubt that strengthened personal convictions become all the more important in the face of objective uncertainties. Witness the rise of various experience-based philosophies which range from inspirational movements such as the charismatic elements found in numerous religious organisations, to the increasingly popular expressive therapies such as Esalen, the 'let's-all-huddle-together' movement whose adherents claim to cure their psyches by bodily contact, and the 'primal scream' groups whose devotees hope to do likewise by re-living the trauma of their birth.

However, the whole idea of subjective truth raises two important questions. First, how is knowledge *'constructed'* and what conditions experience? To what extent are our subjectivities determined by the objectivities of the social world? We must always bear in mind the cardinal influences of socialisation from which none of us can escape. Secondly, we must ask ourselves how knowledge and experience are *changed*. If we think, for example, of the variety of 'subjectivities' that have operated in the area of sexual mores in, say, the last fifty years, we will see that what people 'knew' was right and wrong, appropriate and inappropriate, tasteful and otherwise has changed enormously in recent years. This is something we are going to consider in more detail later (Chapter 7), but at this early stage of the discussion it is worth noting how imperceptibly social norms and personal certainties have altered as far as sex is concerned.

There is too what we might call *didactic truth*. By this is meant 'teaching' truth, although here we are thinking not so much of the 'truths' themselves but of the vehicles whereby certain ideas are transmitted and reproduced. This is a largely unperceived process which has subtle yet potent influences on the culture of society.

Take, for instance, the cultivation and development of the arts. Music and poetry – the music of words – may not themselves 'contain' truth, but they convey impressions and ideas which are both associative and evocative. They reinforce and, in a sense, validate various normative elements in respective cultures. In Classical Greece, for example, youths were taught Hellenic virtues such as honour, fidelity and so forth by reading the works of Homer, and whereas education – especially philosophical education – was the privilege of the few, ordinary citizens were instructed and edified by seeing the performances of the great playwrights at the celebrated public festivals. Inspirational effects are the *raison d'être* of social rituals, particularly religious and political rituals which provide – among other things – symbolic expressions of the relevant ideology. It is considered the legitimate exercise – especially of mass movements – to conduct rituals which heighten awareness and arouse enthusiasm, which insinuate meanings and induce compliance. They may not do this directly, but such things will be implied by the presentation; the context of the rituals may well be more important than their content. The medium may well be the message.

The student of social behaviour is already well aware of *social truth* which incorporates those institutions and practices that operate for the harmonisation of social interests. Take marriage, for instance, which exists for the regulation of sexual practices and thus acts as a foundation for family structures. If defined in broad terms as a contractual arrangement between the sexes, it can be seen as a ubiquitous social institution which is there for the orderly conduct of society. Or we could take the example of religion. This may not have any objective validity, but insofar as people are willing to live and die by it, it is both socially and psychologically true for its adherents.

Truth then has many facets, but the main problem is to distinguish, if possible, between the objectivity of values – really the essentialist position – and the social practicality of values which is implied by the nominalist position. And then to ask whether there is any correspondence between the two, or whether such a question is falsely conceived because the very notion of objective reality has metaphysical implications which are beyond the scope and competence of the social sciences.

The academic legacy II

It follows from the previous discussion that the problem which lies behind so many of our difficulties is one of appearance and reality. What is real and what is mere impression? Can I believe what I see or is this simply another form of illusion? This raises the Idealist-Empiricist spectre again which, in a sense, is another form of the old Nature-Nurture argument. Remember that the Idealists argue that humans naturally possess the basic hypotheses; these are 'faculties' they inherit rather than acquire. It is humans who impose meaningful patterns on the world, and order their own reality. Empiricists, on the other hand, build up their realities from the assimilation and processing of sense-data. Knowledge is therefore constructed on the basis of experience. The underlying assumption behind both approaches is that the external world, the world outside our heads, may be unknown and even unknowable. All we know are the sense-data, the stimuli, the impressions of sight, hearing, touch, etc. The actual source of these sensations may remain forever a mystery to us. This can be easily illustrated from the science of optics. It is well known that the human eye can only respond to a limited band in the light spectrum. It is not sensitive to infra-red, ultra-violet, X-ray, etc. So what does the world look like? We can only know it as it appears to us. It is similar with the audio-spectrum. Again, our senses are not capable of picking up all the world's sounds – something of a mercy for we could hardly live with this cacophony of audio-sensations. All this can only mean that we have little or no idea of what the world is really like.

Our basic problem, then, is what is the nature of reality? And what is – or can be – our relationship to that reality? From our previous discussion, we can rightly infer that there are two main kinds of approach to this problem. The first suggests that reality is the reality of the world of space and time, the everyday reality that we see and feel, the reality revealed by science, the reality that we infer from experiment and experience. This 'answer' implies that the world we know, the world of physical objects, is the real world, and that our dignity and survival as human beings depends on our ability to understand its processes and master and utilise its laws. This is the general position of the physical sciences and of those philosophers that are particularly influenced by the explanatory power of those sciences. The second approach, which is associated with such thinkers as Plato and Kant, holds that the world of appearances is but a pale reflection of the true reality which exists either 'out there' in some para-cosmic sense, or 'within' as a product of the mind. (It is interesting to look at the anomalies of the drug culture in this respect. Are mind-expanding drugs such as the hallucinogenic LSD simply sources of illusion, or do they introduce takers to an external reality or help them to find their 'true selves' as a subjective experience? It is important not to confuse this with specifically religious arguments which emphasise the *significance* of experience. Religionists are generally concerned as to whether what is experienced has any objective reality of a supramundane kind. So they would ask, for instance, whether such experiences as spiritual healing are really charismata: are they natural phenomena or do they emanate from a supramundane source?)

In view of this, it might be instructive to glance briefly at what certain philosophers have made of all this, and see what their 'solutions' were to the appearance and reality debate.

Plato

It has been suggested that the whole of Western philosophy is merely a footnote to Plato. It is certainly true that although the modern reader would find some of Plato's ideas strange and even quaint, there is a great deal in his work which would not look out of place in a current text. In some of the key issues that he addresses he is actually quite avant-garde in his views, especially on such matters as education and the place of the family. These are to be found principally in his major work, *The Republic*, in which he sets out his blueprint for a well-ordered society. In this proto-sociological text, he argues that the just man is produced by the just society which is controlled by well-intentioned experts.

Plato was born into an aristocratic family in *c.* 427 BC and became a disciple, chronicler and interpreter of his friend and tutor, Socrates. It should be pointed out that, as far as we know, Socrates wrote nothing but spent much of his time arguing and discussing ideas with just about anyone who would listen. He was not a formal teacher and liked to distinguish himself from the itinerant 'lecturers' of the time – the Sophists – who charged considerable fees for their services. Much of his teaching took place during the protracted war with Sparta, and toward the latter part of his life he attracted a disparate band of devotees who were interested in his ideas and who, no doubt, rather liked to witness the discomfort that he generated in others. When Socrates was eventually tried, condemned and forced to commit judicial suicide by the restored democracy in Athens, Plato became thoroughly disillusioned with politics which he tended to regard as a fruitless enterprise. He saw that in city-state (*polis*) life political systems came and went with unrewarding circularity. Furthermore, he was tired of the petty wrangling in the Athenian democracy. So, instead, he devoted the remainder of his life to teaching in what we would call higher education. Like Socrates, he taught his students how to think, and how to relate – as he believed – to the ultimate order of the universe.

Characteristically, many of his arguments have a strong metaphysical basis. He maintained (hypothesised?) that beyond the visible world of objects is the invisible world of *forms*, and that these forms are really eternal ideas that are only imperfectly reflected in our senses. They are not to be discovered by mystical contemplation but by the application of rational analysis, as in mathematics and philosophy. These permanent ideas are not, by definition, humanly created but are the work of the gods, and the hope is that one day humans will discover the highest form of all – the good – as this constitutes the pinnacle of philosophical knowledge.

For many – perhaps most – people of his time, external reality was seen as an extension of the known world. The gods were simply humans writ large; they acted like humans but possessed magic powers which they used selectively and often capriciously. It is little wonder that Plato and others (e.g. Xenophanes) felt that there was something almost demeaning and contradictory about divine beings as traditionally conceived. He was not happy with the arbitrary actions of the gods, nor with the all-powerful Zeus indulging his lascivious appetites with coquettish nymphs and sundry mortals while his human subjects were vainly trying to solicit his favours. Plato took the view that what we call the real world was but a distorted reflection of another world which was characterised by a supreme and well-intentioned divinity.

Descartes

René Descartes (1596-1650) whom many regard as one of the seminal minds of Western philosophy, was a mathematician and a scientist who, in his approach to the problem of appearance and reality, adopted the method of doubt. He began by asking himself if there was anything of which he could be certain, and whether the investigations of science yielded such a thing as unassailable knowledge. While Plato questioned politics, Descartes questioned the entire enterprise of science. He then posed the question whether in observing the everyday world he was in some way self-deceived or – as an hypothesis – demon-deceived, and concluded that whatever was the case, these 'deceptions' had a remarkable consistency. Despite the reassurance that appearances always ran true to form – circles were always round and squares always had four sides, etc. – he still doubted that this gave him any *direct* perception of reality. The psychological breakthrough came when he realised that the presence of doubt was itself a kind of proof; it reaffirmed his autonomy as a person. Hence the dictum 'cogito ergo sum' (I think therefore I am).

Descartes doesn't really provide a solution to our difficulties, he merely gives us a reiteration of the problem. But the idea of methodic doubt is useful in that it demands that nothing must be taken for granted. Everything is subject to scrutiny and criticism. Descartes maintained that we must always try to eliminate the unreliable and illusory elements from our minds. But how? Presumably by taking nothing at face value except our ability to think and reflect; in this way doubts can become stepping stones to knowledge.

Kierkegaard

Sören Kierkegaard (1813-1855), a Danish philosopher, reacted against the cold philosophical and theological speculation of his time, and attacked what he felt to be the pomposities and system-building of the philosophical establishment. Instead, he advocated a return to the kind of Idealism which, in effect, contended that the only true reality is inside one's head. He rebelled against two thousand years of Western – though not Eastern – philosophical tradition by denying the link between objectivity and reality. But in his repudiation of the possibility of 'out-there' knowledge, and his insistence on the value of inward subjectivity, one suspects an anti-intellectual avoidance of disciplined thought and rational speculation.

For Kierkegaard, the worlds of politics, commerce, education and institutionalised religion were aesthetic trimmings. The only knowable world was the world of the individual psyche. This was the world in which man became aware of himself, of his future, his longing for faith, his eternal destiny – these were the things that were real to him. But to apprehend them, reason had to give way to the 'leap of faith'.

Kant

If Kierkegaard represents the inward reality position, Immanuel Kant (1724-1804) represents that of moral reality. In fact, he provides us with the interesting possibility of reconciling Idealism and Empiricism. He argued that scientific, i.e. empirical, knowledge is genuine knowledge, but it is knowledge of the *phenomenal* world – the spatio-temporal world of things as they appear to us. Yet he anticipated Einstein by contending that we contribute to our own realities in the very act of observation. He argued that we see things not as they are but as *we* are – in other words, we 'contain' the world conceptually as we endeavour to understand it. But he also insisted that there was another *noumenal* world which is not bound by spatio-temporal considerations. This is the world of things-in-themselves and not simply things as they appear to be. This is somewhat reminiscent of Plato, who advocated the idea of universal moral absolutes, an ideal of goodness that exists quite apart from any specific instances or experiences of good acts. But unlike the world of Plato, Kant's noumenal world is not perceived by reason; insight into ultimate reality is only achieved by moral action, though, like Plato, there is the presupposition of elements that are universally understood as good. Kant maintained that if there were no universal categories, and all was relative, meaningful communication between humans would break down.

Scepticism

Uncertainty about the external world and the possible implications of some over-arching metaphysical reality have led many to dismiss such ideas for all practical purposes. This position, known as Scepticism, has taken many forms and dates back at least to the sophist Gorgias in the 5th century BC and his contemporary Kritias, a one-time acquaintance of Socrates, who later became a notorious oligarch in Athens. They, like others, harboured serious doubts about Greek religion, but instead of entertaining ideas of a 'purer' religion, decided to dismiss it altogether. Later in the 3rd century, thinkers such as Pyrrho added to these systematised sophistic doubts, yet further doubts about the senses themselves. Extreme sceptics doubt arguments from contingency because they regard them as having an endless circularity. They may even question the basis and principles upon which such considerations are made, and when the ground-rules are discarded, it is difficult to know where to begin.

Are there any ways out of this impasse? *Certain* ways out probably do not exist, but traditionally attempts have been made to negotiate the terrain in the following ways:

(1) by adopting the way of science in order to build on everyday empirical reality;

(2) by attempting to discover an internal reality, which can mean espousing anything from mystical religions to Freudian psychodynamics;

(3) by searching – or hoping – for an alternative (external?) reality which really takes us beyond the world of experience.

Can there be such an alternative reality? Should we settle for the here-and-now world, or can we dare to contemplate the possibility of a metaphysical reality? The debate continues, and is not likely to be settled to the satisfaction of the academic community. It is only resolved by individuals in terms of their own faith or scepticism.

Much of this discussion has centred on ideals and how these ideals can be reconciled with everyday experience. But why do we have ideals in the first place? It could be argued that nothing we know in this life is perfect, yet ontologically we have the conception of perfection – of the ideal. Furthermore, in behavioural and intellectual terms people aspire to the ideal, in science, in sport, in the professions and in their relationships, but usually feel that they never quite succeed. Certainly, this is true also of moral issues – we rarely live up even to our own standards, yet we still persist in trying. Why should this be so, and why should we have such a conception at all?

Allied to this is what we might term the problem of correspondence. Are there objective realities that correspond to our subjective needs? At the mundane level, there obviously are. If we are hungry or thirsty or have the need for companionship, there are objective realities that correspond to our subjective needs: food, drink and friends. But if we step up a gear, and ask about the need for justice, for truth, even for goodness, are there – somewhere, somehow – objective satisfactions that correspond to our subjective needs? If there are not, we must ask why is it that we have such conceptions in the first place. Can it be that we are vestigially moral creations?

2

How Are Values Derived?

The question of values has not been extensively examined in the social sciences, and their derivations and possible objective validity have been felt to be problems that lie outside the province of social science. By and large, these matters have been left to the studied uncertainties of philosophical speculation. The possible autonomy of values has certainly not received much attention from sociologists, mainly because it raises questions which do not allow for any very satisfactory answers. Some writers have simply regarded values as products of social usage, others – following Durkheim – have seen them not as autonomous entities but as part of the very fabric of society itself (e.g. Nadel, 1953, p. 17). In fact, this interactive process – if indeed it is an interactive process – between values and society constitutes one of the thorniest problems of all. Even Talcott Parsons, who is usually credited with making numerous priority-statements about the place of values in social integration, has warned fellow theorists about the methodological pitfalls which can attend an undue concentration on 'the unprofitable/ideal/material dichotomy' (Parsons, 1961b, p. 25). This may be all very well if one is seeking 'solutions', but it is unavoidable as an exercise in moral theory.

No one seriously disputes that values are important. They lie at the very heart of social experience. They are implicit in just about everything we do, yet it is extremely difficult to adduce scientifically valid criteria for assessing even the most common social values. What is of particular concern is whether or not they are independent of the material conditions of life: Milton Yinger writes concerning religious values: '[We are concerned with] the point at which ideas and beliefs enter into the field of interaction. Are they prime movers? Can they arise independently of material conditions and help create new arrangements; or do they reinforce, rationalise and preserve the old?' (Yinger, 1946, p. 11).

Ideologies – religious or otherwise – may be seen as constellations of values and beliefs, though it might be argued that any discussions as to the overall and general priority of ideological factors are ultimately fruitless, and that structural arrangements and re-arrangements come about as human necessity requires. Yet these structural arrangements themselves create problems and tensions which need to be resolved, and therefore dispose individuals to believe and act in specific ways. So structural and ideological factors are necessarily complementary. Values inte-riorise social arrangements. As ideology, they 'explain' and interpret social goals. They reinforce both the belief in the goals and the need for their realisation. Furthermore, they justify the kinds of action and machinery necessary to be effective. Therefore sociologists, in particular, have tended to confine their attention to values as empirical variables in social life whose scientific importance is not so much dependent on their 'correctness' as upon the fact that they are *believed* to be true and valid by those concerned. After all, people act as they think, and think as they believe – and belief is informed by values.

Initially, therefore, we are more concerned with the nature and deriva-tions of values than with their social manifestations. So the main question we must now address is how values arise – what we might call the problem of origination. This issue permits – with minor variations – only three types of answer: values must be either personal (innate), or extra-personal (social) or supra-personal (metaphysical), or possibly some combination of these (for a development of this thesis in relation to war, see Carlton, 1990, section IV).

The view that values are largely or exclusively *personal* is something of an idealist legacy. Idealism, remember, has always stressed that it is the thinking subject who establishes the standards of objectivity. Every prob-lem, every 'picture' of reality presupposes a way of thinking about it. Subjectivity presumes principles of conceptualisation which organise hu-man experience. Thus certain categories of knowledge are regarded as given, *a priori*. This view that values are innate has several implications. It can mean that the *need* for values is innate – exactly *which* values being left undetermined. This seems to be something of a casuistic cop-out in that several plausible interpretations become possible. Or it can refer both to the structure of the idea or value and to the context in which it is expressed. This poses the perennial problem of whether or not these value-structures have some kind of universality. This seems to be sup-ported by those who argue that there are deep structures to language itself, and that these indicate innate thought forms that are merely refined and developed by experience (Lyons, 1970). These ideas have been taken up by some educationalists who have insisted that both moral thought and scientific conceptualisation derive innately, and that social life is necessary to stimulate their potentiality (e.g. Piaget, 1970).

A particularly influential version of the 'deep structure' approach can be seen in some anthropological theories where the intention is to reveal the fundamental properties of human society and to relate these to what are held to be the basic characteristics of the human mind. This would presumably establish certain psychological universals which would then constitute the basis of sociological explanations, something that can be seen particularly in the work of the French structuralist Claude Lévi-Strauss (Lévi-Strauss, 1952). By analogy, this kind of analysis bears a strong resemblance to the Marxist substructure-superstructure thesis. The deep or hidden structure, which is to be found by inference and analysis, has to be distinguished from the 'surface' structure – those directly observable relations with which sociologists have traditionally been concerned. Critics of this approach have pointed out that in the two spheres of social life to which Lévi-Strauss has looked for evidence to vindicate his method, namely, kinship and myth, there are serious discrepancies between his interpretation and the actual ethnographic evidence. Edmund Leach, for instance, insists that the 'code' does not produce consistent or identifiable kinds of message (Leach, 1970). Indeed, structuralism has been criticised at several levels, not least that it is more appropriate to the study of simple societies. It has been used with some sophistication – even ingenuity – at the tribal level, but it remains an open question whether it has the capacity to achieve similar analytical results with highly differentiated systems. It is also open to question that even if such a method could succeed eventually in demonstrating the existence of some universal properties of the human psyche, it would not explain either the empirical diversity or the historical evolution of human societies (e.g. Bottomore, 1976). Needless to say, the neo-Idealist insistence that there are some kinds of conceptualisation common to all individuals but disguised by various cultural forms is clearly not attractive to those who see 'nature' as something determined by the circumstances in which it is expressed.

The *extra-personal answer* or 'solution' to the problem of derivation is particularly popular among sociologists. Here, society is seen as the true source of human values. Some theorists have even gone so far as to argue that the very categories of thought are socially determined (note the school of social interaction that stems from G.H. Mead – see Mead, 1934, pp. 6-8; 46-7). But, as far as we can tell, it is the *interpretation* of thought that is social; the claim that the categories themselves arise from experience begs the question of just how experience is structured. Such epistemological exercises have their uses, but they do little to illuminate the meaning and extent of social determination, or to uncover the possible sources of social values.

This view that social life is the primary reality which ultimately determines our modes of thought stems largely from Emile Durkheim, for whom society constituted a constraining force (Durkheim, 1968). It is not unlike certain ideas of Freud, who recognised some inherent universals in the human make-up, especially those related to sexual aggression, which were harnessed by the 'conspiracy' of society (see Freud, 1953; Meyerhoff, 1963).

One particularly influential variant of the Durkheim thesis is the functionalist argument that social categories and values arise from the needs of the group. This becomes reductionist insofar as everything is seen to conduce to the need – conscious or otherwise – for social solidarity. All sorts of multifarious activities from Cabinet meetings to people enjoying a Turkish bath can be interpreted as either directly or indirectly affirming a complicated system of interests and values. Group solidarity is such an amorphous concept that almost anything can be seen to contribute to its realisation. We could take the functionality of religion as an example. To say that religion functions to further or enhance group solidarity is surely not to exhaust the meaning of religion. It is not possible logically to invert the argument and say that the need for group solidarity produces or causes the phenomenon we know as religion. A function of the thing is not the thing. Religion in both its meaning and functions is much more complex than this. There is another related issue: if the role of religion in society is the re-affirmation of values and sentiments, it follows that all religions are 'true' if they correspond to given social conditions, and all are of equal value if they fulfil the same functions. It is then but a short step to the inclusivist position which maintains that any system of belief and what might be broadly construed as ritual which functions as religion *is* religion for all practical purposes. Such surrogates might include almost anything from National Socialism to psychotherapy. This leaves religion without any distinctive credibility; thus critics argue that if religion, as a term, is to have any academic respectability, it must be distinguished from other ideologies by being definitionally linked to the supernatural (see Robertson, 1970).

Just one further point while we are on this issue. There can be an often unperceived logical error in looking at values, practices, institutions, etc., primarily in terms of function. Let us continue with the example of religion which – as we have seen – incorporates a whole constellation of values. There is a well-meaning tendency to try to prove a non-empirical statement such as 'religion is good' (e.g. integrative) by the empirical generalisation 'religion is universal'. This does not follow logically, although – as with so many consensus arguments – it can be persuasive. It is understandable that many sociological accounts of religions and their attendant values are inclined to concentrate on the conditions in which they appear and are sustained, but such assumptions may ignore the creativeness and reflectiveness of their human agents.

The view that values can only derive from social experience does not really explain anything. It merely involves us in an irritating circularity. To say that somehow society produces them of itself is simply to restate the problem in another form. This is one of the particular difficulties with Marx and many neo-Marxists who have expanded the range of determinative criteria for social action beyond crude economic conditions. If human consciousness – the way we think – and the values which inform that consciousness are socially derived, then so are all theoretical formulations which purport to account for those values, including Marxism. Again, we are on an intellectual roundabout.

A variant of the social origins view is provided by Norbert Elias, who argues that social values derive from necessities which had some signifi-

cance in their specific historical contexts even though these are now largely
unknown or forgotten (Elias, 1977). So if we take the customary practice
– at least, until recently – of a gentleman walking outside a lady in the
street, we can trace this back to the days when footpaths were rare, and
carriages were liable to injure or splash water and mud at pedestrians.
But why protect women in this way? Well, one could hypothesise that it
was a way of guarding valuable breeding machines, or that it stems from
the time when women were important as property and status symbols. But
all this tends to discount the felicities of 'good manners' which may have
little to do with the hypothesised functionalities of the past. This 'hidden
meanings' approach would be interesting if it was not so terribly strained.
And if that sounds unnecessarily critical, we should ask ourselves why we
ever open a door for somebody else. Not only is the argument strained, it
is often unclear. We could take Elias's own example of genital display,
which he insists was originally prohibited in order to show respect to one's
superiors. This, he says, generated feelings of shame which became
'moulded according to the social structure ... . First it [was] a distasteful
offence to show oneself exposed in any way before those of higher or equal
rank ... Then, as all became more socially equal, it [became] a general
offence ... and [took] on the form of a more or less total and automatic
self-restraint' (Elias, 1977, p. 139). This is a singularly unfortunate illus-
tration of his own theory simply because it is subject to so much qualifica-
tion and conjecture. Genital display has meant – and still means – different
things in different situations. In the remote past, for instance, among
certain Semitic peoples, it had solemn associations such as the euphemistic
'hand on thigh' of Hebrew oath-taking. On the other hand, it can be a form
of insult, a protest, a provocative or blatantly sexual gesture – or merely
a prank. To try to derive any one implicit value from an act or practice that
could have numerous meanings and interpretations is little more than a
guessing game.

Finally we come to the *supra-personal solution*, which has not found
great favour with theorists. It implies that values emanate from a supramundane source – something which cannot be substantiated, and something upon which the social sciences are unable to pronounce with any
confidence. The very idea of 'revelation' suggests ultimate verities which
stand outside the intellectual orbit of the social sciences, and are more
properly the province of philosophical and theological speculation. Religion
– and that is what we're really talking about – precludes, by definition, the
possibility of full understanding. In the social sciences, religious beliefs
and practices have often been taken as symbolic expressions of something
else: with Freud it was frustration and helplessness; with Marx it was
alienation; with Durkheim it was the need to validate moral behaviour.
Beliefs in external referents – in *actual* supramundane beings – have
rarely been seriously entertained in the social sciences.

However, perhaps such ideas should not be dismissed out of hand. Belief may be defined as the subjective aspect of what is perceived as objective reality, and, with our human limitations, we are hardly in a position to pontificate on the nature of that reality. Belief implies the personal endorsement of values that may exist as part of a cosmic order regardless of their subjective apprehension or appropriation. After all, we are all aware that certain values such as the reverence for life, the promotion of love rather than hate, the need for justice and truth, and so forth, are really critical to our existence. The world works better when they are observed. Without them, we only wreak our own destruction. As Thomas Luckmann has said, 'Belief is not an essential dimension of the human condition, but an historical articulation of a universal element of human existence' (Luckmann, 1971, pp. 22-3).

Excursus I. Philosophy, science and religion

The question whether or not it is reasonable to think of religious ideas as validating factors poses all kinds of problems for philosophers, especially for those who prefer to adopt an intellectually neutral or naturalistic stance. Naturalism – as the term implies – desires to explain the world in naturalistic terms. It does not have recourse to religion to understand what are, as yet, seemingly inexplicable phenomena. Religion itself, therefore, is also interpreted in non-religious terms.

Naturalism has its roots in the writings of Aristotle, Lucretius and Spinoza, and can even be detected in the philosophical fragments of Presocratic philosophers such as Anaximander. In recent times it has been particularly well represented by the philosophers Bertrand Russell and A.J. Ayer, and by the physicist Stephen Hawking. Very generally its position is that of the impartial, reasonable, enlightened person. Its main theses are as follows:

(1) *Only nature exists*, which, by implication, means that supernature does not exist. By nature is meant the spatio-temporal universe which exists independently of the knowing mind. The cosmos is, therefore, the ultimate reality. Naturalism is thus associated with atheism, but the two are not synonymous.

(2) *Nature is non-personal*, which means that whatever order exists within nature is inherent in nature, and is not the result of any kind of special creation by a suprapersonal intelligence. This, therefore, rules out the idea of gods who fashion the world for reasons of their own, or of gods who are part of nature in some pantheistic sense. There are no divine beings who are either transcendent, over and above and apart from creation, or immanent and therefore involved in its workings.

(3) *Anthropomorphism must be rejected* – we can no longer 'see' the world in circumscribed human-like terms. So, for example, such things as love, hate, guilt, fear, satisfaction and aspirations – in fact, moral concerns

generally – may be characteristic of high-grade organisms such as humans, but they are not to be seen as reflections of some ulterior will or divine nature. They are purely human values, and derive from human needs and social exigencies.

(4) *Natural events have natural causes.* There are no *un*caused happenings, i.e. events do not have supernatural causes. There are no miracles or acts of the gods. Creation is therefore not a special event; the universe is eternal, self-sufficient, and indestructible (Hawking, 1988)

(5) *The scientific method is the only natural method for discovering truth.* Indeed, it is regarded as the only legitimate method of arriving at a true understanding of the physical world. Naturalists are concerned with the empirical verification and falsification of hypotheses. Presumably this includes – as in, say, mathematics and physics – the imaginative theoretical constructions that are based upon the additional criteria of simplicity, coherence and elegance.

(6) *The endorsement of humanism.* Human welfare must be – indeed, can only be – promoted by human intelligence and furthered by human ingenuity. The place of religion is merely an aid to psychological adjustment and well-being, an adjunct to social betterment.

It is important to note how many of these propositions are really *metaphysical* assertions, and not the well-established conclusions of the special sciences of chemistry and physics. The sciences, *qua* sciences, do not prove the 'truth' of Naturalism because none of them tries to prove or disprove the truth of anything outside its physical domain. Naturalistic philosophy is not a scientific alternative to supernaturalism; it is really a series of *a priori* metaphysical assertions in that it tries to say something about everything, whereas the physical sciences try to discover limited facts about some things only. And, anyway, how does one set about trying to prove a negative? Scientific method can only give us the facts; it is only indirectly concerned with values. It certainly cannot give us a knowledge of the 'good' or determine our moral goals. A rational justification for particular ideals and values is not the same as 'proving' them scientifically. Science may be able to show us how to implement our ideals effectively, but it cannot give us the ideals themselves.

Whereas supernaturalists (sometimes called cognitivists) believe that religion provides us with an understanding of another reality that transcends the physical world, naturalists or non-cognitivists, as we have seen, deny the existence of any trans-empirical reality. They argue that religion is really the construction of moral systems which are clothed in symbolic language. Some supernaturalists, such as C.S. Lewis, would reply that transcendent reality is such that it can only be spoken of in terms of myth and symbol, metaphor and analogy. How else can one express the inexpressible? Lewis, for instance, suggests that myth is a symbolic representation of a non-historical truth – an unfocussed gleam of the divine which illuminates the human imagination. This is endorsed by J.R.R. Tolkien who contends that whereas speech is invention about objects and ideas, so myth is invention about truth.

Of course, this raises the question whether or not supernaturalists can ever talk of knowledge. Many philosophers would confine themselves to discussions about *belief*, and social scientists would settle for the study of *behaviour*. But then it should be remembered that these are not mutually exclusive. Furthermore, there are different types of beliefs: factual belief (belief *that*) as distinct from dependent belief (belief *in*). I may be quite prepared to believe that the nearest star to the Earth, Proxima Centauri, is four light years away (approximately 23 million million miles). This is a factual belief, and for all practical purposes a few noughts either way doesn't make that much difference. On the other hand, my religious faith (dependent belief) may make all the difference to the way I conduct my life.

So how should the religion-science controversy be resolved? In favour of religion? But then one recalls how institutionalised religion has often stood against all manner of humanitarian and scientific advance, from the use of surgery to views about cosmology. Then in favour of science? Undoubtedly there has been a gradual retrenchment of religion on all sorts of key issues such as immunisation, sterilisation, contraception, and so on. But imperfect as theologians have been in addressing such issues, they still try to answer the most perplexing questions of all – the problems of meaning. Perhaps the most profitable approach is to see religion and science as different universes of discourse. After all, when Beethoven gives us a musical impression of a storm in his Sixth (Pastoral) Symphony no one is seriously suggesting that this is at variance with a scientific explanation of a storm in terms of electrical discharges and precipitation. This is analogous to the relationship between religion and science. Perhaps some reconciliation is possible if both are seen to be 'legitimate' in their own special ways.

The greatest single problem that besets religious believers in their 'confrontation' with the cosmos is undoubtedly that of trying to reconcile the justice of the creator(s) with the sufferings of the creatures. This problem of theodicy, which is probably the greatest general deterrent to religious belief, has generated many answers – none of them wholly satisfactory. Actually, the problem is twofold. First there is the problem of *physical evil*: is there a necessary screen between the creator and the created? The physical structure of the world of which we are all a part appears to have certain inherent defects which give rise to suffering and death. The ineradicable presence of disease on the one hand, and of natural competitiveness and red-in-tooth-and-claw cruelty on the other, present the would-be believer with insurmountable intellectual difficulties. These cannot be attributed to any kind of early 'fall' or loss of innocence, as in the myth of the Garden of Eden, because we know that certain diseases (e.g. tuberculosis) existed in the pre-human world. It is much more likely that the spread of disease – as with, say, modern HIV – was due to ignorance, as is reflected in the Greek myth of Pandora's Box. Secondly there is a problem of *moral evil*. This is less difficult theoretically because it can be argued that the *possibility* of moral evil must exist if people are to be allowed to act freely. Freedom of human action implies a capacity and a potentiality for both good and evil. What we term good and evil seem to be locked in a complex relationship which is variously seen as oppositional or complementary. Good often comes of evil when, for example, a plane crashes with fatal results, but afterwards certain mechanical faults are detected and remedied, which action eventually saves lives. But it must also be said that sometimes evil comes of good. This is evidenced by those well-intentioned actions which have turned out to be disastrous, e.g. war-time operations such as Gallipoli and Arnhem which were strategically sound and intended to save lives in the long term, but which proved calamitous at the tactical level.

Theodicy is not a problem, of course, for the non-theist. Where there are no gods the dilemma can hardly exist. So in Buddhism, for instance, to live is to suffer; there are no gods that are accountable for this condition – it is just the way of things. Polytheism, the worship of many gods, is – for Max Weber, among others – the best 'solution' to the problem especially in its Hindu form which stresses reincarnation. Innumerable successive lives are conditioned by virtuoso self-merit, and make a kind of immortality possible which compensates for the evils of this present existence. Despite caste distinctions, Hinduism promises the hope of post-mortal mobility for even the most modest devotee. The great advantage of polytheistic systems generally is that different gods can represent different facets of experience. Evils can be attributed either to the arbitrariness of particular gods or to the wayward actions of different gods. Thus all contradiction is avoided.

A refinement of Polytheism, Dualism, which holds that there are only two great forces in the universe, those of good and evil, is still not really satisfactory as an explanation. Dualism takes two main forms: it may hold the view of an originally good world somehow corrupted by evil, or of an evilly conceived world which is gradually being perfected by the forces of good. It usually presupposes, as in the ancient Persian religion of Zoroaster, that there will be the ultimate triumph of good, but does not really tell us why it is going to take such a long time to suppress the evil forces, or why they were allowed to exist in the first place.

The problem of theodicy can be avoided by denying the existence of evil, by insisting that it is just a humanly constructed concept to denote those things that we find unpleasant. Many find this difficult, however, especially in the face of, say, the Holocaust, or Stalin's ravages in Russia, or other mindless massacres of the defenceless which have been a feature of so many wars. These at least seem to indicate an overpowering malevolence which surpasses ordinary human failings. Alternatively, it could be argued that regardless of these and other evils, all will eventually turn out for the best. Evil happenings are simply the intersecting lines of chance that seem unfortuitous *to us*. If only we could see the world as it really is, then that which we presently construe as evil will be shown to have existed for some ultimately good purpose. What we call evil is thus based upon a misunderstanding or misperception – even an illusion – regarding the cosmic plan.

A more acceptable view for many, one associated with the 3rd century AD teacher, Irenaeus, and popularised by the modern theologian, John Hick, is that evil is not some kind of divine punishment, but a potential built into the created order to bring humankind to moral perfection. The idea is that if the laws of nature are to work properly, there have to be victims of the system. People were not created perfect but imperfect so that they might develop perfection through a process of moral apprenticeship. A variant of this is the survivalist view that for those that believe, the evils of our present existence are as nothing compared with the glory to come. But critics maintain that these prospective solutions only exacerbate the problem. They argue that no heaven can compensate for the scale of human suffering, and that – philosophically – one obscure problem is being answered by an even more obscure promise, life after death – the proverbial pie-in-the-sky when we die. But believers counter with the insistence that a whole eternity is more than recompense for the pains and frustrations of our fleeting lives.

Theoretically, a world could have been created that was free of human evil because people could have been so fashioned that they always chose what was right. But would this have been a free world? It certainly could not have been a *moral* world because this implies the freedom to make the correct choices; it does not mean being programmed to make those choices. But, as we have seen, the issue of evil as a product of human freedom is only half the problem. What of 'natural' evil? It seems obvious that the created world was never intended as an earthly paradise. In a perfect world, there would be no suffering, no danger, nothing to endure or worry about. But there would also be no ethical concepts, no sense of striving or achievement, no aesthetic values, no white because there would be no black. There would be none of those virtues which are universally admired: no courage, kindness, honesty, fidelity, loyalty, sympathy and compassion. In short, none of those qualities which make for the development of personality. Furthermore – to return more specifically to the implications of science – nature would have to run according to completely arbitrary laws. It would have to obey conflicting human inclinations. All possible sources of danger would have to disappear – mountains, seas, fire, electricity, etc. – or they would have to possess such variable qualities that there would be no sense or consistency in our environments. To prevent, say, a plane crash, we would have to suspend the force of gravity which keeps us all on the planet! It is obvious that such a world would be impossible if it was to serve everyone's happiness all of the time.

We do live in a violent universe, though we can't actually say what the universe *is* – only what we can know about it *in theory*. It is a universe which is characterised by awesome – perhaps contending – forces, but it is also a universe which has an inexplicable balance, where no physical force overwhelms any other. The violence is neutral; it is the *mind*, not matter that is moral. But we just can't leave it there. In our current state of knowledge, there are several outstanding questions which we feel are still unanswered. Why *this* kind of a universe, working to *these* kinds of laws? While acknowledging the uncertainties of quantum physics, how can we explain the 'simplicity', i.e. the elegance, of the mathematical laws that appear to govern nature; or the fact that size prevents the universe from suddenly collapsing under its own gravity; or that spin stabilises the galaxies and their planetary systems; and that the slow rate of nuclear fission ensures the longevity of the universe?

There is a certain inadequacy in the popular scientific picture of the universe. The central inconsistency turns on the fact that this picture depends on inferences from observed phenomena, and unless these inferences are valid, everything is in ruins. Yet those who ask us to exalt the role of reason in arriving at these facts and to believe this cosmic picture, sometimes ask us to accept that reason is the unforeseen and unintended by-product of mindless matter at one stage of the evolutionary process. Perhaps we should not dismiss too easily the idea that we might all be part of a cosmic experiment in which – with all its imponderables – we will be the ultimate beneficiaries.

3

How Do Values Develop?

Theories of moral development

Whether we believe that certain basic values are intuitive or socially created, or even divinely bestowed, it is undeniable that they are developed and structured by experience. It follows, therefore, that moral development is inextricably linked with personality development, and that this necessarily involves such matters as needs and wants, perception and the nature of intelligence. These all impinge on the question of moral maturation. A number of psychologists have formulated models of cognitive development which incorporate the idea of growing moral awareness and responsibility. Predictably, they divide into a number of separate schools whose differences cannot always be resolved, although some are not as far apart as they would have us believe. Perhaps the best way of approaching this issue is to look at these divisions and offer a critique of some of their basic assumptions.

A broad general division is that between what may be conveniently designated the Determinist and non-Determinist theorists. The Determinists, in turn, can be divided into the Psychodynamic school (Freud, etc.) and the Behaviourist school (Skinner, Eysenck, etc.). This is something of a simplification, but it is a useful distinction between what are forms of psychological non-freedom and conditioned freedom.

Psychodynamic theories

Psychodynamic theories may be variously seen as realistic or pessimistic in their pre-suppositions about the human personality. Although these ideas are commonly associated with Freud and many of the neo-Freudians, they were anticipated, in essence, by the 18th-century writer Bishop Butler, who held office at both Durham and Bristol but actually refused the Archbishopric of Canterbury (see Broad, 1962). Butler's scheme can be represented diagramatically (see p. 28).

Butler assumed that all people have particular passions and impulses, and that these must be checked by the twin controlling influences of Self-love and Benevolence. Thus the basic propensities are subject to these two counter-balancing principles, and these, in turn, are subordinated to the ruling power of conscience. This is not dissimilar to Freud's famous triangle of forces that are said to operate in every one of us: the Ego (the conscious self), the Id (the instinctive, uncensorious self) and the Superego (the conscience). This controlling triumvirate has been subject to some criticism. (I think it was Spike Milligan who observed that 'the Ego, the Super-Ego and the dirty old Id, all live together in my Uncle Sid'.) Like Butler's categories these too are simply inferences from experience.

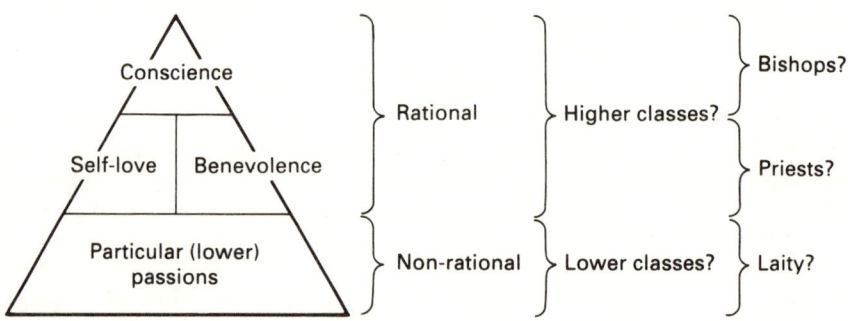

The basic assumptions of the Psychodynamic theorists are as follows:

(1) Individuals are fundamentally at variance with their social environments. Humans, by their very nature, are at war with society. They are egocentric and aggressively self-interested, therefore the task of coming to terms with their environments is unnatural and alien to their basic wishes.

(2) The effort to curb these natural instincts and desires inevitably results in suppression and repression of natural human inclinations. *Suppression* is defined as the conscious control of desire, the deliberate attempt to harness the demands of one's 'lower nature'. So, for example, if a person felt compelled to seek revenge and hurt someone who had humiliated him, he might exercise both discretion and control, especially if the expression of anger was likely to lead to yet further humiliation – particularly if the focus of that anger was someone who was regarded as in some way 'superior'. The suppression of such desires is said to result in possible *neuroses*. Suppression is therefore the opposite of expression. To give vent to these urges – albeit in relatively harmless ways, such as, say, the sublimation of aggression in sport – is said to be preferable to not giving them expression at all.

Repression, on the other hand, is regarded as the *un*conscious control of desire. This is said to happen particularly where that which is desired is forbidden in normal society. This would apply, say, where there are tendencies towards certain forms of deviance such as paedophilia. Presumably, in many cases the sexual taboo is internalised, and the urge or inclination is either effectively or temporarily neutralised. Thus the opposite of regression is recognition. Failure to recognise one's proclivities is said to result in *psychoses* which can have dangerous social repercussions. The complement of this is the believed inability of those who are responsible for these repercussions to perceive the 'true' cause of their condition. So, for example, it has been seriously hypothesised that the megalomania of the early Zulu tyrant, Shaka, and that of the German dictator, Adolf Hitler, was a kind of compensatory outworking of their sexual impotence.

The implications of this are endless. For instance, a great deal of attention has been given recently to the question of what is or is not 'sexual harassment'. It is a popular feminist allegation that sexual harassment betrays repression, possibly beginning in early childhood. While it is undoubtedly true that some men have endured excessive censure from their parents and therefore have strangely ambivalent attitudes towards sex, it is difficult to believe that this is the general determining factor. Certainly research in the UK and the USA is inconclusive on this point, perhaps because some of the questions in the surveys were so vague and ill-defined. After all, how is harassment to be interpreted? Must it consist of actual physical molestation or can risqué remarks and even 'staring' and 'leering' be included? And exactly what is meant by these favoured questionnaire terms anyway? Little was said – and still is said – about women who harass other women, women who harass men, and certainly women who trade off sexual power for, say, economic advantage. Given the ambiguity of the evidence, it could be argued that it was not just male repression that gave rise to such actions, but that some women wished to portray males in a certain light.

The obvious implication of the Psychodynamic approach is that it is largely society which is responsible for these various complexes that result from the unwelcome control of the instincts, although this curbing of the natural appetites is seen as necessary if society is to be ordered and stable. The general Psychodynamic view is that individuality can only find its safe expression within an accepted and acceptable social framework. Conduct is only correct if it enjoys the imprimatur of the community. Rampant and uncoordinated self-expression can only lead to individual breakdown and eventual social chaos.

(3) It is further argued – as we have seen – that human personality, as we know it, is formed in the shadowy half-world of the unconscious mind to which forbidden desires have been suitably banished. What we see of human behaviour is merely the tip of the iceberg, or – if some theorists are to be taken seriously – the powder-keg. This 'real self' is only hinted at in dreams, most of which are seen to be meaningful. There is a tacit assumption that all incidental experiences including dreams – possibly the redundant baggage of the mind – are endowed with some personal significance. It is felt that they must mean something, thus the cardinal importance of dream interpretation as a route to self-awareness, and in the alleviation of complexes and phobias. Significant also may be those inadvertent errors

of speech ('Freudian slips') which indicate temporary loss of control. Was it just a printer's innocent error when, not long ago, a well-known institution of higher education advertised one of its courses as a BA in Pubic Administration, and another as an option in Penile Policy?

(4) Thus the process (ritual?) of psychoanalysis is held to be the method for uncovering the nature of this 'true-self' and for revealing the real causes of one's current traumas. (Note the affinities here with Marxian class awareness. Freudian psychic emancipation is analogous to the liberating transmutation of a class-in-itself into a class-*for*-itself). But in the clinical process there is the ever-present danger that analysts may fall prey to the temptation to impose previously assumed patterns of causation which cannot be empirically verified.

(5) It is maintained that the human personality develops in stages or episodes. Some theorists, e.g. Erik Erikson, have followed Freud quite closely here, while others, especially Alfred Adler and Carl Jung, departed from the 'ways of truth' and founded their own particular schools. But with all of them the underlying assumption is that the personality is shaped largely by childhood experiences, and that these determine future adult behaviour. Freud's is an essentially pan-sexual theory, and he argued that sexual energy (libido), which is a product of the instinctual sexual drives, becomes focused on different bodily regions as psychological development takes place. And he further insisted that if children experience conflict or frustration at any particular stage they might become fixated at that level, and that this would influence their subsequent modes of behaviour. So, for example, he hypothesised that if children experienced a satisfactory First (oral) stage of development associated with breast and bottle feeding, this would probably produce amicable, self-indulgent individuals, whereas if they were denied oral gratification they might turn out to be querulous, resentful people, more given to thrombosis than obesity. Children can pass through the Second (anal) and Third (phallic) stages, at which sexual identities are said to become established, and on to the Fourth (latency) stage where the incestuous longings and the anti-parental, Oedipus and Electra, complexes are things of the past. (It was left to a disciple, Melanie Klein, to out-Freud Freud by 'discovering' pre-genital forms of the Oedipus complex.) They can then get on with being 'normal', self-absorbed children until the recapitulation phase known as the Fifth (genital) stage at the onset of puberty when sexual interests re-awaken and cultural factors at last operate to modify the individual psyche.

Needless to say, this entire schema is open to all sorts of questions: what exactly *is* the unconscious mind, and is it the seat of the most powerful motivating influences? Can we establish these phases of development as authentic stages? Did Freud, in particular, confuse observation with speculation, and mistake correlation with causation? Are these merely interesting insights inflated into a general theory which the evidence does not support? Certainly from a scientific point of view, the extremely interpretative nature of Freud's methodology leaves a great deal to be desired. Take parent fixation and domination as an example: if *all* children experience this the idea loses its explanatory significance in particular situations. For instance, the dilemma of obedience and disobedience: how can we account for the compliance and non-compliance of different children, over, say, drinking even though they are brought up in the same teetotal household? Furthermore, if it can be shown that a child has experienced certain traumas, it is still not possible always to determine the future consequences of these experiences; a trauma in infancy does not have to lead to a predictable pattern of behaviour. Indeed, it could be argued that these are merely *post facto* intellectualisations based upon observed behaviour in the adult. Problems can always be regressed in such a way that psychoanalytic 'explanations' cannot easily be contested.

Another kind of stages model, though still very much in the Freudian tradition, is that of Erik Erikson. He posits an eight-stage psychosocial scheme which stresses the self-conscious (ego) dimension rather than Freud's instinctual (id) self. Erikson's stages are constructed in terms of *progressive contraries*:

(a) *Basic trust and mistrust* (0-1 yrs). At this stage the care of the parents engenders a sense of security in the child. Parental failure at this point may damage the child's personality irrevocably.

(b) *Autonomy versus shame and doubt* (2-3 yrs). Here the child should develop independence. Failure will bring a sense of shame and inferiority.

(c) *Initiative versus guilt* (4-5 yrs). This is the period of dawning curiosity and the acquisition of new skills. This may call for disciplinary action on the part of the parents who regard the child as increasingly assertive – even aggressive. The teaching of right and wrong may then produce moral ambiguities.

(d) *Industry versus inferiority* (6-12 yrs). School training and peer comparison may either develop confidence or a sense of inferiority.

(e) *Identity versus role confusion* (13-18 yrs). A period that is critical for the development of personal, sexual and work relationships.

(f) *Intimacy versus isolation* (19-25 yrs). Here there is the crystallisation of personal identity; the individual's nature becomes 'set'. It is also the period where, statistically speaking, they are most likely to merge their sexual identity with others.

(g) *Generativity versus stagnation* (26-40 yrs). The time of achievement or disappointment. Disillusionment may lead to an immersion in hobbies, work or other extra-curricular activities.

(h) *Ego integrity versus despair* (40 yrs onwards). The natural development of (g). A time of reflection and accounting. Everything will depend upon the 'success' of stages (a)-(g).

Many of the questions we have raised about Freud apply also to Erikson.

Can these stages be clearly identified? Have they any explanatory potential, or are they mere descriptions? Does Erikson underrate physiological factors in determining the development of the individual? In particular, it can be argued that to construct a scheme of contraries is to ensure that every continuum effectively covers every behavioural contingency. Do they therefore tell us anything?

Psychodynamic theories, then, stress the pull of strong, inner, unconscious forces in shaping the personality. These inherited tendencies are primitive and powerful – but often unrealised or unacknowledged. Yet they are manifested in behaviour as compelling urges and desires which are potentially destructive, but which may be modified by therapy or perhaps by society. They are therefore determinist in that they assume that individuals are victims of their own past experiences. Therefore certain specific elements of personality development, especially moral development, present the subject with a *fait accompli*. There are severe limits to the possibility of change, and personal responsibility is minimal. With the prescribed therapy, where the vital components are unearthed and analysed – often taking months and even years, at no little expense – some improvement may be possible.

Behaviourist theories

Behaviourist theories are really another form of determinism, but the focus of investigation is different. What the Freudians and neo-Freudians regard as the tip of the iceberg, i.e. actual observed behaviour, the Behaviourists regard as the real area of study – in fact, the *only* area of study. They too make number of basic assumptions:

(1) Humans are animals who are subject to much the same stimuli as other animals, and can therefore be studied in similar experimental fashion. Thus, for example, there is an assumption that the behaviour of rats in mazes in some ways corresponds with the behaviour patterns of humans in analogous situations. Perhaps we have here another instance of the common confusion between same and similar. It is most likely that humans and rats do have some things in common, but their reactions cannot be the same. Some recent experiments, for instance, have shown that rats can be treated with tranquillisers to ease stress, and – as with some humans – this reduces their capacity to cope with the *next* stressful situation, but, as far as we are aware, there is no way in which rats can analyse problem situations and remedy matters by a combination of reflection and alternative strategies.

(2) The Behaviourists' approach to the pursuit of knowledge is scientific because it is based on empirical, experimental procedures. They assert that humans have basic drives, such as survival, satiation, reproduction, etc., and that these are unalterable biological 'givens'. We are all, therefore –

to some *un*determined extent – at the mercy of our phsysiologies. Behaviourists are not primarily concerned with hypothetical unconscious forces, instead they assert that behaviour is simply a series of responses to known stimuli. Change the stimuli and you change the responses. Thus control of the subject's environment must lead to control of his or her responses through either negative or positive reinforcement.

(3) There is a de-emphasis on mind as distinct from the brain. The *mind* is a subjective entity which is not directly amenable to examination. Thoughts, feelings, fantasies – the stuff of the Psychodynamic theorists – are not open to experimentation. The *brain*, on the other hand, is a physical entity, and the behaviour which presumably derives from its activity *is* examinable. Science, it is argued, is not primarily concerned with non-examinable phenomena. Admittedly, there is much about the brain's functions that we do not understand, so it is better to concentrate on what we know and can *see*. The non-examinable dimension is probably best left to disciplines such as philosophy.

(4) Some Behaviourists (e.g. Eysenck) maintain that as far as therapy is concerned, recovery rates of patients using psychoanalytical methods are no higher than those of patients who wait for normal recuperation. Yet for certain conditions they have shown empirically how successful behavioural therapy can be. For example, in the area of sex therapy, considerable improvements have been effected for those suffering from various forms of sexual dysfunction. Whatever reservations one may have about these techniques popularised by Masters and Johnson (Szasz, 1981) they can be shown to have worked in an impressive number of cases. By concentrating on the symptoms instead of the causes, they have been able to alleviate anxieties for many of their patients (Carlton, 1980).

Behaviourists, then, are not unconcerned with causes, but insist that for practical purposes, the mental (mind) implications can wait; what matters is the capacity to understand and, if necessary, *change* observed behaviour. To this extent, they too are deterministic in that they believe that with the right inducements humans will respond to given cues. It is just a question of introducing the appropriate stimuli in order to induce and control the required reactions.

A highly modified version of Behaviourism can be found in Learning theory. Again, there is the stress on the manifestations of behaviour rather than the believed generating sources, but the Learning theorists put considerable emphasis on observational learning. Behaviour is not explained simply in terms of biological pre-dispositions, but is learned by initiation and imitation. So, for example, a person learns to drive a car not on a stimulus-response basis (which really means an untutored trial and error basis) but by instruction and demonstration. And so with morality, which is not normally left to chance: the young are socialised into the norms and values of their particular culture.

Personality is said to develop by following *models*, and these vary with class and culture. What is not satisfactorily explained is why any particular individual will follow one model rather than another, even within the same community or family. It also raises interesting questions for the media. If, for instance, we got away from the current obsession with social realism on TV and portrayed life as some would like it to be, would it lead to higher ethical standards? Doesn't Plato's injunction to seek 'the good, the beautiful and the true' demand authenticity as well as idealism?

What of course is missing in Behaviourism is any serious consideration of values. All kinds of distinctly human characteristics such as hopes and ideals seem to be discounted. The whole concept of mind has been undermined by Behaviourism, and the controlling significance of the *conscious* mind has been complicated – even downgraded – by the Freudian emphasis on the dominant importance of the *un*conscious mind. This is why Cognitive psychologists such as Walter Mischel (Mischel, 1973) have tried to restore mind to its 'rightful' place in the complex of personality, and have even attempted to reconcile Behaviourism with the phenomenological tradition of subjective introspective cognition. Cognitivists regard humans as capable of intelligent decisions; they are not just victims of a stimulus-response world. They are complex, problem-solving creatures who collaborate in the construction of their own worlds.

Humanistic theories

A general dissatisfaction with the earlier conditions of Behaviourism and even its more refined offshoots has led to counter-theories of what is broadly termed Humanistic psychology. These maintain that human behaviour is intelligent and purposive, that individuals are unique creatures who cannot be thought of in purely mechanistic terms. Humans act in accordance with knowledge and pre-determined goals; this implies that the potentiality for behaviour modification may ultimately be conditioned not by changing the stimuli but by the calculated self-interest of the subject.

The late, great high-priest of Humanistic psychology, Abraham Maslow, advanced a hierarchy of needs theory which argued that all individuals must satisfy certain needs in order finally to realise their full potential as human beings. He suggested that people are – either consciously or unconsciously – striving for 'actualisation', i.e. self-fulfilment, although it has to be admitted that Maslow was not always clear as to what actually constituted a self-actualised person, or who these people really were. (It's rather like asking a Buddhist how many fully enlightened people there are.) In one college sample, he claimed to have found only one out of 3,000 students; and in a retrospective glance at historical figures, he unsurprisingly included Einstein and Beethoven among the chosen few.

Despite its weaknesses, it could be said that this approach does have important moral implications. It concentrates on the positive potential of the human personality rather than emphasising – as did Freud – its more negative aspects. It therefore assumes that this potential exists and that human 'growth' is possible. Perhaps Maslow's best known disciple is Carl Rogers, who takes the view that the self cannot be known in any objective sense; it is intensely personal and subjective and can only be known as a phenomenon, i.e. as something that is perceived. These perceptions are 'real' for the perceivers, so we must try to understand (tolerate?) each other's perceptions (realities), and this can only be facilitated by open, honest communication. In this, we must freely acknowledge our failings, but try to minimise them and then strive to realise our true potential.

Laudable as this sounds, by scientific standards its claims are not open to experimentation *as a theory*. Its strength lies in its attested virtues as a *therapy* in that some people have undoubtedly been helped by it. By being prospective rather than retrospective, by telling people to disregard past failings – unlike the Freudians who always seem to be looking for them – and to set their sights on the future, many have come to see themselves as more able and more worthy than they originally thought. Its weakness by ethical standards is in the tendency to dismiss the idea of guilt as something which is emotionally debilitating rather than a necessary precursor to self-improvement. It does not actually help us to understand the structure of personality, and there is little exploration of possible unconscious motivations and urges – or what Carl Jung might have called the darker side of our natures. Neither – complementarily – is there any concerted attempt to relate behaviour patterns to the norms and values of the wider society, especially when that behaviour is what some would euphemistically call 'dysfunctional'.

The Humanistic school is an understandable reaction to the determinism of the Behaviourist and Psychodynamic theorists. The Humanists want to liberate people from their pasts and even from the indelibility of their own natures. They want to see people not as controlled by either biological urges or environmental conditions, but as individuals who are free 'to be', whose 'true' identity and potential are realisable. They exude an optimism about the human condition which may be as worthy as it is almost certainly misconceived.

Cognitive theories

We can see the close affinities between Cognitive theorists – to whom we have already briefly alluded – and the broad spectrum of humanistic thinking. Cognitivists are not primarily interested in biological determinants, psychic forces, or even social pressures. Instead they stress the importance of the ways people abstract and process information, and how it is then utilised in everyday decision-making. They look for regularities and consistencies of behaviour, and they are concerned with *explanations* and *interpretations* of that behaviour by others as well as the subjects themselves. This involves the notion of *attribution*; to what do people attribute their own actions, and those of other people? And what can they expect in given sets of circumstances? Those who feel that the locus of responsibility is in themselves, and who believe that they have control, tend to be highly motivated and achievement-oriented. On the other hand, those who feel that their lives (fates?) are largely out of their control often lack this kind of dynamism. For them, it is 'circumstances' that are accountable for their condition, and some studies have shown that externally-motivated children tend to be more impatient with delay or deferred gratification whereas internally-motivated children are said to experience less frustration and – by implication – are better behaved than their discontented counterparts.

This controversy is really one variant of the nature-nurture argument. Another variant which is relevant to our general discussion is the trait-situation dispute. Have we specific inherited traits or is behaviour determined by its social context? There is actually no clear evidence for unambiguous traits, but there is some support from longitudinal tests that certain personality characteristics remain consistent for the same people over time. Trait studies, therefore, confirm the presence of general characteristics but are unable to predict specific modes of behaviour in given circumstances.

By contrast, situationalists emphasise the importance of the *context* in which behaviour is expressed. This is well attested, for instance, from studies of sexual dysfunction. Men who have sexual difficulties such as impotence are usually not hormonally deficient or otherwise physically impaired, but are often affected by the circumstances that prevail at the time. Similarly, some studies of the relationship between moral beliefs and behaviour have concluded that honesty, for instance, is much more likely to be determined by the situation than by the belief itself. So, in the army, it is common knowledge that soldiers never mind appropriating anything – clothes, food, etc. – from 'them', i.e. the army authorities; taking extras from government stocks is regarded as fair game, and certainly not as stealing – though the authorities themselves would take quite a different view. But to take from 'mates' is altogether another matter. A thief would be hard put to it to justify such a reprehensible act, which would be seen not in terms of the act itself, but in terms of the context or situation in which it took place. It is difficult, therefore, to avoid the conclusion that because each individual has a unique interaction with his environment, no matter how marked the trait in question – if, indeed, it can be clearly identified – acts will usually be conditioned by the circumstances themselves.

Perhaps the most notable of the pioneer Cognitivists was the Swiss psychologist, Jean Piaget, who maintained that individuals pass through reasonably clearly defined stages of conceptual development:

(1) *The sensorimotor stage* (up to 2 yrs of age): this is when children begin to distinguish between themselves and others, and also take the first steps in organising their experiences. As far as moral development is concerned they begin to learn about intentional behaviour, and that actions have consequences.

(2) *The preoperational stage* (2-7 yrs): here children learn to anticipate, but find it difficult to retrace steps whereby they have reached a conclusion (Piaget's 'irreversibility'). They develop an increasing ego-centricity – a kind of furrowed mentality about themselves and their relationship to the world.

(3) *The concrete operational stage* (7-11 yrs): during this phase of development, children learn how to see things in more than one dimension. They can begin to appreciate another's point of view, and even correct themselves when they are mistaken.

(4) *The formal operational stage* (12 yrs onwards): this is the time for problem-solving. Children begin to think in abstract terms and even to test intellectually hypotheses about the external world. Morally, they become clearer about issues of praise and blame.

According to Piaget, cognitive development requires that individuals are able to assimilate and accommodate information. *Assimilation* involves being able to interpret new information in terms of what is already known. However, if this proves difficult, the information in question will either be ignored, or it will produce a cognitive change, i.e. a process of *accommodation* (Piaget & Inhelder, 1968).

These ideas have, needless to say, been questioned in a number of ways. For instance, are children entirely consistent in their behaviour at particular stages? How instrumental are they? It can be shown that even pre-school infants will temper their conversation to particular audiences. Piaget later modified this theory to indicate that individuals reach stage (4) by the time they are twenty, though other studies have shown that even in Higher Education this is only characteristic of a minority of students. But then maybe his theory refers to capacity and not necessarily to habitual strategy (Davidoff, 1980, p. 284). Furthermore there may not be an unhindered progression from one stage to the next. Mental abilities may reach plateaux of dormancy before they move on to the next level. Certainly children differ tremendously in this respect, and perhaps Piaget tended to emphasise the genetic (natural growth) factor rather than the influences of culture and environment, and the innate perceptual abilities of the child.

One development of Piaget's ideas – a development specifically related to moral reasoning – is to be found in the work of Lawrence Kohlberg. In his seven-stage scheme, he tries to encompass a development from pre-morality to ethico-religious beliefs. This may be summarised as follows:

Level I. Preconventional – where rules are given by others.

Stage (i) is orientated towards punishment and obedience. Goodness and badness are determined by the physical consequences of action.

Stage (ii) Instrumental relativist orientation. Elementary notions of reciprocity, but moral attitudes are predominantly ego-centric and instrumental.

Level II. Conventional – where the individual is prepared to adopt the rules of others, indicating a general acceptance of society's norms and values.

Stage (iii) Learning to be 'nice'. Good behaviour is that which is approved by others.

Stage (iv) Law and order orientation; a stress on duty and respect for those in authority.

Level III. Postconventional – where the individual follows the rules which he/she has chosen to recognise.

Stage (v) Social contract orientation. That is right which is agreed on by consensus. Rules can be modified in accordance with changing social needs.

Stage (vi) Universal principle orientation. Ethics related to abstract general principles such as the Golden Rule to treat others as you would hope that they would treat you, rather than obedience to specific commandments.

Stage (vii) Cosmic principle orientation. Ethics defined in terms of religious ideals.

Kohlberg speculates that cognitions are the key ingredient in socialisation. He assumes that people strive to maintain a coherent conception of themselves and their place in the scheme of things. They look for consistency in values, beliefs and actions. Conscience is seen as a set of internalised rules which reflect the norms and values of society. Ideally, it is these values, which may be informed by inculcated religious principles, that – in theory, at least – govern the individual's modes of behaviour. Kohlberg's view was that most people (in his sample of 24-year-olds it was 90%) do not operate beyond Level II.

Kohlberg's view that action is primarily based on belief has been contested; the empirical evidence is still ambiguous. Indeed, other studies (e.g. Feldman & Feldman, 1967) have shown that many people will contravene the rules if the likelihood of discovery is encouragingly remote. In an experiment, students were given the opportunity to mark their own examination scripts from a key but kept unaware that the scripts had already been marked. As part of the experiment the invigilator was 'unexpectedly' called from the room, and cheating was found to be as high as 50%, with boys scoring considerably more highly than girls.

Stages theories are often interesting and insightful, but they are open to the obvious criticism that their categorisations are very general and are thus subject to very many possible exceptions and variations. So many of the arguments are reversible in that they rely upon a 'read-back' method from effect to hypothesised cause. In the context of our discussion, this implies the possession of a believed personality trait that is typically manifested at a particular stage of development. The whole idea of personality is somewhat untidy and extremely difficult to conceptualise. It is not easy to disentangle values and their development from other facets of personality, such as disposition, abilities, temperament, etc. – in short, what we call identity. Some psychologists tend to regard personality as *the* area of study, and divide their attention into attempts to assess and measure it, attempts to understand and explain its mechanisms and – not least – attempts to mould, modify or actually control it. As we have seen, there has been some success in behaviour modification, but not much joy in other respects. Thus we have had to make do with the sorts of classifications we have been considering, but these are mere substitutes for the ability to assess and understand personality that we would really like.

No matter what view we take of the derivation of values, there is little doubt that they are screened and shaped by the socialisation process. The trouble with Personalism, the view that individual personality should be the main focus of psychological enquiry, is that it may degenerate into Personalistic Psychology, the idea that all behaviour is determined by personality characteristics which are largely inherited (e.g. see H.J. Eysenck, 1979) rather than moulded existentially by life experiences. In fact, research has shown that seemingly self-evident virtues, such as, say, 'responsibility' and 'truth-telling' do not correspond with any single quality in the human character (see Samborn, 1971). Nor do they describe or represent anything fixed and specific in human behaviour in general. Although most people would admit that they were desirable, they would not always agree on what it means to tell the 'truth' in any particular situation, and whether or not it was 'right' for this to be modified to suit the occasion. It is not surprising, therefore, that many educators have been happy to see moral issues transferred into ones of mental health with subjects being enjoined to seek 'adjustment' in their personal lives. But it is also little wonder that other educators, who may even be convinced relativists, grow impatient with this vagueness and confusion, and find themselves directing the behaviour of the young – perhaps more out of expediency than conviction – in accordance with carefully prescribed standards.

Situationalism, then, in one form or another, would seem to reign supreme. Research is very uncertain about self-imposed objective standards from which people will not deviate regardless of the circumstances. Yet ideological imperatives can be such profound motivating forces in the lives of some individuals that their potency can withstand the most rigorous intellectual assaults. The process of value-inculcation may well begin in childhood and crystallise into firm belief during adolescence. Alternatively, it may come as the result of ideological conversion which revolutionises the entire intellectual and vocational orientation of the subject. The operative agencies are pre-eminently religious organisations; there is more than a grain of truth in the Catholic dictum, 'Give us a child until it is seven ...'. Experience shows that no matter how far that child-turned-adult eventually strays from the faith, it is rarely able to escape completely from its influence. This can be shown to be true even where sophisticated belief-cum-behaviour modification techniques are employed, as is the case with certain political prisoners. And where there is an ostensible switch, say, from Catholicism to Communism (as in the post-Second World War Soviet satellite states of Poland, Hungary, etc.), it is all too obvious that those concerned are surrendering themselves to another system with very similar demands and organisation. The content of the ideology is different but there are remarkable similarities in its structure. Consider the case of Theodore Maly, who it is now virtually certain recruited some of the young Cambridge intellectuals in the 1930s such as Kim Philby, Donald Maclean and Anthony Blunt, and induced them to spy for the Soviet Union. Maly was a one-time Hungarian priest who had converted to Marxism in the 1920s, and who became so undeviating in his allegiance to the Soviet system that when he was recalled to Moscow in 1937 at the height of the notorious treason trials during which untold numbers were either imprisoned or executed (Conquest, 1990), he returned willingly knowing that he was going to his death. Before leaving England he said philosophically, 'They will enjoy killing a Communist' (Poretsky, 1963, pp. 128, 214). He was completely committed, so whatever the system decreed, had to be right. And in this he was not alone. This dichotomy of thinking is not unusual; it is a form of cognitive dissonance which can actually confirm rather than neutralise the subject's faith. Situational relativism has its limits; for the ideologue belief is the reason for his existence.

Perception and conceptualisation

It is taken as given that moral development must be related to social influences – the family, education, the peer-group, the media, etc. – but we need to ask in what ways the individual appropriates from society, and what is it that conditions the nature of this appropriation. Learning and intelligence must play a crucial role, but these, in turn, are very much affected by the phenomenon of perception. So why do we 'see' things as we do, and what shapes the nature of our understanding?

First of all, we must make the simple but important distinction between sensation and perception. In everyday experience, they are normally part of a single process, but technically they can be distinguished. We can *think* of sensation and perception separately, but in humans it is difficult to see how they can be separated *in practice*. Sensation is the reception of a stimulus from a sense organ, a receptor, which is selectively sensitive to changes in the environment. Thus we respond automatically to noise, to touch, to images, and so forth. We are continuously being fed with sense-data of one kind and another which are then processed by complex neurological mechanisms. More subtle still is the way these operate to maintain the body in a constant state of unconscious well-being; a delicate sense of balance, a steady temperature, finely-tuned physical and mental coordination (kinaesthetics), all of which contribute to what is technically called homeostasis.

The brain which controls all these infinitely complex operations is – as far as we are aware – the most amazing mechanism in existence. The body contains some 10-12 thousand million nerve cells (neurons), about 75% of which are located in the higher brain centre (cerebral cortex). The human foetus accumulates nerve cells at the rate of about 1,300 per second, but one day just one Martini might kill upwards of 10,000! The baby brain is already 12% of its body mass, and by six years of age the brain is already 90% of its adult size. Each nerve cell has anywhere between one and ten thousand synapses, i.e. links with other nerve cells, and each synapse acts as a micro-computer. This makes an incredible variety of behaviours possible. Data are processed at about a hundred 'bits' per second, and this means that each neuron is much more densely packed with information than any known computer.

Intelligence does not seem to be directly related to brain size. Einstein had an abnormally small brain, and recent scanning techniques have shown – quite exceptionally – that considerable intelligence may some-times exist even when the brain 'matter' is minimal. The brain hemi-spheres make up about 70% of the entire brain and nervous system. But Karl Lashley (Harvard) has shown in experiments with rats that even a 10% removal of the brain does not seem to affect their behaviour. Perhaps we do have what Ralph Gerard (University of Michigan) refers to as 'redundant storage' – a kind of excess capacity which holds knowledge that is no longer relevant.

We cannot pretend to know much about the brain; in fact, we have to admit that none of its functions is clearly understood, let alone the interaction of those functions in the determination of behaviour. If we take memory as just one example, we are not sure why some people learn more quickly than others, or why some develop specific abilities that are out of key with their other abilities, say a low IQ child who can play a piano well 'by ear'. Why have some people got photographic memories? And exactly what does this mean? Why – very commonly – do some learning experi-ences last for life, such as being able to swim or ride a bicycle, and others, such as recalling telephone numbers or people's names, disappear quite quickly? Is it a matter of age, or circumstances, or importance, or what? We are learning more all the time about these things, but we are still only on the fringes of real understanding.

When we speak of memory, we are, of course, thinking about the operations of the Central Nervous System (CNS), but we are not certain exactly how this interacts with the Autonomic Nervous System (ANS). What precisely is the relationship? For instance, if we go to the dentist, and the brain (CNS) – despite a natural apprehension – commands composure, yet no matter how insistent its instructions to the body, it is often unable to prevent certain automatic physical responses; the clammy palms, the sweaty armpits, the seemingly inevitable intestinal butterflies just as he is going to drill or even inject ... This is just one override effect among many that we cannot control.

Sensation, then, is a response of the Autonomic Nervous System (ANS), but perception is more complex than sensation. In texts on Psychology, perception is customarily related specifically to the act of seeing, and knowing that which we see. We often use the false analogy of a camera projecting little pictures of an upside-down world to the cerebral cortex. Actually, each retina is sending the cortex about a million simultaneous streams of electro-chemical data transmitted by some 125 million rods and cones. A better analogy would be the dots on a printed page. The mosaic of dots from the retina is transformed into something that has *meaning* for us.

But the term perception can be used more broadly than this. It can be used to denote the act of *interpreting* the stimulus – of seeing, hearing, or whatever. Perception is to do with making sense of the world.

Sensation is reinforced by associations of learning, by past experiences, by ideas, images, memories, etc. For example, on the longest-running BBC radio programme, 'Desert Island Discs', the guests, who have to choose eight favourite records, are frequently faced with the dilemma of deciding on the *criteria* by which these discs are to be chosen. Do they want records simply because they like them or because they mean something special to them? Are they to be fun or are they to represent a recollection of some incident or experience? People do not want to hear mere sounds (sensation) – (though one is left wondering about certain forms of popular music where sensation appears to be everything) – generally speaking, they want these sounds to be enjoyable because they are familiar and *evocative* (perception). The experience of sound is just sensation, but *ordered* sound may be interpreted as music or language, and therefore have a special symbolic significance.

It is perhaps worth noting that damage to certain areas of the brain, particularly the association areas of the cerebral cortex, either through accident or perhaps by certain operations, may not result in any marked reduction of sensation, but in a considerable impairment of perception. Patients are often restless, lacking in concentration, and very easily distracted. So much so, in fact, that certain routine tasks may actually have to be *re*-learned – and often with frustrating difficulty. We can, therefore, describe and – within limits – analyse the psychology of sensation, but we can only hypothesise something of the psychology of perception.

The process of perception, as we shall see, is subject to distortion, ambiguity, paradox, and various kinds of 'fiction'. The Gestalt emphasis on holistic interpretations reflects the view that the brain develops a number of 'analogues', i.e. preferred forms or desired ways of seeing things. This process consists, first, of the *organisation* of innumerable nerve impulses into meaningful brain 'pictures' or percepts, and, secondly, the *utilisation* of these percepts to facilitate the most appropriate responses. Of course, there is always more information available in the environment than the brain can deal with at any one time, so a process of *selection* takes place, and it chooses that which is most valuable for its immediate needs. It has to be discriminating in its choice of 'digestible' material such as sounds from the environment – so it is not at all uncommon to hear wives complain that husbands never hear what they say! I knew, for example, of one eminent scholar who – in his earlier years – did much of his studying in a noisy living-room where children were playing and the radio was on much of the time. Most of us would find this very nearly impossible to cope with but his concentration was such that he could ignore all distractions and get on with his work. Suffice it to say that he ended up with four degrees including a doctorate.

Psychologists commonly use the term *attention* for this selection activity which takes place according to several criteria, the most important of which are: (a) *Appetite and need*, which encompass a variety of forms from pre-occupation with food or health or sex to all-absorbing economic concerns. (b) *Interest*, which more or less speaks for itself, and can be expressed as a furrowed mentality. I am reminded of a long-term unemployed mature student who told me how 'shocked' he was on one of his rare visits to London. I immediately conjured up visions of dirty streets, tatty buildings or even possibly the engagingly seedy attractions of Soho, but I was quickly assured that it was none of these. No, it was affluence. He couldn't take his eyes off the cars, the shops, the prosperity, the *spending*. He saw everything in economic terms. To him, it was just one huge sybaritic display of unashamed consumerism. The other attractions of the metropolis were lost – perhaps because he simply couldn't afford to enjoy them. (c) *Expectation and association* are also fairly obvious, although experience can play tricks on us in that it is easy to make pre-judgements which are actually *mis*judgements. Generally speaking, attention is engaged when information is *unusual*. Strange or peculiar sights and sounds immediately command our attention: the unfamiliar; that which is a change from the habitual and the customary; occurrences that are *reminiscent*, a scene or face, a reminder – welcome or otherwise – of something that is long past. How many of us, for instance, who experienced the Blitz don't still react momentarily to the whine of a factory siren?

The *principles of perception*, that is to say the characteristics or capacities of the perceiving process, are almost certainly *inborn* (the nature argument) although they are patently refined by learning and usage (the nurture argument). The perception of space, for example, seems to be innate and experiments with very young babies appear to confirm their ability to make certain kinds of conceptual judgement. This has been demonstrated in the work of Jerome Bruner who, in a series of experiments, presented babies 3-4 months old with dummy-sucking mechanisms wired to strain-gauges which, in turn, were connected to a large screen. In Experiment A, extra sucking gave them no milk but brought the facial image on the screen into clear focus, whereas in Experiment B extra sucking gave them milk but took the facial image out of focus. The result was that most babies turned away from the unfocussed image and used the dummy that would restore it; they preferred the correct image to the comfort of the milk. From this it was deduced that they already possessed an inbuilt model of how the world should look – and they obviously wanted to keep it this way.

Such experiments compare with others that underline these abilities but also highlight the capacity for *learned* behaviour. In a well known and repeated experiment attempts have been made to assess human abilities to focus sight and hearing, and especially what is termed figure ground separation. The subject of the experiment was fitted with specially designed head-gear – rather like an elaborate diver's helmet – which gave a visual field of 180 degrees, a reversal of left and right, and a reversal of up and down. This equipment was worn during daytime for eight days, and the subject was blindfolded at night. He experienced almost complete confusion during days 1 and 2, and this was accompanied by disorientation, depression and even nausea. Days 3/4 brought some degree of adjustment and by days 5/6 he had established a new set of motor-visual relations. When the equipment was removed, bewilderment lasted for several hours during which normality was gradually re-learned. Such experiments confirm the capacity to group and organise information in relation to such principles as similarity, proximity, symmetry, continuity, completeness (pattern), constancy and regularity, etc., despite the fluctuations in sensory stimuli. We can 'create' what are, in effect, computer models in the brain, so that if, say, someone mentions damage to a car, providing we know the make and model well, we can turn it round in our heads and 'see' the situation as a whole even though it can never appear as such to our senses.

How much these findings tell us about our innate or learned capacities for moral behaviour, we are not quite sure. They certainly point up something of the futility of the continuing nature-nurture debate. Both perspectives are obviously relevant – we are not dealing with an either/or dichotomy. Equally pertinent is this complex capacity to see and assess situations graphically and imaginatively. This means that we have the ability to put ourselves in the position of the 'other', to adopt multiple perspectives, to view a problem from all angles, and to make judgements that take account of a variety of possible scenarios, as we shall see when we come to look at the ways in which values can be studied (Chapter 4).

Having considered something of the processes and principles involved in perception, we should now look at some of the factors which influence 'correct' perception. The first is the obvious persistent *problem of misperception*. This may come about because we receive wrong or inadequate information, or – and this is what really concerns us – it may happen because of misunderstood, misconceived or generally misinterpreted information. If we take, as a matter of special interest, UFO phenomena, and try to analyse what it is that people see, or purport to see, that has given rise to UFO reports, we will have to distinguish between a UFO *event*, i.e. the generation of an unusual image by a physical cause, and a UFO *sighting*, which is the claim to a perception of this image by a witness or witnesses, which is what will concern the scientist. In all this, we are immediately involved in matters of clarification and interpretation. We have to study not only the most 'significant' sightings, but also the reactions and motivations of various groups – scientists, the military, enthusiasts and cultists – who will all have a stake in the findings. Speculation will be accompanied by a clarification of reports into a hierarchy of reliability (Vallee, 1974), and these, in turn, will coalesce into a corpus of plausible theories. Much ultimately depends on the trustworthiness of the witnesses; failures of memory, misjudgements about velocities, heights, shapes and dimensions, are all crucial to the investigative enterprise. As with so many problems, not least moral ones, it is very difficult to arrive at normative judgements without a reasonable appreciation of what are regarded as the facts. One suspects that innumerable issues in society could have been resolved if there had been a correct perception of the situation in the first place.

Secondly, we frequently encounter the *problem of non-accommodation*. This is the situation where there is an unwillingness to receive information when it does not fit or conform with one's existing ideas and values. For example, there has been a spate of literature which purports to 'disprove' the Holocaust. Some maintain that atrocity stories are false or grossly exaggerated; others soft-pedal their arguments and are prepared to concede the substance of the accusations, but minimise or exonerate certain individuals in the programme (e.g. see Irving, 1983). These protestations, which, one suspects, have come about because they serve particular political purposes or conduce to some kind of quasi-political ideology, have been ably refuted by serious students of the Holocaust (see Seidel, 1987). But in some cases, the atrocities have been denied by well-meaning – sometimes devoutly religious – people because they would not, or could not, accept that some human beings could actually do these things to other human beings. It was information that simply could not be accommodated.

The third – and perhaps less familiar – problem is that known as *psychological dualism*, i.e. the situation in which the self is effectively divided against itself. Theoretically, this means that we distinguish an ideal and an actual self, and that we perceive the self we are as somewhat different from the self we would like to be. And this, in turn, influences the way we see – or wish to see – others as well. Should we, therefore, learn to accept ourselves as we perceive ourselves to be, or should we try to change ourselves into something – an image – that we think we ought to be? For instance, one of the main tasks of Alcoholics Anonymous is to get clients to see the real nature of their dependency; only then is there any real possibility of doing something positive about it. Only when they compare the self they are with the self they would like to be, have alcoholics any reasonable chance of success.

Perception, then, is an active process. We are constantly extracting data from the world of our senses and processing them in such a way that they become familiar and – for all practical purposes – comprehensible. But there are still enormous gaps in our knowledge. We can never fully explain perception in purely clinical terms. Not only do we need to know more about the neurophysiology of perception – how the neurons register, retain and transmit information – we also need to know more about human motivation, why we respond to some stimuli more than others, and to what extent perceptions are influenced by emotions, predispositions and values.

Learning and intelligence

We have already noted that some theorists emphasise the perceptual as opposed to the purely sensory approach to the acquisition of knowledge, and that some (e.g. Piaget and Kohlberg) further argue that *moral* development involves the ability to make finer distinctions and more comprehensive generalisations. This means that a necessary – though not sufficient – condition for principled morality is general intelligence, the ability to reason abstractly and analytically. We should, therefore, look at learning and intelligence in more depth and ask first of all how we learn and how knowledge is actually acquired.

Researchers usually measure learning by observing changes in a subject's behaviour. This is called *performance*. A term which – within an institutional framework – makes certain assumptions about standards and what exactly is expected and required. What is improvement, and by what criteria are these things measured? The difficulty, at all levels, is that so much learning takes place without any observable responses. It is concealed or latent learning. Certainly the inculcation of value-ideas is often indirect, and the internalisation of those ideas may be largely unconscious. Furthermore, if tests are deliberately contrived to determine the degree of learning, or learning capacities, they may give a distorted picture of actual skills. Intelligence tests, for example, though generally useful, can give a misleading impression of a particular subject's abilities. So should research be directed towards the testing of specific abilities and responses, as the Behaviourists might argue, or should it concentrate on forms of 'whole person' analysis? This would be the opinion of the Gestaltists (Gestalt here means 'completeness' or 'wholeness') who reject the mosaic hypothesis of learning, i.e. the view that knowledge comes from random associations and impressions which are somehow fortuitously coalesced to become what we call the personality. For the Gestaltists and those of a more humanistic persuasion, the whole is held to be greater than the sum of its constituent parts – people must be studied as people, not as factorial isolates.

However, acquiring knowledge is not just a passive activity. From our earliest years a subtle reciprocal process takes place involving accommodation and adaptation to the environment – the process we generally call 'socialisation'. Learning to cope stimulates our mental capacities. We assimilate information from the environment, categorising it and organising it into meaningful and accessible patterns. Piaget distinguished between what we learn and the ways in which we learn it. But it is also important to consider *why* we learn as we do. We obviously select and organise our knowledge strategically. We have to determine what is appropriate and – perhaps more important – what is relevant. After all, learning of whatever kind is a sort of survival mechanism.

All learning theories make certain basic assumptions. As we have already noted, they presuppose that the content of our knowledge is largely given in experience (nurture) and that the formal patterning of that knowledge is a capacity that seems to be inherently given (nature). So, for example, we find that ballistic skills appear to be part of our physical make-up, though few would dispute that such things as timing and the judgement of distance must be refined by practice. Even these can be variable in the trained athlete, as the fascinating problem of 'form' – which may have important psychological dimensions – eloquently demonstrates. It is also worth noting the limits of both nurture and nature in this respect. The naturally gifted child will almost certainly not reach the higher standards without training; even such natural athletes as, say, Kenyan distance runners need to hone their talents through disciplined effort. It is amazing too what the former DDR (East Germany) with a relatively small population was able to produce by way of Olympic medals and world records from a highly organised system of talent-spotting, careful selection, privileged rigorous training schedules and – so it is rumoured – a little surreptitious drug-taking. Alternatively, it should be stressed that all the training in the world is not going to produce a glut of world-class runners. Generally speaking, you've either got it or you haven't. In moral behaviour also there are those with naturally nice dispositions, and people who are intelligent enough to see the issues. But as the poet Ovid reminds us – if, indeed, we need much reminding – to know is not necessarily to do. It has surely been an error of many well-intentioned philosophers since Plato to believe that education leads to moral betterment. If we ever had any doubts about this, it is instructive to look, for example, at the role of the SS intelligentsia in the unspeakable crimes of the 'final solution' programme. (Carlton, 1992). Education sometimes helps people to be evil more subtly and systematically. Clever or not, we have to work hard at morality – it certainly doesn't come easily to most of us.

It follows from what we have just considered about inherent qualities that learning theories presuppose that we have the capacity to 'organise' reality. So, for instance, space and time 'exist' even though their properties, their relationship with each other and their cosmic significance are not clearly understood, but for practical purposes they can be 'contained' conceptually insofar as they can be measured and utilised. Most units of measurement – inches, centimetres, minutes, hours – are contrived for human convenience; they have no correspondence with the real world. We can extend this argument to the conceptualisation of values, social practices and institutions, for some would contend that these too have no place in the physical universe but are simply contrived for social purposes. Yet this tends to leave out of account those values which we retain but which do not serve any biological purpose, such as kindness to the weak and incurable. The Nazis tackled this issue with the kind of logic which the world has rightly condemned. Yet it is interesting to ask exactly why it did so, and why it continues to have strong views about the preservation of sickly children and the old and infirm in circumstances where population is probably the single greatest problem facing the planet. Perhaps there still exists a more then vestigial humanity, though society has not always been so sensitive about these matters. In ancient Rome, unwanted children were sometimes thrown on rubbish dumps, and one wonders if one of these days circumstances will generate a 'Soylent Green' scenario* and there will be a reversion to type.

Learning theories also imply a capacity for problem solving which involves 'seeing' a situation from several angles at the intellectual level. We have already considered the ways in which we can complete pictures in our heads; we seem to have this inherent capacity for solving problems by supplying the missing elements, as it were. In simple ways this can be seen in the solution of word-puzzles and picture-puzzles, or in the everyday experience of, say, driving a car where we have to 'read the road' – we anticipate possible dangers in advance by completing 'pictures'. We utilise this capacity for 'closure' all the time without being aware of it. Humour is a good instance of this; a joke consists of elements that almost make sense plus some kind of punch-line which completes the sense implicit in the original statement(s). It may be as someone once suggested – that

* In the film 'Soylent Green' the problem of food shortage is solved by the consumption of products made from human flesh.

there are only six jokes in the world. Presumably what was meant was that there are only six *types* of joke or six basic principles on which jokes are constructed. Freud favoured ambiguity, Arthur Koestler liked incongruity, and Woody Allen tends to specialise in disparity ('I'm going to be executed at 6 o'clock; I was going to be executed at 4 o'clock but I've got a good lawyer'). The analysis of humour is fascinating in itself, and we find in practice that every variant requires a perceptual leap; possibly all humour involves closing a cognitive gap and in a flash, as it were, bringing all the elements together. There is little doubt that the wider the learning, the greater the capacity for appreciating a wide variety of humour.

The question of learning cannot really be studied without some discussion of the much-debated problem of intelligence. The basic question here – and one that is still not satisfactorily resolved – is exactly what we mean by intelligence. Is it simply what intelligence tests measure? Or is it cleverness, inventiveness, the capacity for judgement and discrimination, or – as some critics of the examination system have complained – merely the ability to recall and organise past experience and learning? (This is reminiscent of some arguments about art – that 'true' art is not simply the ability to reproduce what you see, but is essentially a form of self-expression. Yet the ability to reproduce *accurately* what is seen is no mean feat.)

Earlier approaches to the problem tended to view intelligence as an assembly of superior mental elements that were believed to be measurable. Donders, a Dutch physiologist in the last century, constructed a number of experiments to test subjects' reaction times as an index of intelligence. This involved trying to assess the differences in time between automatic reflex movements and voluntary actions. We can find this sort of thing today in simulated driving proficiency tests in which the 'road' is quickly scanned, possible hazards are selected and discriminated, distances and timing computed, and the choice of avoiding action is taken. The main flaw with this type of test is that if it is broken down into component elements, it is still uncertain what is meant by 'pure' perception, 'pure' discrimination, 'pure' choice, etc. These may not actually exist as separate entities, and therefore cannot be measured *independently*. Another fairly obvious difficulty is that reaction times can be improved even by apparently *un*intelligent people. So again the so-called basic or native intelligence is still a mystery.

This kind of test was complemented – some might say superseded – by the sort of test with which most of us are familiar, based upon the Intelligence Quotient hypothesis. This is sometimes called the clinical psychometric system, and it was presented by Alfred Binet in collaboration with Theodore Simon in 1905. Using children as subjects, they contended that intelligence could be measured in terms of the levels of judgement required to solve certain puzzles. Items were selected for difficulty and the degree of discrimination involved, and relative cleverness was measured by the ratio of mental age (MA) to chronological age (CA) thus:

$$IQ = \frac{MA}{CA} \times 100$$

The validity of the tests was established by correlating the test scores with eventual examination success.

This form of testing has been developed with increasing sophistication; some tests are very broadly based, e.g. school tests, but others, such as Army Signallers tests, are very highly specialised and are designed to assess very specific aptitudes. Such tests are still subject to many criticisms: do they take account of changing levels of intelligence? Are they too culture-bound? Can subjects learn how to pass them with coaching and repetition? But whatever their weaknesses, they have come to be regarded as useful general indicators of ability. The problem again is how to know just how specific abilities relate to 'primary' (i.e. native) intelligence, and what weight can be given to the developmental processes. The measures obtained have to be seen in relative, not absolute, terms, therefore we can only be confident in making qualified statements when we try to correlate intelligence with other factors.

Intelligence and age

This is a subject which has occasioned considerable debate. What we can say is that by the mid-teens, the bases of intellectual ability appear to be set. Studies have shown that in Performance (speed) Tests, there is a general decline after the age of 30 regardless of the content of the tests. Working against the clock seems to be a particular forte of the young. On the other hand, in what are termed Power Tests, i.e. tests that are not time-governed, mature people often do better than the young. My own impression – and it is *only* an impression – is that in Higher Education mature people, especially if they do not have orthodox entry qualifications, tend to comprise the very best and very worst students. However, older students seem to have a general aptitude for in-depth studies, and this is evidenced by the fact that many do so much better working at the graduate than at the undergraduate level. Writing a thesis *in their own time* is often much more to their liking than undergraduate examinations.

It is worth wondering if there is some correspondence between keeping the mind in trim and continuing ability. Is the mind like the body in this respect? Does lack of exercise encourage deterioration? Perhaps we have to modify the stereotype of the elderly person who lives perpetually in the past, whose old memories are clearest because they were 'taped' in youth. (Birren & Schale, 1977). Despite all that has been written about senile dementia and intellectual failure with increasing years, there is *some* evidence to show that the faculties do respond to training, and that those who exercise those faculties do stand more chance of retaining many of their intellectual capabilities as they grow older. (I once knew a professor who learned a new language every year after he turned 40, but then he had been an ancient languages specialist since he was a young undergraduate.)

Intelligence and sex

Here again the relationship is long-debated and still uncertain. It is true that men have achieved more historically, but this may well be accounted for in social terms; there is no evidence here for differences in innate intellectual ability, only differences in socio-cultural advantage. In *moral* terms, however, some feminists have argued – quite accurately – that women have harmed the world less; again, this may have nothing to do with innate differences between men and women but may also be attributable to social and possibly physiological factors. To suggest otherwise is to fall into the same kind of trap as the racists who, for various reasons, *see* some people as inferior and therefore conclude that they *are* inferior, *innately* inferior. True, men do act aggressively, but there is precious little evidence to indicate that they are inherently more aggressive than women. It has to be said that women have not been notably more humane than men when, in a variety of situations, whether as Ptolemaic queens or Nazi concentration camp guards, they have been able to exercise arbitrary power over others.

Some general points can be made about intelligence and sex that probably have little or nothing to do with the inculcation of accepted educational values or the emulation of particular role models often associated with purported docility (girls) and aggression (boys). At puberty girls tend to score higher than boys in IQ tests although boys catch up in their later teens when their pace of IQ development appears to be faster than that of girls (but research findings are admittedly still ambiguous on this issue). It seems too that girls appear to have certain superior perceptual abilities. They excel at tasks requiring co-ordination, and are noted for their verbal and clerical skills. Boys, on the other hand, are more perceptive in matters of spatial relations (sports and driving) and, in general, may have greater scientific mathematical abilities – although some research disputes this. There is, however, no reason to suppose that there is any significant difference in moral development although some tests have shown that girls do seem to have a greater awareness of many value-issues than boys, or, at least, display a greater moral concern (Le Francois, 1983, pp. 351-2).

Intelligence and race

This too is a matter of continuing debate, and has been clouded by persistent uncertainties about tests, emotional attitudes and political issues. Race and ethnicity, as we now know, are not easy to define. Are we using biological or cultural criteria – and what exactly do these terms mean anyway? And when it comes to intelligence, tests of validity vary: after all, it is not really possible to compare, say, the hunting skills of Dinka tribesman with the computational skills of a Dane. A Nigerian student is always going to perform differently from a West Indian street cleaner or an Irish labourer. We should never confuse the problem of race with that of colour because when it comes to the essential social issues, colour may be largely irrelevant. Current conflicts in, say, Sri Lanka, Kashmir, or Papua New Guinea or even the more parochial troubles of the West Indians and Asians in Handsworth, Birmingham, have little to do with pigmentation and more to do with power and economic advantage.

Some past studies which appear to show the intellectual superiority of whites, notably the work of Arthur Jensen (Jensen, 1968) which has put considerable emphasis on inherited characteristics, have been largely discredited (see, for example, Scarr & Weinberg, 1976). But there are still some disturbing questions that have not been satisfactorily answered. In Jensen's studies, blacks scored consistently 10/20 points below whites. Of course, it could be argued that these tests contained an in-built culture-bias, but try as they may, it is probably true to say that researchers have never been able to devise a completely culture-free test. Jensen stressed that this disparity did not occur with Chicanos, American Indians or Eskimos. Some studies undertaken in the UK are similarly ambiguous. In the Rampton Committee Report which was based on the study of six Education Authority areas, only 2% of blacks of West Indian origins got 'A' Level passes compared with 13% of Asians and 12% of other leavers. In another study on black pupil attainment that was undertaken by Michael Rutter and published in 1982, the results were similarly inconclusive. Professor Rutter looked at the examination results of 844 pupils in twelve inner London schools over a period of three years. He found that 19% of blacks left school with 5 or more 'O' Levels compared with 11% of whites, and 18% of blacks left without any qualifications at all compared with 34% of whites. Impressionistically, this seems to bode well for black pupils – but there were snags. The samples were questionably too small and were taken from deprived areas of South East London. Furthermore, the black pupil results may have looked better because 28% of the whites left before the exams took place – though arguably these would have been the least able pupils anyway. More disturbing is the fact that when most sample pupils started school in 1971, the selective system had already creamed off the best whites for the Grammar schools. It should be said too that all pupils – both black and white – were low achievers; only 41 of the 844 went on to obtain any 'A' Levels at all. Perhaps this tells us more about our system of schooling and the cultural divide than it actually tells us about innate or developed intellectual abilities. Underachievement as opposed to intellectual wherewithal must be largely a cultural product.

Intelligence and environment

This is hardly less controversial than the question of intelligence and race – indeed, in many ways the two are related. Again, we are firmly back with the nature-nurture issue. The most advanced experiments have been done with identical (monozygotic) and non-identical (dizygotic) twins reared either in the same or different environments (e.g. Henderson, 1982). In broad terms, we can say that identical twins reared apart still show high score correlations in tests. Adopted children tend to show high correlations with their natural parents despite being reared by social (i.e. foster/adoptive) parents. It should be emphasised that twin-studies may – especially in the case of monozygotic twins – constitute a unique phenomenon. They often seem to have an intriguing *sympatheia*. (I once knew an identical twin who, as a child, swallowed an open safety pin; his twin now has the scar.) Fascinating as twin-studies are, it is only with some caution that we can extrapolate to the population at large.

In general, then, it would appear that highly intelligent people reared in an unconducive environment will not develop as well as they might have done, but will not be entirely 'neutralised' by that environment. Alternatively, people of low intelligence will not improve appreciably with the 'right' environment, although some studies show that the environment has a definite stimulatory effect. This, of course, has to be highly problematical. How can we usefully define 'stimulation', and how can we calculate its effects as an independent variable? In particular, from our point of view, how can we assess the effects of specific aspects of the environment, family, peer group, media, etc., on the whole question of value-determination? There is little doubt that theorists are in some disarray on these issues, which have yet to be satisfactorily resolved. Whether they ever will be is in doubt, mainly because they are vitiated by strong sentimental and ideological associations. One suspects that even the researchers themselves are cause-motivated. It is infamously difficult to maintain a value-free stance on such highly emotive issues.

It remains arguable whether a factorial analysis of intelligence is possible. In testing, we have to differentiate between operations, contents and products, and, if we just take operations as an example, this in turn has to be broken down into cognition and memory, besides divergent thinking and convergent thinking. Any evaluation must be vitiated by the complexity of the variables. But as we cannot measure intelligence directly, perhaps we can only depend upon looking at its assumed components. Yet this must not preclude an attempt to look at the 'whole person' and try to uncover what is meant by 'native' or 'natural' (primary) intelligence. We have to ask, too, whether the criteria used in tests are arbitrary, and whether the results depend largely upon the contrived nature of the test itself? And certainly, we must always take into consideration the possibility that performance may be ultimately related to other, extraneous factors such as motivation, interest, desire for status, even habit, which must influence not just the performance but – as with exams – the actual *taking* of the tests themselves. Those of us who have taught children despair when they are not sure whether Charles II came after Cleopatra, but never cease to be amazed when they reel off the minute details of the professional soccer tables.

We can say, then, that there is an indefinable relationship between intelligence and values. This really means a relationship between intelligence and an *awareness* of values. It implies a greater ability to engage in moral discourse and appreciate the subtle nuances of moral debate. But it does not, and cannot, mean that intelligent people – however defined – are nicer, more moral people than others. It can only mean either that they know the arguments already or that they have the intellectual capacity to grasp the arguments and their implications once they are presented. It certainly does not mean that having 'seen' the pros and cons they cannot go wrong; history is littered with the consequential debris of those who did the wrong things for the right reasons and the right things for the wrong reasons. Worst of all, some people – either as individuals or as governments – may deliberately choose what they know to be either contentious or patently wrong, and then try to justify their actions with unconvincing and specious arguments. Humans have long mastered the psychological alchemy of transforming evil into good if it serves their own ego-centric interests.

Human needs and motivations

Having looked at the ways in which values may be perceived and how this is related to learning and intelligence, we must now at least glance at how this, in turn, may be tempered by needs and desires. So, first of all, let us define our terms. The word motivation is an abstraction; we do not observe motives, we observe behaviour from which we infer motivation. For instance, when social anthropologists first set out to study the religious systems of primitive peoples they assumed that certain beliefs and values constituted the motive force behind those systems. But on investigation, they have often found that participant responses varied and were even confused, so they concentrated on the ritual *practices* which were *assumed* to indicate the nature of these beliefs and values.

Psychologists are interested in behaviour that changes in relation to a situation or condition, or, as they put it, a variation in object-attraction, where normally recognised goals and/or incentives (rewards) are disregarded or reversed. To use religion again as an example, we could take the relatively common phenomenon of the convert to a religious order or sect who will forego what are considered to be normal worldly appetites and pleasures for the sake of spiritual goals. When this kind of radical change is observed, the presence of a particularly powerful motive is implied.

Motivation, then, in Psychological theory refers (1) to *selectivity* of particular responses and (2) to *directionality* of behaviour and *adjustment* of that behaviour in response to the goals in question. As a means/end issue it also implies (3) the capacity to *adduce* reasons for the selection of the means and/or ends concerned. After all, the cause may 'exist' in an unacknowledged and unarticulated way but does not become a motive until it is identified and chosen as a reason for future actions. The goals in question will probably be the satisfaction of certain needs, and the drive to satisfy these needs may be a persistent stimulus which demands this adjustive response.

Not unusually, however, motives are not clearly identified, notoriously so when it comes to moral issues. And the motive and the need may become unclear because need and desire become confused. When is a need not a need? Some might argue when it is not related to actual survival. If you were ever held underwater as a child in the swimming pool, you will have experienced what is said to be the most urgent of all needs, which is to expel the excess of carbon-dioxide and take in oxygen. There is no confusion here between need and desire. There is complete complementarity between the need for sheer physical survival and the consciousness of the possibility that you could lose that which you most desire – to live. Confusion between need and desire becomes clearest when the issues are not so stark, although the relationship can still be puzzling. There was an interesting experiment conducted a few years ago in which a group of male rats was put on one side of an electrified grid, and food, drink and some female rats were placed on the other side. It was hypothesised that in time, the males would satisfy their appetites in a drink/food/sex sequence despite the hazards of the grid. This proved to be correct, but what the researchers found somewhat disconcerting was that when the males were sated they still wandered idly back and forth across the grid seemingly oblivious of the pain. No one knows why. It could hardly have been need, nor even desire. Perhaps it was just curiosity – or maybe they were masochists.

So what is meant by needs? Some see a need as a kind of deficiency although we know that it is possible to evoke a need by either internal or external pressures which stimulate modes of behaviour that bring satisfaction to those concerned. This again brings to mind Maslow's 'hierarchy of needs' in which he stipulated an ordered sequence of:

Physical needs
Safety/security needs
Love needs
Esteem needs
Self-actualisation needs (Maslow, 1970)

Underlying this scheme is the assumption that all physiological problems have psychological implications. It is intuitively attractive, but difficult to test empirically. Some people would surely prefer a different order. Some people prefer, say, honour above survival, and others might opt for esteem rather than affection. (One is reminded of the Roman emperor Tiberius, who on being told of the disquiet of the people, said, 'I don't care if they don't love me, as long as they respect me.'). It is self-evidently true that we all have *physical needs* – food, warmth, shelter, activity and so forth. Much of the time – as we have noted – our basic physical needs, such as digestion, respiration, etc., are controlled by the central nervous system in such a way that we are largely unaware of them. We also have *social needs*, such as security, acceptance, recognition and respect, which can hardly be reduced to physiology and which appear to be fundamental to the species. These physical and social needs may be complementary in operation. The physical impinges upon the social, as when temperature determines the need to dress in order to keep warm. But the social also impinges on the physical, so that the issue of *what* we wear and *when* we wear particular garments raises questions about fashion, style, and – more intangibly – respectability, acceptability and modesty, all of which have value overtones. This highlights the problem once again of whether moral behaviour is determined by social conditions, and how important the cultural context is to moral activity.

Needs must also be *differentiated in terms of dimension*: it is necessary to distinguish between the needs of the individual and those of society, and even of the species. For example, in what sense can we regard sex as a need? It may be enjoyable, desirable, an overwhelming urge, or – as Malcolm Muggeridge once observed – quite hilarious. But is it really essential? Obviously, *procreation*, i.e. sex as a need, is critically necessary for the species, but sex as *recreation* may be a pleasurable pastime which is hardly vital to the survival of humankind. This again raises the issue of needs and wants, a dilemma as old as philosophy. Plato (in *The Republic*) provided a blueprint for the society that he thought people *needed*. Aldous Huxley (in *Brave New World*) satirically extended this idea to the kind of society that people *want* or are conditioned to want. In western industrialised society these terms, quite erroneously, have become almost synonymous. Wants have changed to needs. There are certain basic requirements beyond those required to live which have come to be seen as the unquestioned necessities of a civilised society – TV, radio, fridges, running hot water, electricity, central heating – which a mere 50 years ago would have been regarded as the last word in luxury. Wants have become necessities that must be supplied immediately. Desire demands instant satisfaction. And there is no need to wait providing you have the merest of prospects and can manage the statutory signature. The very idea of saving to buy is undermined by extensive credit schemes which are ostensibly designed for the benefit of the customer – not the profit of the companies. A national bank's recent circular to its customers is fairly typical: 'It happens to everyone. You see something you want, a suite of furniture, a new television, a carpet, but you haven't got the money there and then ... we've changed all that. Our Instant Credit Scheme gives you the freedom to buy what you want when you see it.' This scheme, which is 5% over the base rate, is regarded as generous (compare the 30% plus offered by many department stores and multiples) and is said to obviate the 'humiliation' of asking for a loan. Suffice to say that averaged out over the population, the current debt burden (1991) is running at about £1,100 per person in the UK (excluding mortgages).

Needs and needs-satisfaction imply the operation of *positive incentives* which indicate a particular directionality to behaviour, and *perceived disincentives* which are occasioned by aversion. Furthermore, needs-satisfaction has an important *affective* dimension. It is barely possible to satisfy needs without feelings and emotions which may take the form of elation or depression. This is an inevitable ingredient in the human response. Indeed, humans alone have this reflective capacity to feel sad/pleased, disgusted, enthusiastic, embarrassed, etc. Those who do not appear to evince these characteristics may actually be derided as 'cold' and 'unfeeling', and it is interesting that in so much activity today – especially in music and the arts – we are enjoined to *experience* rather than understand the activity or artefact in question. But how valuable is emotion without cognition? And without cognition what happens to values?

The whole idea of need is often associated with that of deprivation, and deprivation is frequently seen as a 'cause' for the breakdown in moral behaviour. This initially plausible hypothesis poses three sets of problems. First of all there is the *concept of deprivation itself*. This expression, which is bandied about so freely, especially in what we now call the caring professions, raises certain doubts. It almost goes without saying that deprivation is a relative term. Most of us are deprived and few of us are deprived, depending upon one's position in society. It is all a question of the reference point; do we compare ourselves with an oil magnate or an Indian peasant? This is something that hardly needs to be laboured. What is more pertinent is that the concept of deprivation is really too inclusive. It can be used, especially in the social sciences, to cover too many contingencies. Glock and Stark, for example, have suggested five categories of deprivation (Glock & Stark, 1965):

Ideological: the need for a sense of purpose
Ethical: the need for a moral code
Organismic: the needs which arise from physical deficiencies
Social: the need for friendship and communal support
Intellectual: the need for knowledge and self-development

It is argued that deprivation in any one or combination of these areas will almost certainly lead to problems. But it is not always possible to specify the *kind* and *degree* of deprivation. By these criteria we are all deprived in one way or another. The concept of deprivation is also too prescriptive. Like Maslow's 'hierarchy of needs', it is value-loaded and suggests that a clear ranking of needs is possible and/or discernible. The order of needs may well change in different circumstances. Finally, on this point, the concept of deprivation is quite unscientific. Though we know it exists, it is something that is rarely possible to quantify or test to everyone's satisfaction. Furthermore, the concept is not always easy to apply. What are we to make, for instance, of the idea that people turn to religion as a compensation for various kinds of socio-economic deprivation, when we find that religious adherence in the West is strongest among the middle classes where there are fewer *felt* needs?

Secondly, the term has *conflicting subjective/objective implications*. People who do not feel deprived may well be told that they *are* if, say, they have only one car, don't drink Smirnoff, have no sense of class awareness, or whatever. They are not allowed their cosy – and perhaps mistaken – subjective certainties. Instead, they are assured by the respective agencies that they are deprived according to certain arbitrary but controversial criteria. The very idea of need is subject to control and conditioning – so much so, in fact, that 'needs' are artificially created and become so much part of our thinking that we rarely stand back to question them. Psycho-chemical needs such as alcohol, tobacco and sedatives – the accepted social drugs – have been shown to be far more dangerous to society as a whole than the hard drugs which attract so much media attention. Alcohol now contributes to about 40,000 premature deaths in the UK: the nation spends about £17 billion a year on drink (Rutherford, 1988); tobacco, although not so much in demand as it once was, is still a disturbingly popular drug among the young. In the UK, tobacco-related disease kills about 2,000 people a week, about the same number killed in a year by the effects of the bomb dropped on Hiroshima in 1945. It is estimated that this costs the NHS some £200 million a year, a huge figure, but still considerably less than the tobacco industry spends on advertising and sponsorship. And what does it tell us about society in general to learn that Valium is now the most prescribed drug in the world? The extent and degree of drug-dependency in one form or another is impossible to estimate.

We might also mention, while we are about it, those less obvious psycho-social 'needs' which we are told we have, pre-eminently the needs to own and consume – something we are going to consider in more detail. Our society is based upon production and consumption, but are things getting out of hand when we have to have razor-blades that will shave us closer and closer, shampoos that 'moisturise' and 'hold', deodorants for every possible orifice, and sanitary towels that must be worn for the 'whole' month – just to keep us 'fresh'?

The third set of problems relates to the question of need and cause. This is an important theoretical point. Needs may be *associated* with causes, but they should not be confused with them. If we say, for example, that 'good housing reduces the incidence of juvenile delinquency', this does not mean that the 'need' to reduce the incidence of juvenile delinquency has given rise (i.e. caused) the development of good housing. Similarly, the statement 'material prosperity neutralises political insurrection' cannot mean that the need to neutralise political insurrection has 'caused' material prosperity. This is to confuse the origins and development of a thing with the *functions* of a thing – not an uncommon error in the social sciences.

We can see then that the whole idea of needs is subject to a number of very important qualifications, especially those relating to values. Our view of a sense of need is often largely conditioned by those apparently non-reducible values that we tend to regard as part of the natural order of things. Sometimes these can be actually set against each other, for example, hedonism and altruism which are both related to the problem of need and desire. In all societies, people accept certain values *a priori* – they are regarded as being self-evidently true and as enshrining ideals that are worth pursuing. These values have become part of a shared reality within the community, so that even where people flout or ignore them, they are really giving tacit recognition to the existence – even the worthwhileness – of these values. But do people observe or fail to observe these values from rational calculation or instinct? And are those instincts basically ego-centric? Undoubtedly some responses are instinctual. In many situations – even where there is thought to be a clear moral dimension, people still react unthinkingly and do what they have always done in such circumstances – buy a flag for charity, fudge their tax returns, or whatever it happens to be – though this often means that they settle for short-term satisfactions which militate against their long-term interests.

Acquisitiveness, the desire (need?) to possess and the desire to display, appear to be ubiquitous social phenomena. They may be regarded as expressions of hedonism, and are commonly associated with the consumerism of modern industrial societies, but they are actually found in one guise or another in all societies. They are bound up with territoriality and status, and can take quite *non*-rational forms. Bronislau Malinowski, in his classic study of the Trobriand Islands in Melanesia, tells of a practice known as the Kula in which the tribespeople perform a sort of la ronde among the islands exchanging particular sets of red shells for sets of white shells. The interesting thing is that the shells have no intrinsic value, but while any tribal group possesses them that group is accorded special status. It is all rather contrived, but one can see how it serves to maintain a kind of balance between different tribal units (Malinowski, 1922). In its own way this makes more sense than rich connoisseurs who hoard art treasures – which admittedly *do* have an intrinsic value – simply for their personal delectation. But is hedonism the prime motivating fact governing all need and desire? It is doubtful whether people invariably seek their own unadulterated pleasure. They do not always make calculated decisions of a rational self-interested nature, and will often deny themselves for others.

Of course it can always be argued that egoism masquerades as altruism in order to achieve its ends, but would we be aware of the imitation if the genuine article nowhere exists? Can there be counterfeit money without the presence of real money? There are just too many instances of benevolence where there is no obvious benefit to the actor to deny the presence of altruism, much as we may feel that it is in rather short supply these days. But when have things ever been different?

There is a fourth set of problems tangential to our discussion: is the phenomenon of religion also generated by human need, as suggested by Marx and others? The argument is that humans feel alienated in an uncaring world, and are at a loss to explain or account for the puzzling antinomies of their existence in a seemingly friendless universe. They feel that life is therefore empty and purposeless, so they resort to peopling the cosmos with beings of their own creation. Marx, following Feuerbach, maintained that seeing through all this and thus becoming 'fully human' rendered the gods unnecessary. He felt that people simply devise myths as a form of consolation. They bestow a coercive autonomy on these objectified beings and worship them as though they really existed, whereas they represent only (as Freud argued) the subjective unfulfilled longings of inadequate individuals.

There are a number of problems with this thesis, some of which we have already touched upon, but the main one is that if the objects that satisfy religious need do not exist, it is hard to see how the existence of the need to believe *per se* can be properly explained – certainly it is difficult to understand why its fulfilment should take the form it does. It is, therefore, not unreasonable to suggest that the demand for religious faith must be based upon the real nature of things. This does not mean that supramundane beings have to correspond to any ideas that humans may have about them, but it does pose the question, are we so constituted that we can only survive by believing in something that isn't true, or, at least, something that doesn't represent the truth?

Behaviour modification

If, as we have just discussed, need and desire and, therefore, behaviour are conditioned by values and interests, we must ask to what extent that behaviour can be modified. Initially, we can say that there are several ways in which people can be induced to change their patterns of behaviour. Change can be *socially imposed* in that people can be re-socialised in ways which can effect considerable alterations in their way of life. This hardly needs stressing; joining a political or religious organisation, even a club with particular rules and requirements, can bring about a change in attitudes and in behaviour itself. Change can also obviously be brought about by *coercion*, but this may *only* apply to behaviour, not to attitudes. When a conquered people is experiencing pressure from an occupying power, it is often only changes in *behaviour* that take place – rarely is there any change in actual values unless the occupation continues over a very long period (Carlton, 1992). Change can also be *legislated*. This may be seen as coercion, but if done in the right way it is rather more subtle and usually less demanding. This can be seen clearly in the implementation of seat-belt policy. In the UK this was a carrot-and-stick affair that, by and large, has worked quite successfully despite early resistance, because drivers and passengers came to see it as generally beneficial. The promotional campaigns convinced the majority; and eventually – with time – old habits were forgotten, the new routines of 'belting-up' became instinctive and unquestioned: what was imposed has now come to be seen as normal, common-sense behaviour.

Change can also be *psychologically induced*, notably by a method or series of techniques, collectively designated Behaviourism, that have generated considerable controversy and hostility in recent years. Behaviourists have, to some extent, been joined by the Learning theorists who maintain that behaviour may be modified by changing the conditions in which it is expressed. These ideas, which were developed in the 1920s and particularly the 1930s, in fact have quite a long pedigree. The Roman writer Pliny the Elder described some proto-behaviourist methods of curing alcoholism, ranging from physical punishments to the simple expedient of putting spiders in the bottom of drinkers' wine-cups – really a form of primitive aversion therapy. As a modern scientific theory, Behaviourism is associated with Ivan Sechener (d. 1904) who argued that all animal and human acts are reflexive. Sechener consistently applied these ideas even to intellectual and artistic achievements because he took the radical view that thought itself was an inhibited reflex. He believed that philosophical deliberation should give way to rigorous experimentation, because for him human action was not volitional; willed action was an illusion.

Perhaps the best known name in this field is still that of Ivan Pavlov (1849-1936). Pavlov was originally a physiologist who gained the Nobel Prize in 1904 for his work on the physiology of digestion, and it was not until his middle years that he turned to psychology. While he was studying the digestive glands of dogs, he discovered that the animals actually salivated *before* the food was given – indeed as soon as they heard the footsteps of those that came to feed them. After further experimentation, he developed the theories of the *conditioned (primary) stimulus*, i.e. the naturally elicited reflex, in this case the sight or smell of food, which might be anticipated by the *unconditioned (secondary) stimulus*, which might be almost anything, a light or sound which could eventually be made to elicit the response itself. He found too that even *tertiary conditioning* was possible, say recognition of a colour, which was only obliquely related to the secondary stimulus. This involved the power of association, but there were limits to associative responses, though in humans *recollection* can be quite a potent adjunct of association. In general, unless there was *reinforcement*, a secondary or tertiary stimulus could lose its strength (extinction), although it might still be revived by using the appropriate techniques.

Pavlov contended that these phenomena were subject to *generalisation* and *discrimination*. The effects of a general stimulus might break down if the stimulus was presented in an unfamiliar or distorted way. The subject 'filters' the stimulus in a discriminating way and either accepts or rejects it. So, for example, we find that kittens who are reared with white mice will often not kill them, but as cats, when fully grown, they will attack brown mice. Neuroses may result if the stimuli are introduced in such a way as to confuse the subject. This can be done by alternating positive and negative stimuli; one can see this, for example, with inconsistency in the disciplining of children. Intensifying the stimulus or increasing/decreasing the time between the stimulus and its 'reward' can be very effective, as can also providing stimuli which cannot produce the intended response, as when children/adults are given tasks which are definitely beyond their capacity to complete. Such techniques come into the category of what is loosely called 'brain-washing'. They neutralise the capacity for discrimination and reduce or eliminate the subject's ability to make correct judgements or predictions (Sargant, 1959). In its most extreme form, by generating a sense of uncertainty and unpredictability, brain-washing can render the subject incapable of ordering any kind of consistent reality.

B.F. Skinner and H.J. Eysenck have modified the earlier and more questionable forms of Behaviourism by de-emphasising crude classical conditioning, and stressing instead what is called *operant conditioning*, i.e. conditioning related to results. The underlying assumption here is that stimuli in the real world – the world outside the laboratory – may be too complex to analyse or control or predict. Naturally, a stimulus is subject to certain conditions. There must be both *recency* and *frequency* of stimulus application for the process to be effective. This can be seen particularly well in TV advertising where the same very expensive advertisement may be screened three or four times in one evening. Modern Behaviourists have laid a greater emphasis on *reinforcement* and *rewards*, on effects rather than causes. Reinforcers can be positive (rewards, privileges, etc.) or negative, which usually means the withholding or withdrawing of rewards as a punishment – a practice found in many Detention Centres. They can also be intermittent or continuous or fixed or variable: what matters is that they have been introduced as factors in motivation.

Of course the connection between a stimulus and a reward may be purely adventitious, as when lucky charms appear to 'work'. In a way, this can be detected in the commercial world. Think for a moment about the insidious nature of tobacco and alcohol advertising which 'connects' consumption with youth, wealth, glamour, etc. (one popular cigarette advertisement in *Time* magazine showed a young couple wandering on a sun-drenched beach which promised idyllic privacy and sexual possibilities). Well-known but slightly up-market alcohol advertisements imply that it is the smart set that indulge, and that *this* brand is enjoyed by those on the route to achievement and success. Any *actual* success 'validates' the advertisers' claims. This is an example of Skinner's programmed 'superstitious behaviour'. Advertisers use the technique of 'shaping', i.e. choosing from a repertoire of reinforcers (inducements) those that work in given circumstances (pragmatic promotion).

Behaviourists, then, are saying that given the application of the appropriate stimuli, there would be the appropriate and, they hope, predictable responses. But this can fail if the long-term goals are not clearly determined in advance. One can see such ideas in practice within the context of a total institution such as a prison because here there is (a) an established regulative system with controls and sanctions; (b) a way of ensuring that these conditions are set and stable, i.e. there can be no change in the possible stimuli; and (c) a tariff of rewards and punishments to confirm (reinforce) behaviour. These act as incentives and therefore – in theory, at least – generate the correct motivations.

Convincing as some of these ideas appear to be, they are open to a good deal of criticism.

(1) *The negative-positive response problem*: a certain stimulus will produce a certain reaction, but can effective controls ensure which form the reaction takes? For example a TV advertisement – especially if it is singularly moronic and repetitive – may make some viewers determined *not* to buy that particular product. A negative reaction is generated every time the commercial is shown. Pressure to buy can well evoke mistrust of the product itself. Perhaps there is no such thing as *a* stimulus. There are different stimuli and reinforcers for different people for different situations. Suppose that the stimulus is a 'Rambo'-type film; it is extremely difficult to predict just how anyone in the audience will react, or to know if they would have reacted differently on a different occasion. In very few cases, the reaction may be one of *imitation*; perhaps a high proportion will not copy but quietly admire the qualities displayed by their hero(es); perhaps it will be by *sublimation* – some will choose other ways of exercising their emotions; or it may be that the reaction of many may be *denigration*, ridicule or even disgust. There is no sure way of knowing just how any one person will respond.

(2) *The efficiency versus enjoyment issue*: Skinner has shown empirically that his techniques can work, for example, with some mental health patients by timing (restricting) their access to dining halls; and with delinquents by controlling their environments. For example, at the Robert Kennedy Youth Centre at West Virginia, 'patients' were awarded points for positive acts such as picking up their books, and with these they could 'purchase' benefits such as a private room, their own TV, etc. But in some such centres, e.g. one relatively recently established in the UK where the

ratio is two staff to one 'patient', each of whom costs the tax payer about £35,000 per year, the results have not been so impressive. The drain in resources can be very considerable in these homes, where the inmates are so undisciplined that they can destroy property without due restraint. They lose points, of course, but this doesn't seem to concern them greatly – they are obviously determined to enjoy their delinquency.

Skinner has also made much of the introduction of learning techniques into the educational establishment for subjects such as Mathematics. Here the student is praised by the computer for the successful completion of set projects. The only snag with this is that it has been found that after a while these pedagogic innovations wear thin. The process is regarded by many as solitary and boring; admittedly computers are efficient, but the novelty has a limited appeal. Talk-and-chalk may be old-fashioned but, if it is well done, it does at least continually engage the student's attention. The trouble with so much programmed learning is that the machine is under the student's singular control and can therefore allow him to relax or turn off whenever he pleases. Basically it is an undisciplined approach for those who are not that anxious to please.

(3) *The control versus freedom issue*: one of the commonest accusations levelled at Behaviourism is that where it should be using its techniques to further understanding and prediction, it can be – and perhaps is – used to promote increased control in society. Psychology, particularly in its Behaviourist form, probably has more success in the *mechanics of control* than in the actual explanation of human action (Louch, 1966, p. 36). Skinner is altogether sceptical of democracy, and insists that conventional education and training are not making for a better (i.e. more ordered/stable) society. Perhaps this is a little unfair, but one can see shades of *Nineteen Eighty-Four* and *Brave New World* in the mind-manipulation techniques that are to be found in greater and lesser forms in so many societies. Arthur Koestler, one of Behaviourism's most bitter critics, has suggested that it is nothing more than a pseudo-science – a monumental but dangerous triviality – that has sent psychology back into a modern version of the Dark Ages because it has abandoned mind and imagination.

(4) *The creativity problem*: the linguistic specialist, Noam Chomsky, has asked how it is that we can ever do what we have not specifically learned such as sentence construction? He maintains that Behaviourism cannot account for the act of creation. If all is stimulus and response, what precipitates the conceptual leap? (Lyons, 1970).

(5) *The question of values*: unlike non-humans, people are motivated by deeply-held values. Can these possibly be erased or altered by simply modifying the stimuli as Behaviourism implies? The evidence, for example, of many captured American GIs in Korea suggests not. Where the values are not deeply held, a subtle reiteration of a new or different value may be effective, but there can be no fundamental or lasting character change if

the values in question are, or have become, a basic element of the personality.

We may, then, draw certain conclusions about Behaviourism. Its fundamental assumption is that all behaviour is *learned*, and therefore, by definition, all behaviour can be *un*learned – using the appropriate techniques. We therefore have to decide whether these techniques work, and if they do, what is their proper application? Then, from a moral point of view, we must ask whether they should be employed in the first place.

Although Behaviourism is very pre-occupied by the possibilities of behaviour-modification, its techniques are not to be equated with brainwashing, although brain-washing is a form of behaviour-modification. Behaviourist techniques have a reasonably sound experimental basis, though in some ways the concentration on effects rather than causes has sometimes made them appear to be (a) superficial, in that they do not always seem to be addressing the 'real' problems, and (b) trivial and even banal. Linda Davidoff cites the case of Robert, a child who had recently recovered from a long illness and who had become impossible at bed-time. The family took the view that he could not be left, and decided to look after him on a shift basis. Eventually, a Behaviourist was brought in and he advocated leaving the child in a 'relaxed' fashion and when he screamed to ignore him. Unsurprisingly, this worked. But is this any more than applied common-sense? (Davidoff, 1980, pp. 152-3)

The techniques certainly have commercial applications, e.g. in advertising, though they are not unambiguously successful. On the other hand, they have proved to be quite effective in some para-medical areas such as sexual dysfunction involving controversial therapies, and in the alleviation of some health conditions such as asthma, hypertension, etc.

We must give some credence to Behaviourism, and realise that its practitioners and devotees are not quite as academically hidebound as some of their critics make out (e.g. Heather, 1976). For example, a modern behaviourist, David Broadbent, has indicated that the merit of objective (experimental) study is that it provides a means of testing intuitive knowledge (Joynson, 1974, p. 33). Others, such as N.E. Miller and Hans Eysenck – although experimentalists – are actually quite close to the Cognitivists in certain respects. Eysenck gives considerable credence to attitudes and values in his own research questionnaires, and even Skinner is ready to acknowledge such matters as feelings, intentions, and so forth, but tends to discount them as *causes* of human behaviour. Skinner has expressed concerns about the nature (possibility?) of the ideal society, but the logical problem concerns the sources of the standards of good and evil in that society. Who decides what constitutes pleasure and pain, reward and punishment? We are back with Plato – who controls the controllers? It really amounts to this: the behaviourists are willing to admit the 'presence' of the phenomena that concern more humanistic psychologists but they do not give them the same *meanings* or credit them with the same *relevance* as others (Broadbent, 1974). No matter how objective tests and experiments appear to be, the respondents invariably interpret their experiences and impressions in mentalistic (i.e. subjective) terms.

It doesn't take very much to see some of the moral problems posed by Behaviourism. The laws that govern behaviour modification are neutral in themselves, but people fear their possible applications whether it be in the hands of the unscrupulous, as in the engineered 'confessions' in the so-called Soviet treason trials of the 1930s (Conquest, 1990), or as a less insidious adjunct of the advertising industry. Moral values tend to be ignored or conveniently rationalised when political and economic interests are at stake.

Excursus II. Science, sociology and the paranormal

Having touched on the subject of the paranormal (UFOs, religion, etc.) a little earlier, it is perhaps permissible to look at it in some more depth, and ask whether parapsychology, the study of the paranormal, is a science, a pseudo-science or a supra-science? Parapsychology had been regarded by many as at best misguided, and at worst as the pursuit of tricksters and charlatans. The view that it is, in fact, a kind of fledgling science is only now being seriously entertained. In the last thirty years or so, many scientists have shown an increasing open-mindedness on the subject of extra-sensory perception (ESP), and have given greater credence to the apparent human capacity for the paranormal experience (PSI).

Parapsychology involves the study of a wide variety of phenomena which are not amenable to normal scientific investigation. These range from psychical investigations of mediumistic activities, ghosts, poltergeists, apparitions and out-of-body experiences, all of which are held by some to support the survivalist hypothesis, to research into telepathy and clairvoyance, and even to such fringe phenomena as unidentified flying objects. The allegation that ESP is preoccupied with the far-out and the bizarre has given rise to a growing concentration on controlled experiments, which have at least a gloss of scientific respectability (Mauskopf & McVaugh, 1980). In the 'trade' there has been a great deal of debate as to exactly what the term ESP should signify. As it stands, it has a number of not always compatible connotations. It may be regarded as prejudiced in that it is thought to relate vaguely to phenomena 'outside of the senses' (Neppe, 1984), yet, at the same time, it is said to be radical in that it does not appear to allow for alternative explanations in terms of physiologically based mechanisms. Furthermore it is judgmental in that it implies a form of unconscious communication or perception which is not conducive to other accepted modes of cognition. It can also be seen as anachronistic in as much as it is antagonistic to modern conceptions of psychobiology and self-regulation. Obviously, some observers would welcome a more neutral term which allows for the possibility of naturalistic explanations which, as yet, have not been convincingly formulated or generally accepted. Perhaps a suitable working definition would be that ESP concerns 'information acquired about the external world other than through any of the known sensory channels' (Beloff, 1977). This allows for hypotheses which are consonant with accepted scientific parameters while, at the same time, leaving the door open for explanations of a more speculative kind.

The problem of definition immediately raises the whole question of parapsychology as a science. The natural sciences are usually taken as the models of what a 'proper' science should be; but should a science be defined in terms of its aims, its methods, or its content? Scientific investigation, as normally understood, involves the classification of materials, the framing of testable hypotheses, and the capacity for measurements, verification and prediction. Such criteria inevitably raise doubts when applied to parapsychological research. Furthermore, the entire issue of the control and repeatability of experiments, which is particularly pertinent to parapsychological investigation, is very much open to question. Indeed, where attempts are being made to establish the reality of paranormal phenomena, it is disputable whether the usual scientific canons of evidentiality are even appropriate.

The key problem is that paranormal phenomena rarely conform to regular patterns. They are usually spontaneous, and occur without prior planning or preparation for observation, control and experimentation. Researchers have to depend upon the *witnesses* to these phenomena to describe as carefully as possible what they believe occurred – something which is very evident, for example, in numerous UFO reports. Indeed, it is only after all the evidence has been analysed and all normal explanations have been rejected, that the judgement can be made that a particular phenomenon can be reasonably categorised as paranormal. In most cases there is inadequate supporting evidence, and it has been estimated that out of every 100 reports received, only one or two are found to be worthy of publication (Ashby, 1972).

It could be convincingly argued that the problem of scientific credibility is even more acute for parapsychology than for other 'marginal' pursuits, as in, say, the behavioural sciences. Paranormal concerns are so outré that they probably require *more* evidential support than orthodox investigations; their very implausibility makes them that much more suspect. It is a matter of record that many claims to the possession and exercise of PSI have been shown to be fraudulent, and in a number of notable instances, controversy still rages as to whether particular individuals have this capacity or not. Similar mysteries surround the activities of even the best known mediums. Indeed many mediums have undermined their own claims by their unwillingness to consent to scientific examination under controlled conditions. Nevertheless, there are still some remarkable unexplained cases (Gregory, 1985).

The 'paranormal' covers a very wide range of phenomena which may be simplistically classified as either physical or mental, and the documentary or witness evidence which is held to support either type may be flawed for several combinations of reasons. There are questions about the quality and quantity of the witnesses themselves involving problems of reliability and faulty recollections; there is the matter too of the conditions in which the incident(s) occurred which may preclude accurate reporting; and then there is the interpretation of the data, which is often no easy matter. Such phenomena are normally neither repeatable nor statistically measurable; they are not always controllable, and are rarely free from some degree of – albeit unconscious – human bias or error. To complicate matters further, reports are often subject to sensationalism and trivialisation and – as we have seen – they can provide the basis for downright fraud and deception. It is therefore little wonder that the whole grey area of the paranormal is treated with some scepticism by the scientific community. Consequently, this has resulted in a move away from anecdotal reports and witness-dependency generally to an increasing reliance on controlled laboratory experiments which, it is hoped, will give parapsychology a greater scientific respectability (McConnell, 1983).

The intriguing debate concerning what is science and what is pseudo-science, especially in relation to parapsychology and its associated themes, is related to the more general discussion about science *per se*, and the emergence of a new order of 'companion sciences' such as the behavioural and social sciences. Any aspiring science will be assessed by the standards of scientific conventionality. All disciplines have their own 'reception systems', and the scientific community is no exception. A reception system constitutes the criteria whereby one discipline, in this case science, judges an alien or intrusive discipline to be worthy of consideration either of inclusion or simply of credence. Parapsychology makes implicit and explicit demands for recognition, if not for actual acceptance. How, then, is it received?

There are two reception models which may help us to conceptualise the problem (de Grazia, 1978). The first we may call the *rationalistic model*. This represents the position of scientific orthodoxy with its emphasis on scientific method as the exclusive determinant of scientific development. 'Truth' – as we have seen – is arrived at by empirical procedures based upon the verification principle. The stress is on controls, quantification and prediction. All findings must be open to investigation and falsification, and these should be available for applications which are themselves a form of further validation of the procedures employed.

In relation to parapsychology, this model of positivistic orthodoxy is well represented by the eminent scientist Francis Crick, Nobel prize-winner in 1962 (with James Watson) for his work on the structure of DNA. Crick writes, 'The most striking thing about the work of the last thirty years on ESP has been its complete failure to produce any technique whatsoever which is scientifically acceptable ... Not one truly reproducible experiment has been devised although the record is thick with fakes and sloppy experimentation ... We must conclude either that the phenomenon does not exist or that it is too difficult to study by present methods ...' (Crick, 1973).

By implication, therefore, a discipline such as parapsychology must remain suspect; it is not actually outlawed because much as it respects the scientific approach, it also holds to the possibility of other, extra sources of knowledge.

Publication and investigation are also constituent parts of this model. Science is a communication system for the advancement of truth. Findings must therefore be made available for critical comment. (To some extent the superordinate nature of the discipline can be seen in the international conferences of Soviet and US scientists where the unifying ideology of science will sometimes supersede that of the political system.) Honesty and fairness are enjoined within the intellectual community, as is also radical innovation and open discussion. The assumption is that science is a universal medium of exchange, a known conceptual universe, which can be appraised by all who have the requisite academic training and are tutored in the correct scientific codes.

This has several implications for parapsychology. By definition, much that is subsumed by the term 'paranormal' is outside the scientific orbit of debate. Its theories are not always open to validation and its assumptions are largely *a priori* and unfalsifiable. Of course, they are open to a level of discussion, but even this is circumscribed because scientific language – the recognised mode of discourse – is not accessible to the uninitiated. Yet, despite this, the *concerns* of parapsychology – as opposed to the *methods* whereby these concerns are addressed – are in a real sense open to all. In fact, it might be said that they have a universal and simplistic appeal. The questions they raise are not difficult to understand. Indeed, given their ubiquity in all ages and in all cultures, unlike the closed esoterica of science, they have a common experiential currency.

The rationalistic model must also include the question of acceptability by the scientific establishment. There will be an understandable reluctance to accept anything that threatens the scientific community. Everything will therefore depend upon the credentials of the intrusive discipline. Competing cognitive systems will not simply be judged on the basis of their 'truth' or otherwise; their explanatory possibilities are not the sole criteria for acceptability. What also matters is whether or not they disturb the academic status quo; if the verities of the scientific community are questioned, the establishment may well unite to resist innovation. Theoretically, they are open to challenge, but in practice there is a reluctance to disturb the air of canonical certainty. Parapsychology presents science with a countervailing or, at least, complementary ideology. It is doubtful whether it can ever be fully accepted because it undermines orthodox science as a total – or potentially total – explanatory system.

In considering the relative imperviousness of the scientific establishment, it is worth noting that many respected academics have been traditionally associated with parapsychology, from philosophers such as Henry Sidgwick and C.D. Broad to medical practitioners such as D.J. West, and natural scientists such as A.J. Ellison and Sir Alister Hardy. But esteemed as these and many other devotees are, they still only represent a tiny minority, and their views – which are by no means unanimous – are little more than tolerated eccentricities. Their voices are insistent but hardly strident, and, as such, are unlikely to disturb the entrenched positions of the scientific hierarchy.

The second reception model may be termed the *indeterminacy model*. This is quite a different kind of construct in that in it there are no prescribed scientific procedures, only 'creative hypotheses'. Science fiction, magic and the occult, astrology, and certainly parapsychology, all find their place alongside logico-empirical acts and procedures. 'Success', as such, is largely a question of popularisation and chance; what really matters is the creation of an intellectual environment from which practical accomplishment emerges. The system is 'open'; everything is feasible. Meanings about the 'state' of the universe are extended and simplified, joining the pool with other cosmological possibilities such as, say, Hoyle's panspermia thesis concerning the origins of life on Earth (Hoyle, 1983).

In such a model, where there are no certain rules, people order their own realities. The phenomena that are the concern of parapsychology cannot, therefore, be lightly dismissed, and the hypotheses which are provisionally held to account for them can be included among the melée of contenders for 'meanings' and explanation. But their reception will still not be easy because the overarching claims of scientific orthodoxy will almost certainly relegate them to supernumerary status. As one writer has ably put it, 'So long as the pursuit of psychical research is given neither the economic resources nor the basic academic respect that any field of knowledge needs in order to flourish, it cannot possibly flow and develop like a subject not in that predicament' (Gregory, 1983).

Not only are parapsychologists on the defensive vis-à-vis their physical science counterparts, they are also rather wary of those social/behavioural scientists who – one might think – would be more favourably disposed to their endeavours. Indeed, it is not uncommon for them to be accused of not really getting to the heart of the matter and minimising the real significance of the paranormal. This is reminiscent of the somewhat analogous reactions by some theologians to sociological studies of religion. They maintain that many sociologists rarely display any true appreciation of the content of religion, and that they are merely skirting the subject when they concentrate simply on the social determinants of religious *forms*, and ignore the implications of belief. A similar kind of essentialist apprehension is often very evident among parapsychologists who allege that socio-logists, *qua* sociologists, have little real understanding of what ESP is all about, and are simply trivialising it by their 'investigations' (Gratten-Guinness, 1985).

These suspicions are even more evident – indeed, justified – when the social scientists in question are markedly relativistic in their approach to parapsychology. By the very nature of their training they find the tendency to reduce parapsychological phenomena to psychological states or social circumstances virtually unavoidable. A case in point would be the very interesting work on 'entity' phenomena and UFOs by Hilary Evans (Evans, 1984). Here the author has adopted a Kuhnian stance and argues that belief in the paranormal is not primarily a matter of evidence and objective evaluation, but is largely influenced (determined?) by cultural factors such as political and religious ideologies, and the prevailing ethos of accept-ability in the societies concerned. Evans maintains that psychic pheno-mena are largely rejected by science for much the same reasons that they are ignored by the public generally. New ideas must accord with the normative expectations of intellectual elites in particular and society in general. A further issue raised by Evans' work is that of the disparities not just between parapsychologists and others, but between contending para-psychologists who can be just as reactionary about unsettling findings within their own subject area. The cognoscenti themselves are not always agreed about what can and cannot be explained naturalistically, or even what is or is not to be regarded as suitable material for investigation. It is, therefore, hardly surprising that their critics often have a field-day at the expense of this fascinating but uncertain discipline, which after all these years is still struggling for recognition.

This entire issue is vitiated by the problem of knowledge. How is knowledge derived, fashioned and authenticated? Presumably it must derive from experiment and experience, but what *counts* as 'knowledge' is very much a social construct. 'New' knowledge or 'proper' knowledge will be conditioned by the intellectual ethos of the culture concerned. The climate of opinion will influence the generation and reception of new knowledge and – not least of all – the mode of legitimation of that knowledge. Cognition is a social concern, and the entire issue of plausibility is bound up with social acceptability. Certainly what was regarded as valid knowledge was once culturally relative, but with increasing convergence the dominant paradigms of science are coming to be regarded as the only legitimate forms of knowledge.

This all raises an interesting and contentious issue. Is there a highly qualified sense in which all knowledge – and implicitly all values – can be seen as objective? In what senses can they have meaning and rationality? There are three related positions or perspectives that can be taken here. The first is that explanation is elusive simply because we are confronted with the problem of conflicting rationalities, different frames of meaning which are 'true' in their respective ways for those who formulate them. Different theorists are locked into their own paradigms which, in effect, comprise a set of incommensurable logics. Yet these have their distinctive rationalities no matter how bizarre or extreme they may appear. So, for instance, witchcraft – although having little appeal for the modern western realist – becomes a closed and unassailable system for those prepared to accept its basic presuppositions. This comes dangerously close to maintaining that any thought-system which has its own internal coherence must qualify for social recognition. Needless to say, this could encompass such questionable pursuits as, say, astrology or scientology, and is reminiscent of some defensive treatments of theology where attempts are made to present an apologia for theology as a legitimate scientific enterprise simply because it can claim to frame and use its own categories. This independent rationalities position is also endorsed by those who advocate an extreme social reductionism in terms of 'self-contained socio-cognitive systems' (Collins & Pinch, 1982). Substantially, such theorists are arguing that different people have different meaning-systems, and as long as these make explanatory sense to those who endorse them, then, *ipso facto*, they have their own special kind of validity.

The second position maintains that 'truth' is not so much paradigmatic as relative. This can mean relative to social experience – like Durkheim – where collective social life determines all modes of cognition, or it can mean relative to *differences* in social experience – like Marx – which are conditioned ultimately by the pattern of socio-economic relations. Such views are restrictive for the sorts of reasons we have already considered. Not only can total relativism run the risk of total anarchy, it can – under given conditions – run the even greater risk of endorsing a form of doctrinal tyranny. The third position, which is really a variant of the first, is simply that all 'truth' is complementary. All knowledge is valuable; different perspectives incorporate a range of useful insights. Perhaps all are partly right – so no one can really lose. Thus parapsychology is not to be seen as a discrete paradigm, but as an additional avenue to understanding and explanation.

A reasonably impartial consideration of the evidence suggests that parapsychology is best seen in terms of a complementary perspective. It is not an alternative to orthodox science because it does not encroach upon the scientific preserve or presume to pronounce on matters outside its particular sphere of competence, although – as we have seen – orthodox science, understandably, ventures into ESP territory not only to verify its procedures but also to explain paranormal phenomena naturalistically. Parapsychologists are prepared for this and often actually welcome it as a necessary preliminary exercise. Indeed, where possible, they are wholly in favour of utilising the methods and technology of science if this will help to further their own investigations. But, essentially, they are exploring a dimension of experience which is largely outside the scope of accepted scientific parameters. They are using increasingly sophisticated techniques to investigate age-old concerns. Despite the present uncertain currency of their findings and the recognised limits of their success, they are at least addressing themselves to what many regard as intriguing and fundamental issues.

Whatever the scientific status of parapsychology, it interests itself in some important facets of man's perennial quest. The reductionist sciences portrayed humans as little more than passive automata, a view that was encouraged by the emergent activities of the behavioural psychologists. But this approach will no longer do. People are moving away from purely mechanistic orientations, and groping for new syntheses and new meanings (Koestler & Smythies, 1970). We are still confronted by the fundamental question of being. A cognitive vacuum still remains. Natural science – as we now understand it – will only take us so far, and behavioural science can only complement this by examining the phenomenological implications of the problem. In all this, parapsychology surely has a place. To rephrase Marx: 'Science has changed the world, the problem now is to understand it.'

4

How Can Values Be Studied?

In this section of our discussion we are going to ask two questions:

(1) What exactly is an ethical statement?
(2) By what criteria can we make ethical judgements?

An ethical statement is a proposition that incorporates moral values. And in any discussion of ethical statements we must bear in mind the basic distinction between substantive statements – those which refer to what is factual, empirical and thus verifiable – and normative statements which concern that which is thought desirable and obligatory – those things which we think *ought* to be. Related to this is the distinction between fact and value. If I say, 'That man is a bank clerk', this is simply a statement of fact, but if I then add, 'Being a bank clerk is very dull work', I am proffering an opinion which is really a statement of value. It is not uncommon for this kind of statement to be confused with statements of fact, indeed, advertising thrives on such a confusion. A further distinction of which we must be aware is a variant of the fact-value dichotomy, namely, the distinction between aesthetic and moral judgements. This entails the possible failure to distinguish between subjective opinion (a) what *I* like, and subjective opinion (b) what I like is good, and subjective opinion (c) what I like is good and therefore others should like or must learn to like it too. This kind of preference statement is a form of psychologism. It is very similar to the tendency to generalise from a particular. A person may say 'I am (or I think I should be) a teetotaller'. Does this mean that others should not drink either? Pontifical as it sounds, it is understandably difficult for those of us who feel that particular disciplines such as healthy eating, exercise and abstemiousness are desirable, not to want to impose such rigours on others.

One last point on this matter of moral judgements. There are those who feel that we should not make judgements about others' behaviour, although, in practice, most of us find this very difficult to do. Much depends on whether we are making moral judgements or judgements of a substantive nature, say a person's suitability for a post. The idea that we must abide by the rule to 'judge not that ye be not judged' is often misunderstood. We tend to forget how the quotation continues: 'lest with what judgement ye judge, ye shall be judged'. In other words, if we are going to judge the behaviour or opinions of others, we must be prepared to be judged ourselves *by the same criteria.*

When we ask how values – particularly moral values – can be studied, we are, by implication, asking by what criteria we can make ethical judgements. Thus we must start by looking at the main types of ethical theory. The texts distinguish between *teleological theories*, which stress the consequences of action (i.e. how much good or otherwise will result from this action? – this is the sort of problem we will encounter with Utilitarianism) and *deontological theories*, which emphasise the intrinsic nature of the act (i.e. that acts should be good in themselves, and not necessarily designed or carried out to achieve some purpose).

Another way to approach the problem of analysis is to distinguish between subjectivist and consensus theories of ethics. Subjectivist theories focus upon individual responses, upon personal evaluations. This might involve some deprecation or repudiation of society's norms, and even a degree of selective moral deviancy, though usually it merely indicates no more than a quiet and not very effective intellectual departure from the 'rules'. In practice, one finds that such subjectivism finds expression in nothing more offensive than mild cultural eccentricities. Indeed, it is questionable just how personal these personal moralities actually are. Non-conformists have a disillusioning habit of getting together with other non-conformists and thus conforming to the vaguely alternative codes of a recognised sub-culture. We are therefore going to look at two 'philosophies' of a subjectivist type, namely Emotivism and Existentialism. In their own ways, these act as justifications of the subjectivist bases for making ethical judgements.

Both Emotivism and Existentialism are naturalistic in their approach to ethics. Naturalists maintain that moral values can be reduced to non-moral terms. That is to say, certain acts, say acts of violence, can be interpreted – even explained – in terms of biochemical reactions, or psychological states, or social circumstances, or whatever, and imply that people are not entirely responsible for their actions.

The problem for Naturalists is that if a moral value is seen to derive from another 'source' – say, our biochemical natures (x^1) – how can this then be reconciled with those who insist that it is merely a conditioned psychological response (x^2)? So can violence be seen in terms of x^1 or x^2, or, for that matter, x^3 or x^4 and so on? To complicate the matter further we find in practice that $x^1 \neq x^2 \neq x^3$, etc., in other words the x's are incompatible. Add to this the fact that the value in question may be such a complex phenomenon that even a sum total of the x's (Σx) may not exhaust the meaning or significance of the value, and the investigation reaches an intellectual impasse. Consequently, Non-Naturalists argue that moral values are not reducible in this way, and that values can only ultimately be interpreted in terms of themselves. We will see this more clearly when we come to discuss Moral Relativism.

Emotivism and its critics

Emotivism has a long pedigree stemming notably from the eminent philosopher David Hume (1711-1776), although it was anticipated to some extent in the work of the early Greek writer and politician, Protagoras, who was a contemporary of Plato. Emotivists maintain that all acts possess only those qualities which we *assign* to them, and that these are assessed in terms of emotion rather than reason. They argue that when people make moral judgements, they believe themselves to be talking about the quality of the acts in question, but in reality they are talking about their feelings in relation to those acts. Hume, in particular, argued that it was an error to think of morals as though they were self-evident because it is not possible to establish their truth or falsity. His conclusions, followed perhaps by most Emotivists, were based upon the following arguments:

(1) Moral values are not subject to verification by experiment or even by reflection. One cannot 'prove', say, that murder is wrong in the same way that $2 + 2 = 4$.

(2) Self-evident arguments for morals cannot account for preference. If murder is so obviously wrong, why have there been societies/individuals who have equally obviously thought that it was right?

(3) Reasoning about these issues can only apply to the *facts* upon which so-called moral judgements are made. Facts can be disputed, and are rightly subject to verification of some kind. But reason alone cannot lead to moral judgements because these are matters of value – indeed, of *opinion* not fact.

(4) Moral judgements then are merely matters of approval or disapproval. To use Hume's terms, they are expressions of 'disinterested passions'. He argued that morality has no *intrinsic* properties, only those properties that we *assign* to it. So there is no objective 'good' or 'bad', only those acts we designate as such.

(5) It follows from this that the institutionalised forms of morality which we call conventions are approved because of their *social utility*. Morality exists because people are disposed to do that which is socially useful. But here we have departed from uncomplicated emotional reaction; reason has been introduced. How else are we going to decide what is or is not socially useful. How is this determined? By a consensus? And if so, how is opinion formed and how are social values structured? These are issues which are particularly pertinent, say, to the study of war and politics and have serious implications for the problem of military action.

One of the most respected modern philosophers, Bertrand Russell, although very critical of Hume in certain respects (Russell, 1948), is a true successor in his Emotivist views. Early in the century in some of his essays he maintained that moral judgements were subjective and variable, but conceded that difficulties in discovering truth did not prove that there was no moral truth to be discovered. Many years later, in his studies of science and religion, his views appear to have changed. He said that he felt that there was no way of deciding between differences of value, and concluded that it must all be simply a matter of taste. In writing about punishment of crime, for instance, he asserted that it cannot be justified on the grounds that the criminal has done something 'wrong', only on the basis that he has done something which should be 'discouraged' (Ginsberg, 1965, p. 24).

Having been a conscientious objector in the First World War, Russell came to see the war against Nazism as a virtual crusade, and in his post-Second World War writings his Emotivist views were seriously modified. He said that he found it difficult to believe that opinions about Nazi persecutions were analogous to opinions about 'eating oysters'. In other words, it wasn't just a matter of taste. He went on to say that this feeling of difference – though not decisive – deserves respect and 'should make us reluctant to accept that all ethical judgements are wholly subjective' (quoted by Ginsberg, 1965). He has had to admit that atrocities have an entirely different quality – a *moral* quality, that marks them off from matters of aesthetic taste.

A more recent and particularly eminent exponent of the Emotivist position was Sir Alfred Ayer, who regarded moral propositions as merely 'pseudo concepts', i.e. expressions of feeling associated with the act (Ayer, 1946). So to say 'He killed that man' is a statement that can be confirmed or disconfirmed on the basis of the evidence. It is a potentially factual statement. But to say 'He was wrong to kill that man' has for Ayer no factual meaning. It is merely an expression of disapproval – it is neither true nor false. Questions of facts can be disputed, but moral disputation is meaningless because it permits of no conclusive (i.e. objective) answers.

There are a number of ways in which we can criticise this approach to ethics, and show that there is something more to morality than mere approval and disapproval. To begin with, if moral approbation is just a matter of feeling, how can it be distinguished from other feelings? And what if our psychological makeup is such that we are – or have become – insensitive to particular feelings, and are therefore unmoved by violations of certain kinds? Does this mean that we are not guilty of psychopathic acts and that we cannot therefore be held accountable for our deeds? There is ample evidence that this was the experience of a number of guards at the Nazi extermination camps. At first they were physically sickened by their work, but gradually it become a morally numbing routine.

A further difficulty for Emotivists is the chicken-and-egg problem of which comes first, the emotional reaction or the rational discernment that something is right or wrong? The mind needs experiences to provide it with occasions in which it can recognise that of which it approves or disapproves. Few would dispute that moral facts cause moral emotion, but if there is no *prior recognition* of the facts, why the emotion? So in the case of atrocity, either witnessed or reported, specific emotions accompany the moral judgement, but the emotion itself is not the judgement, nor need it invalidate the judgement. Undoubtedly, Emotivists make judgements too subjective. What happens when there are different shades of feeling about a particular act? Can it be equally right and wrong depending on the emotional reactions of the observer? Surely reasoning – *moral* reasoning? – must play some part? After all, if a crime has been committed, we would normally expect *reasons* to be given either to condemn or to exonerate, or – failing that – just to understand what had taken place.

We are faced with real problems if we take the view that moral reasoning is simply a product of the emotions. What of those complex situations where the reason and emotions are actually in conflict? Where people have done things out of emotion that they afterwards come to regret? Even more confusing is the situation at, for example, My Lai in Vietnam, where American troops carried out an atrocity on the basis of one set of reasons which some have now come to question on the basis of a quite different set of reasons.

One of the most important issues raised by Emotivism is that of the relativism of values. Emotivists take the view that values are conditioned by cultures. What is right in one culture may well be wrong in another. So moral responsibility is directly related to one's perception of the situation. It follows, therefore, that there are no objective values, nothing that is right and wrong for all time regardless of opinion. This is a very persuasive view and appears to accord with common experience, but it is open to several lines of criticism. First, the relativist position is infinitely regressive. If a value is relative, what is it relative *to*? If we take, say, the obligation to preserve human life, is it relative to states, to cultures, to groups, to individuals or simply to situations where killing is justified and even applauded in certain circumstances (war) but condemned in others (murder)? The problem here is that if *everything* is relative, nothing can be *known* to be relative without a fixed point of reference. Unless a value is established, there is no bench-mark for any possible variations or deviations. Indeed, these may serve to confirm the validity of the value. Despite considerable cultural variations, it is difficult to believe that some universal (objective?) values such as truth-telling, fidelity, reciprocity, etc., do not exist. And as far as war is concerned, surely most people recognise an atrocity when they see one?

The second and perhaps more important criticism of relativism is that it confuses ends with means. That is to say, it does not make a careful distinction between the objective of an action and the means whereby it is achieved. For example, the traditional warfare of many Mesoamerican peoples involved predatory raids on enemy villages with the express purpose of taking captives for sacrifice. In the West, on the other hand, the convention of holding periodic festivals of games became established. Now any resemblance between these quite different developments seems very remote indeed. Yet they were both engaged in what was essentially the same exercise, namely, seeking status. Both were ways of gaining prestige, earning reputations in status-conscious societies. The means whereby these goals were realised were totally different – culturally relative – but the goals themselves and the values enshrined were virtually identical. The goals of most human actions are remarkably similar, it is simply the means that vary. It is the *forms* of behavioural diversity that are subject to social determination.

It may be, therefore, that certain values are ends in themselves and that it is not possible to see them in any other terms. We can see this again in relation to sport. Take shot-putting: a shot can be reasonably easily transferred from point A to point B without having to throw it. So why do it? Obviously not for reasons of functionality. The reason seems to be inherent in the sport itself. If people are pressed to give reasons, they may maintain that they play sport because it has a health/strength value. This gives it a certain tangible instrumentality; the purpose is clear. But some may argue that this is not the main objective, and insist that sport is really about inculcating a sense or spirit of sportsmanship. This too expresses a purpose, but we are here moving into the realm of the *in*tangible – sportsmanship has a rather nebulous quality which certainly cannot be quantified nor always appreciated. But what are we to do about the people who simply say that they play/watch sport because they like it? There is really no answer to this. When sport is fun, then sport has become the means to enjoyment, and enjoyment is such an amorphous aim and signifies such different things to different people that we can virtually regard sport as an end in itself.

Whatever the pursuit, we all know what we like and dislike, but it is often extraordinarily difficult to say why. Perhaps there are some values that just *are* – and we must leave it at that. To say, as some sociologists do, that they exist to promote social harmony and cohesion in the group merely begs the question why we should want harmony and cohesion, and why in this form? To reply that the world works better that way is almost to imply a metaphysical response. Group values are important, but individuals may *adopt* them for self-interested reasons, simply because it can pay to conform. On the other hand, in other circumstances they may ignore group values for similar hedonistic reasons. As a general rule, people do what it pays them to do. But behaviour isn't as simple and predictable as that. It is subject to emotional over-ride. Sentimentality still has a place, and its expressions often defy academic rationality.

Existentialism

Existentialism is a convenient collective term to indicate a particular kind of subjectivist approach to philosophy. Many of those who are designated Existentialists will not own the term, and insist that their particular orientations represent a revolt against traditional philosophy and what they regard as its imprisoning labels. They maintain that they are less concerned with philosophy as a set of rather abstract axioms than as a useful guide to life.

Existentialism, like some other philosophies, has its roots in particular situations. Interestingly, the situation in which a philosophy is first formulated may be quite different from those in which it is popularised; one thinks of Marx and later Marxism. Very many great thinkers actually act against the spirit of their age. Existentialist ideas were first expressed in the relatively prosperous conditions of the 19th century in Denmark by Soren Kierkegaard, and in Germany by Friedrich Nietzsche. But these and similar ideas had little resonance until the crises of the Second World War and the fratricidal Algerian War (Behr, 1961). It was doubtedly the climate of uncertainty and insecurity that facilitated the popularity of Existentialism, which – curiously – appeared in both atheistic and non-atheistic forms, traditions that have been perpetuated ever since.

What then is Existentialism? Jean-Paul Sartre defines it as the principle whereby existence precedes essence (Sartre, 1957). This sounds suitably obscure, but the expression 'existential' is neither accidental nor pretentious. The 'essence' is the conception of something, an image and purpose, that is formulated in the mind. Sartre, for instance, talks of the paper-knife – though it could apply to any other artefact – which exists in the mind of the designer but which does not achieve its 'existence' until it is actually made and is used for its intended purpose. Its function is pre-determined before its manufacture. It is the conception or idea that comes first; only experience will tell if its actual existence will be realised and its intended functionality vindicated (Warnock, 1963).

With 'things' their essence precedes existence, but with *humans* existence precedes essence. There are no prototypes and no stereotypes because all are distinct, unique. Life is not cast according to some pre-determined mould. There is no pattern or allotted role. This is something that humans must find for themselves. We all construct our own life-patterns, we realise our own essence. We are, we *exist*. Apart from death, which is the negation of existence – the final irony – this is all we know. Our essence – what we become – can only be determined (discovered?) by experience. The implication is that we have no 'nature', as such, all each of us has is his personal history.

The central ideas of existentialist thinkers differ considerably but, for our purposes, it is possible to give a composite view based on the central themes that most have in common. Martin Heidegger, for example, writes of 'forlorn-ness', the conviction that we are beings alone in the cosmos. No gods have ordained our condition; we are abandoned (but who is supposed to have abandoned us?) and we must find our own way through life. Soren Kierkegaard takes up a similar theme, and says that we are condemned to a certain 'solitariness'. No philosophy or state system or political credo can give us any useful clues as to the meaning of life. There are no text-books with the answers at the back. Life is tragic in that it can only be understood backwards (i.e. retrospectively), while it can only be lived forwards.

Sartre follows suit, but takes the argument a stage further. We are nothing but what we make of ourselves, and this comes about by continuing acts of choice. We are increasingly becoming what we are not, because as we become aware of what we are, we have already moved on – we have transcended ourselves. Acts of choice express our essential humanity. There is no objective morality, no ultimate principle. Therefore, we can choose neither good nor evil, neither right nor wrong, because these do not exist in any pre-determined forms, nor are they given by tradition or the state. No values are *a priori*. We impose values on ourselves by repeated acts of choice, an idea that was anticipated by Nietzsche, who maintained that morality is personal rather than social, self-determined rather than other-determined. Therefore it is 'heroic' in that *we* have to make our *own* morality and take the full responsibility for our actions.

This is all reminiscent of the Genesis story of the picking of the fruit of the Tree of Knowledge of Good and Evil which – among other things – is an Everyman (and every age) story about the responsibilities of choice. To have the freedom to choose is to have the freedom to make the wrong decision. Hence morality is heroic – it takes courage to make our own rules and stand by them regardless of others' opinions. The ability to choose, to make intelligent decisions, is seen as a cardinal virtue by the Existentialists because the very idea of choice implies a certain conception of freedom. Kierkegaard speaks of making choices in fear and trembling, and Sartre supports this when he tells us that we are condemned to be free. There are hints of Marx in Sartre's distinction between free beings-for-themselves and beings-in-themselves. This seems to echo Marx, who distinguished between the unaware, 'unawakened' class-in-itself and the aware and politically active class-for-itself. Freedom, for the existentialists, is awareness, and awareness involves making choices that must inevitably concern others because other people define our subjectivity. We are told that we are free to choose anything except the surrender of our own freedom, an injunction that should be contrasted with the equally persuasive view that people have no greater freedom than the freedom to bind themselves – a view that suggests that *commitment*, say, in political, religious or even in matrimonial terms is the ultimate expression of freedom.

Awareness also involves a particular kind of resignation. Heidegger argues that only by thoughtful acceptance of the apparent meaninglessness of life can we become 'authentic beings'. The unauthentic being is the platitudinous, commonplace man who does nothing because he does not *think*, he allows his choices to be made for him. Virtue is integrity but vice is self-deception. It is all very reminiscent of the Greek oracular injunction to 'know thyself', and Socrates' maxim that the unexamined life is not worth living. Sartre talks of people who are like characters in bad plays; he says they are 'living clichés' and guilty of *mauvaise-foi* (bad faith). They simply follow the bidding of others and make excuses to cover their slavish actions. To be aware also means being sensitive to the difficulties and disorderliness of the world, and to our own feelings of impotence when we contemplate its seemingly insoluble problems. Sartre says these things generate a sense of 'anguish' and 'nausea'. The pointlessness and futility of existence bring feelings of despair and incomprehension, and incomprehensibility increases our conviction of the 'absurdity' of it all.

In their own way, the Existentialists are highlighting what they feel to be the inadequacies of accepted academic disciplines as explanatory systems. They, like current Postmodernists who owe much to Nietzsche and the general Existentialist tradition, are questioning the validity of such disciplines in purporting to give us a 'true' understanding of things. The social sciences, in particular, try to make sense of social experience by 'containing' it conceptually and by attempting to order its complexities. But in trying to bring this experience under intellectual control, what we want to contain eventually contains us. These organised intellectual exercises lure us on, promising some measure of fulfilment, and just when we think we are beginning to grasp the real nature of things by using these explanatory patterns, what we want eludes us. Sartre suggests that it has a kind of deceptive 'viscosity' in that it escapes from us at the very moment that we feel that we have found our answer. It is rather like language, which is the vehicle of all our conceptualising, yet as we use it, it is also using us. It is a human construction, but it, in turn, shapes our thinking and directs the nature of our cognition. We suppose – perhaps rather vainly – that we have successfully imposed some order upon reality, but in the end we become victims of our own intellectual conceit (Warnock, 1962).

Presented in this way, Existentialism – for many – is a heady concoction of intellectual freedom and personal morality that has a considerable appeal. But, like the other systems we have considered, it is open to a number of objections. There is a fundamental flaw in the whole idea of existential individualism. If our individuality – our authenticity as persons – depends upon personal, perceptive decision-making, how can we take account of the decision-making of others and still retain our essential individuality? There has to be a conflict of interests. Some years ago there was a somewhat unusual question on the Finals Philosophy Paper at London University which asked if Robinson Crusoe had any social obligations before Man Friday joined him on the island. One implication was that no matter how much two people try to reconcile their interests, there has to be a time when they will clash. Complete personal autonomy becomes impossible. If Existentialism is saying that we must take into consideration the consequences of our actions on others *before* we act, it is certainly saying nothing different from other ethical systems.

We must also ask if our choices can really be free. The crucial and unquestioned axiom of Existentialism is that we *are* free, but does the evidence of experience really support this? What about our natural limitations? How can anyone tell a person who is physically disabled, handicapped or in some way disadvantaged that he/she is free to 'become', in the fullest sense of that term? And what about inhibiting psychological factors – the determinants that we have already considered? We don't have to go all the way with either the psychodynamic theorists or the learning theorists to accept that there may be ineradicable elements in our natures that preclude the possibility of really free choice or any kind of appreciable personal development. Not least of all there are inescapable socio-economic factors which vitiate the possibility of choice. It hardly needs to be said that for the underprivileged, the unenfranchised and the persecuted, life does not present many viable choices. Could we tell a Dachau Jew or an Indian shanty-town dweller that they were really free because they were fully aware of their unfreedom? The notion that freedom is really about awareness or authentic living would sound rather hollow in the circumstances.

Existentialism also makes much of its value-freedom. It claims that it does not pontificate about values or prescribe other people's moral behaviour. Yet in a theoretically value-less system, one value is implicit, individual awareness, and another is pre-judged, individual choice, both implying the possibility of authenticity (Gellner, 1963, p. 62). And what exactly does authenticity mean anyway? What is, say, an authentic socialist or an authentic sinner or a saint? Is one free to choose illusion, social disengagement or even an authentically *un*authentic life if one wishes? Are Existentialists therefore in a position to condemn the choices of others? They are quick to accuse others of bad faith, but in what senses can bad faith exist? Different systems diagnose the problem differently. What Existentialists see as bad faith, the Marxists might see as ideological self-deception, or the psychoanalysts as 'truth' obscured by repression. Bad faith does not always imply dishonesty, but a mistaken assessment of one's own situation. Furthermore, if all values are relative, and therefore equally valid, no philosophy or moral system can be right or wrong in any objective sense. So doesn't moral criticism constitute a form of hypocrisy? Relativism also implies that there can be individual moralities. Is this possible, or do socialisation processes preclude the possibility of personal or singular moralities? Codes and rules tend to be common to particular communities and cultures, and where there is deviation from the recognised or prescribed norms, it nearly always takes similar forms. Deviance is often acceptably institutionalised. Whether it happens to be outré fashion or deviant sex makes little difference. The differentiae are often inconsequential. (One thinks of the 1960s alternative life-style 'revolution' where even such trivia as folk songs came to be seen as expressing some deeply significant world-view.) Either the individual moralities tend to be disconcertingly similar, or – as so often happens – the avant-garde is overtaken by society in general. Existential norms merge with contextual norms.

Contrived differentiae may simply be ways of reinforcing the suspicion that there are essential similarities and a certain commonality in periodically resuscitated social tactics.

It is intriguing to consider how one could apply Existentialism to the practical realities of everyday existence. How does it fare as a guide to the necessity of actual policy-making? Praiseworthy as ideas about autonomy and personal responsibility obviously are, what happens, say, in emergency – perhaps wartime – situations when there have to be certain severe restrictions on individual choice and freedom? What does the well-intentioned legislator do? Tell the citizens that despite economic stringency and the loss of political liberties they are really free if they thoughtfully accept their condition? (It is a little like the prostitute who insists that men may rent her body but they never own her mind.) We have already seen that this problem may also pose problems about commitment – something that may be either desirable or necessary in particular sets of circumstances. It is interesting to see how this can all be reconciled with the original philosophy; it would appear that any attempt to do so must come perilously close to 'bad faith'. Sartre himself had a long flirtation with the Communist Party, to which he was reluctant to commit himself, but he eventually capitulated on the rationalisation that he could improve it with the interiorising philosophies of Existentialism.

One wonders if, in some of its formulations, Existentialism is rather too given over to despair. As an ethic it seems to be preoccupied with notions of 'anguish' and 'meaninglessness', and – unlike some religious philosophies – it doesn't even help to be an habitual loser. The emphasis on futility can degenerate into a 'why-was-I-ever-born' outlook, with grievances against all and sundry. (It is instructive to glance at the subsequent careers of many of the 'angry young men' of the 1960s whose protests have now become muted by prosperity.) The world doesn't 'owe us a living', the world really owes us nothing. Just because we happen to have been born does not automatically endow is with certain inalienable rights. On this point the Existentialists are surely right. It is a privilege just to live – to exist. Even if life is nasty, short and brutish, it is both biologically and statistically a miracle that we as singular individuals have even seen the light of day. As human creatures we have no natural rights, only expectations. Existentialism is an actor-oriented philosophy rather than a spectator-oriented philosophy, and whatever its shortcomings it is correct to stress that we must take responsibility for our own actions.

Utilitarianism

The consensus approach to ethics is quite distinct. It assumes, very persuasively, that two heads – or preferably more – are better than one. For the consensualist, there is safety in numbers. Long ago, Plato had indicated that by looking at, say, blue garments we gain some idea of the nature of 'blueness', and that, similarly, if we observed good acts we would essentialise something of the nature of goodness. Much later, Butler followed suit and contended that we construct the ideal in terms of a *series*, that is to say, if we look at round things such as coins, we gain some notion of what perfect roundness would be. And by the same process of reasoning, he also argued teleologically that we conceive the ideal in terms of *purpose*. For what purpose is a watch made? To tell the time. Yet no watch does this absolutely perfectly – only nearly so. But on the basis of the known (the imperfect) we can discern some idea of the unknown (the perfect), even though our everyday experience involves choices which necessarily modify our conception of the ideal anyway.

The most popular and persuasive consensus theory of ethics is undoubtedly Utilitarianism. Ethics, as a subject, usually implies certain normative ideals because, among other things, it is the study of *obligatory* behaviour. But Utilitarianism claims that it is not like this. It is not a contrived principle of action, and is not concerned with what ought to be done, but what actually *is* done. Therefore it is not intended for academic wrangling or theoretical application, but is concerned with practical activity. It is further argued that Utilitarian ideas lie behind current public thinking on broad issues. Indeed, it is the justifying principle behind democratic government. Probably most surveys on moral issues – certainly in Western society – would record people as being knowing or unwitting Utilitarians.

So what is Utilitarianism? Succinctly, Utilitarianism holds that that is good which promotes or enhances the greatest happiness of the greatest number, and in its classic formulation happiness is seen as pleasure and the reduction of pain. It is therefore a consensus ethic in that it tacitly supports popular morality and encourages the well-being of the majority, and, as such, it is undoubtedly an extremely plausible and engaging doctrine.

Historically, it is usually associated with Jeremy Bentham and James Mill, and particularly Mill's more famous son, John Stuart Mill, who refined and popularised these ideas, though it can be found in embryonic forms among the Greeks. The principles enshrined in Athenian democracy as presented to us in the writings of Aristotle display a highly qualified kind of Utilitarianism. Over the years, Utilitarianism has taken three main forms: the classic or traditional form that we have described, sometimes known as Hedonistic Utilitarianism; a modified form of this, Ideal Utilitarianism, which retains the 'greatest number' principle but extends the criteria to include not just happiness but also such aims as fairness, justice, etc.; and Attitude Utilitarianism, which maintains that people will never seek others' happiness and well-being until they have developed the correct 'respect-thy-neighbour' attitudes.

Persuasive and pragmatic as Utilitarianism is, it is open to a number of very cogent criticisms. In its traditional form it may be regarded as too hedonistic, too concerned with personal gratification. Indeed, hedonistic ideas generally are subject to some debate. A thorough-going hedonist cannot really entertain the idea of altruism because no matter how selfless an action appears to be, it can be interpreted as a kind of self-gratification. So, to take an extreme example, a martyr or a person who displays sacrificial selflessness, say, in wartime, can be seen as doing it for his or her own personal – and perhaps perverted – pleasure. Needless to say, few people would go along with this. The argument is not very convincing. It hardly needs to be stressed that the sense of well-being derived from martyrdom is usually pitifully brief. And who is to say that there is no such thing as altruism? Can selfishness really masquerade as selflessness? As already intimated, can there be a counterfeit if the real thing does not somewhere exist?

It could also be argued that Utilitarianism is too psychologistic in that it extrapolates from the particular to the general. It assumes that what one individual likes, needs or wants is what others must like, need or want. So if I want happiness above all else, others must necessarily want it too. Perhaps humans do want happiness most of all – though that has to be an assumption. But do *all* individuals want it, and – what is more to the point – do most individuals want it in all circumstances? There are so many recorded instances of people putting other considerations *before* their personal pleasure – again, especially in wartime situations – that one wonders how valid this contention is? What is more, it can be shown that what is good for the individual is not necessarily good for the masses and vice versa. One could take a wide choice of examples, from buying on a wartime black market to the operation of private medicine. When the act or value is 'universalised' the whole system may be put in jeopardy.

It hardly needs to be said that happiness means different things to different people, and different things to the same people at different times. And what brings happiness to different people varies enormously. Few would surely argue that different kinds of pleasure could be expressed in terms of each other. In general, pleasures are incommensurable. But implied in Utilitarianism is the notion of *quality* besides quantity. It is not just a question of the greatest happiness for the greatest number; in Ideal Utilitarianism the *level* of pleasure involved is also important. John Stuart Mill certainly went along with the idea that there are 'higher pleasures' that are the preserve of a minority, a higher culture as opposed to a mass culture. It may be better to be an unhappy Socrates than a happy pig, but it does not accord with Utilitarianism's original premises. It smacks of an elitism which is not to the liking of every devotee.

This brings us to the thorny issue of how the Utilitarian principle can be suitably distilled for the formulation of social policy. How is the principle to be applied in specific circumstances? This may not sound *that* difficult, but it actually presents very real – sometimes insuperable – problems. To begin with, there is what is termed the 'judge-legislator' problem. This necessitates making a distinction between the formulation of laws/policies (legislation) and their particular applications. The former, say criminal law, may well be constructed on Utilitarian principles, but the bases of particular applications of the law by a judge and the implementation of the law by the police, and certainly the reasons for observing it by the public, may have little or nothing to do with Utilitarian principles.

If greatest happiness is what people want, how much do they want? As we have seen, most people probably do want happiness, but is it the happiness of the greatest number? Is it even possible to promote individual and collective happiness equally? If so, what are people prepared to forego to get it? And are we here thinking of the short term or the long term? What are we to do, for example, about those things which some – perhaps the majority – find pleasurable but which are actually bad for us, such as tobacco and alcohol? What sort of legislation is appropriate or – better still – practicable? This needs and wants problem extends to just about every aspect of government fiscal policy affecting such things as wage restraint, interest rates and that age-old menace, inflation. It certainly affects the whole area of military spending – often a matter of serious contention with the general public. The difficulty is that it is just not possible to give people what they desire *and* what they need – or think they need – at the same time.

Another serious difficulty is the whole complex question of minorities. The greatest number principle must mean that minorities take a lesser priority than majorities. Perhaps that's how it should be, but they could fare rather badly in a consensus oriented society. This problem has been posed in the writings of many theorists, from Plato's *Republic* where – as we have seen – a blueprint society is created to give citizens what they need, to Aldous Huxley's *Brave New World*, where citizens are moulded to fit a pre-determined kind of society where their needs are psycho-chemically conditioned – the ultimate in social control. For where the state is said to 'represent the People' – often a convenient fiction – there is always the danger that the principle could be used for illiberal purposes.

This also raises questions about the limits of application for the principle. Within what areas does the principle apply? If we look for a moment at a society such as classical Athens, what constitutes the greatest number in this particular city-state (*polis*)? Is it the greatest number of the inhabitants? Or is it the greatest number of the inhabitants less resident aliens (metics). Or is it the greatest number of inhabitants less the slaves who comprised perhaps a fifth of the total? Or is it the citizens themselves – the enfranchised minority who also constituted only about a fifth of the population? Here again we must invoke the normative-substantive distinction. What *was*, as distinct from what might or *should* have been. It is interesting, either way, to see how the principle might be applied. And one does not have to go back to classical society for examples; there have been, and are, parallels in the modern world.

It is obvious that the pleasure principle is not quite as plausible as it sounds, not least because of the far-reaching implications of some of its hidden assumptions. It assumes a *capacity for prediction* which is rarely possible in actual situations. Those who wish to apply Utilitarian principles are really being asked to weigh up the possibilities for good and evil (pleasure and pain) *in advance*, and make a judgement on the basis of that evaluation. But this – in turn – assumes (1) that all the necessary facts are available, and (2) that these are at hand before the decision has to be made. In practice, we usually have to make judgements on the best information we have – but it is often extremely difficult to assess the balance of *possible* good over *possible* evil. Perhaps the most notable case in the history of warfare was the decision to use the atom bomb on Hiroshima. The Americans had already seen how the Japanese were defending the occupied Pacific Islands – sometimes to the last man – and they had every reason to believe that they would fight even more tenaciously to protect their homeland. It was estimated that the Americans might lose about a million men in the assault, quite apart from the enormous casualties to the enemy, which would also include civilians. The final decision to use the bomb was taken on Utilitarian principles, not knowing in advance quite what the results would be, and certainly not knowing what they would have been with a conventional invasion. The results, of course, were appalling, but possibly not as bad as they might have been in other circumstances. This we shall never know.

Utilitarianism also assumes the *capacity to make rational choices*. It takes for granted that people can sit down, dispassionately weigh up the facts, and arrive at a sensible decision that will satisfy all parties. It tends to discount – or, at least, underrate – the possibility that the well-springs of human action may be more emotional than rational for both individuals and collectivities. For instance, at the individual level, does the potential suicide calmly contemplate death on the basis of Utilitarian principles? One suspects that in the majority of cases those concerned are just not able to think in rational terms. Possibly most people would take the view that except in cases of terminal illness, there has to be a solution to their problems short of death. Similarly at the collective level. Does war, for example, always begin as the result of a totally rational decision? Or is it often the outcome of fear and suspicion – a precipitate action that might never have taken place if there had been more rational calculation? The American decision to go to war in Vietnam might well fall into this category, as does also the Argentinian decision to attack the Falklands. A little less emotional flag-waving, and a little more sober thought, and history might have been a little bit different.

Finally, Utilitarianism also assumes that the *consequences* of moral action are what really count. Results matter: it is important that the greatest happiness is actually brought to the greatest number. Naturally, this is all very laudable, but what about the motives and the means behind the action? This is the kind of thinking which, taken to its logical – or illogical – conclusion, allows the end to justify the means. It is the kind of thinking that can – and has – sanctioned some of the very worst crimes in history, such as massacre and even genocide. A very high percentage of the indigenous Indian population of the United States was obliterated in a few decades in the belief that this would eventually serve some hypothetical greater good, and, in the early days of occupation, this was often a cause for rejoicing because the settlers regarded it as another setback for the heathen. Indeed, the entire Nazi Holocaust was premised on the assumption that a world free of Jews would somehow be a better place to live in.

When the consequences are all important, the means employed to achieve the required ends can sometimes be too terrible to contemplate. Yet in so many historical instances they *have* been contemplated and worked out in fine detail and put into operation by so-called sane men. Utilitarianism is not, of course, the justifying principle behind such acts, and it must be said that Utilitarians have often been liberal and generous people. But the system, *qua* system, can lend itself to less than generous practices. Its intentions are to be applauded, but its very emphasis on results, and results seen pre-eminently in terms of human happiness, calls its central tenet into question.

5

Are Values Culturally Relative?

This question can be considered in terms of five main issues (note the related treatment with specific reference to war and aggression in Carlton, 1990, section IV).

The problem of correlation

Attempts have been made to try to correlate specific values with particular types of society. One very famous study done many years ago was especially concerned with the idea of moral progress and endeavoured to correlate religion as well as moral values to modes of social organisation (Hobhouse, 1906; Hobhouse, Ginsberg & Wheeler, 1915). This has been followed by others which have tried to show that values and their development might be directly related to the nature of the societies in question. Their brief was to determine the general character and specific varieties of the moral order by comparative studies, and to enquire how moral systems might be related to the nature of – and changes in – the various types of social structures. They then tried to relate this to the growth of knowledge in the hope of discovering whether these correlations could indicate anything that might broadly be called development. Morris Ginsberg, writing of L.T. Hobhouse, endorses the view that the key to this synthesis is to be found in the idea of evolution and the belief in the power of rational thought to direct and control the course of human life (Ginsberg, 1956).

These earlier writers were well aware of the difficulties inherent in such enterprises. They knew that their classifications of societies would not be acceptable to everyone, and they were quick to acknowledge the limitations of the Comparative Method. They realised that certain institutions which are found in different societies, or at different levels and times in the same society, may resemble one another in outward form only, and that they might also differ considerably in meaning and value, and that these differences could well be more important than the resemblances. Social structures too many have a superficial similarity, but actually have little affinity with each other.

As far as moral values are concerned, there is always the perennial problem of evaluation: are socially 'higher'/'advanced' civilisations also morally 'higher'/'advanced' civilisations? What do these terms mean, and by what criteria are they to be assessed? (Wells, 1970). The researchers recognised that any relationship would have to be conditioned by the scale of organisation, by ecological and economic factors, and by the degree of effective social unity and cooperation. All-round development was deemed to be development that satisfied all the criteria. But they also had to admit that development in one area was often defeated by failure elsewhere. For instance, the Roman legal system was very sophisticated by contemporary standards, but the same society still persisted with the indescribably barbarous 'games', in which beasts and humans were butchered for entertainment. Efficiency, too, in many societies – say, in the use of natural resources – was often purchased at the cost of political freedom because it has so often proved the case that increased power over nature has meant increased power of man over man.

There are many problems with this kind of comparative exercise. It is very difficult to determine whether there are common generic factors behind the differences between societies and their institutions, and if there are, whether these differences can be attributed to specific causes, economic, military and so forth. Furthermore, it is also necessary to see if the differences in moral development are due to ethical values *per se*, or to some other external factors as with, say, the moves for the abolition of slavery in the last century which may have been due as much to changing technology as to the powerful moral objections that were offered at the time.

The whole idea of progress is fraught with definitional snags. The very conception of progress is really a form of *pre*-judgement as it implies a direction or goals of a particular kind which are assumed to be good or right. To this extent, it has a rather ephemeral utopian quality. Retrogression can be progress for those who would like a return to the past. Some kind of ostensibly idyllic island paradise, say Tahiti in the 18th century, might be seen as the acme of community living for those who crave that kind of thing. Perhaps the common practice of human sacrifice in Polynesia could be offset by the untrammelled sexual freedom, and the absence of medical facilities by the hope that more 'natural' diets would inevitably mean less illness. In other words, progress can mean whatever people want it to mean. And even if we can agree on what is meant by progress, it cannot be sustained that progress is uniform or has maintained a constant 'rate' over time. Ginsberg feels that there has been a slow, unsteady movement forwards, but it is probably more accurate to describe Western society in particular as one in which progression and retrogression exist side by side. How else can we 'see' a society that can legislate against capital punishment, flogging and slavery, and *at the same time* produce weapons of mass destruction of which our forefathers never dreamed? To insist that society is becoming more rational, and to imply that rational is to be equated with moral, is to overlook the gross moral (rational?) inconsistencies in the world. Does it make moral or rational sense for India and Pakistan, for example, to insist on producing costly nuclear weapons when the bulk of their populations are still hungry? Or consider the Iran-Iraq war where in just one 12-hour battle £40 million was expended in ammunition.

Progress in general implies the abandonment of any notions of determinism; there can no longer be any inexorable 'fates' or inevitable historical 'processes'. It also suggests that there is an underlying unity of humankind, a faith in its common interests and aspirations, and therefore a willingness for possible cooperation. This must involve common value systems which are applicable to all, and the assumption that there is nothing in 'human nature' that cannot be solved by human reason – nothing which admits of ultimate defeat, even if efficiency can only be gained at the cost of certain much-prized freedoms. Such ideas have dominated European thought since the Renaissance, and especially since the growth of science and technology. Few people would dispute that whatever their reservations there has been scientific advance. But has there actually been moral progress? Despite the cynicism generated by two World Wars, the vision of humankind courageously going from strength to strength is still with us today. But, as far as morality is concerned, this idea is supported by precious little evidence, and what evidence there is, is vitiated by ambiguity.

The problem of prioritisation

How are values chosen and reproduced, utilised and perpetuated? The prioritisation of values may be calculated on a number of criteria, including whether they are held to be socially useful, or the extent to which they are regarded as socially workable. It is even possible to settle for an uneasy combination, and to construct systems which are based primarily upon the criteria of social utility, but which contain other elements as well. Underlying all such systems is some implicit notion of rationality. This may assume that the values themselves, or at least some of them, are rationally chosen as, for example, in Utilitarianism. It may be a negative assumption that the values are essentially non-rational and are not really the proper subjects of philosophical debate, as in Emotivism. Perhaps most commonly, the values themselves are seen as non-rational, but the means whereby they can be realised are rationally chosen. Values, *per se*, are non-rational because they possess properties such as 'worthwhileness' which are not susceptible of naturalistic or reductionist explanations. It hardly makes sense to ask why what is worthwhile is worthwhile. It is difficult to see how there can be any derivation of values from facts alone, or from actual values regarded simply as facts. We want certain things because we believe them to be worth wanting.

All the essentials for prioritisation of values can be found in the seminal sociology of Max Weber, elaborated and systematised in the work of Talcott

Parsons. Weber was fascinated by the problem of values at two levels, namely, the relationship between values and scientific investigation, and the determination of values *in* scientific investigation. At the first level, he held that the relationship between scientific objectivity and value-judgement involved a subtle process of interaction. Scientific investigation had to begin from some standpoint in the realm of values. Selection of the study area was based ultimately on some implicit or explicit value system (Weber, 1949, p. 78). However impartial the investigator tried to be, his choices still reflected – however obliquely – his own personal values. Thereafter, the investigation could, in turn, illuminate the range of value choices. It might demonstrate what values were consistent or inconsistent with each other; it could determine the consequences and implications of particular courses of action and assess their 'cost' in terms of the values concerned; and it might even confirm or disconfirm the original choice of subject and the method of study. In short, 'an empirical science could not tell anyone what he should do – but rather what he *can* do – and under what circumstances – what he wishes to do' (Weber, 1949, pp. 22-3, 53-4). Ultimately it is only the values that are held by individuals which give meaning to social existence.

At the second level, on the determination of values, Weber could not say why men came to entertain particular beliefs. Values necessarily incorporate beliefs, and in the Protestant Ethic thesis, Weber 're-creates' the kind of Puritan who holds certain doctrines, but he offers us no really convincing explanation as to *why* some people came to believe in them. In the thesis, he is not primarily concerned with the 'essence' of religion, but with the conditions and effects of a defined kind of social action which can be understood in terms of the subjective experience of the believer. Weber's assumptions are not based upon any hypothesised supernatural dimension, but upon the possibilities inherent in the *belief* in that dimension. It is the value and the operationalisation of the value in socio-economic terms which form the basis of his discussion.

Weber's concern was with the independent causal significance of religious ideas and values, and his studies demonstrated some of the ways in which variations in these corresponded with variations in socially sanctioned goals and values in the secular sphere. They were critical causal factors which arose independently of changes in the social structure, and made their own impact upon society. Religion, therefore, and the values it embodied, was itself an operative cause of social change. For Weber, this confirmed the importance which must be attached to both the empirical effects and logical validity of values (see also Parsons, 1957).

Weber's emphasis on the consensus of value which derives from a belief-system has been controversially developed by Talcott Parsons. It is evident that Parsonian Sociology takes the existence of values and norms for granted; it says a great deal about their nature and function, but little about how they originate or evolve. Indeed, he has been accused – certainly as far as moral values are concerned – of never having really explored how such values actually operate (Gouldner, 1971, p. 140).

Parsons maintains that in any system of human action, individuals are 'controlled' by the norms of interaction prescribed by the social system, and this, in turn, reflects the cultural system of values and symbols. Like Weber, with whom he shared a similar sociological orientation, he is extremely concerned with the 'grounds of meaning', i.e. the basic perspectives around which groups and societies organise their lives – not least of all the elemental cosmological conceptions and their relation to human existence. Not that Parsons regards religious symbols as having any *known* external referent. Symbols represent those aspects of social reality which are outside the range of scientific analysis, yet are significant for human life and experience (Parsons, 1937, p. 421). It would seem, therefore, that for Parsons, the pivotal concept is that of shared symbolic systems, of which religion is one type. In this he is stressing the meaningfulness of human action contrary to positivistic and behaviouristic theories. His view is that man does not relate directly to people and objects; all relationships with other objects and with himself are symbolically mediated. The actor, in any situation, reinterprets things and invests them with meaning. 'As humans we know the physical world *only* through the organism. Our minds have no direct experience of an external physical object unless we perceive it through physical processes and the brain processes information about it ... Similar considerations apply to ... the "ultimate reality" with which we are concerned in grappling with the problems of meaning – e.g. evil and suffering and the temporal limitations of the human life. Ideas in this area, as cultural objects, are symbolic representations (e.g. gods, totems, the supernatural) of the ultimate realities, but are not themselves such realities' (Parsons, 1966, pp. 8ff.). For Parsons, this is how human action differs from the behaviour of other animals. The sphere of values and beliefs represents a great break in the chain of evolution. The cultural sub-system of values and symbols is a source of meaning for the social actor (Rocher, 1974, p. 159).

Such a view has its problems. It does not explain why symbols take the forms they do, or why they do, or should, have a transcendental dimension. Similarly, it is hard to see in the general hierarchy of cultural values which ones are to be meaningfully regarded as 'ultimate', or, indeed, which are to be unambiguously categorised as 'religious'. Yet Parsons makes it clear that values – which he defines as moral orientations towards the problems of life in this world – are never the whole of religion, or even its most central aspects. These, he suggests, lie in the realm of faith and meaning. Parsons does assume certain universal modes of cognition, and – by extension – some universality of values. It is difficult to know to what extent the primacy ascribed to values should be seen in metaphysical terms, but it is clear that the ultimate values which religion represents determine social action. As Thomas O'Dea expresses it, 'religious (normative) ideas become substantive causes' (O'Dea, 1970, pp. 266-7). On this interpretation, it is not so much religion that is a social phenomenon, but society that is a religious phenomenon. It follows, therefore, that all societies manifest religious beliefs and values (Parsons, 1961a, pp. 963ff.), and it is these shared values – whether they are regarded as religious or otherwise – which constitute the basis of social order.

It has often been argued that social order is Parsons' main preoccupation (Giddens, 1976, pp. 96-8) and that his treatment of values implies a society dominated by consensus, harmony and stability. It is said that he ignores the difficulties posed by such distinctions as 'positive' and 'negative' consensus, and disregards the 'content' of the values he so applauds (Mennell, 1974, pp. 123ff.). Certainly little is made of the manipulation of values by, say, government agencies, or of value screening by socialisation agencies such as the 'family'. But Parsons simply takes the existence of order as a point of departure; his view is not that order is an ideal, but a *problem*. He is surprised at the degree of social order given the inherent nature of human competitiveness. A reasonably successful resolution of the problem is achieved by the internalisation of the appropriate values which are then perpetuated in the social sphere. This complementarity between internalisation and expression brings a measure of stability and social harmony (Rocher, 1974, pp. 159-63).

In Parsons' work the prioritisation of values is clear, but what is not certain are the criteria for determining the infrastructure of the value-system. Why *these* gradations in a whole hierarchy of values? Furthermore, the actual operation of these values is unsure. How any particular action can be directly attributed to any particular value is probably beyond scientific demonstration.

The problem of rationality

On what bases are values constructed? Are they formulated simply on the basis of their functionality or otherwise? So, for example, truth-telling is regarded by primitive and sophisticate alike as essential for meaningful communication. Without observing its rules – if only in the most general terms – all sensible communication would break down. Thus it has become as near a universal value as we are likely to find. But are all values so rational? Here we have a form and substance problem all over again. For example, we need order and control in society, that is the principle, but do we need it to be mediated via a monarchy? Presumably too we need – for a whole variety of reasons – to avoid an unrestricted sexual free-for-all. So marriage has evolved to regulate sexual activity and provide a basis for the socialisation of children, but the principles underlying marriage do not necessarily determine its many forms.

The problem of resolution

The problem of values tends to be resolved pragmatically. There is no satisfactory answer to the vexed question of origination; the problems of correlation and prioritisation likewise admit no satisfactory solutions. The arguments are illuminating and often provide the basis for further discussions, but there is no indication that this can be done with any sense of finality. The only practical course of action, therefore, is simply to accept values as part of the human condition and as necessary components of the social process. In effect, this seems much like the response that people make to the most fundamental issue of all – the matter of human existence. Most people spend few of their waking moments ruminating about the imponderables of life and its possible meanings – they simply live it. But values, unlike life, may be part of a humanly constructed world, or, at least, shaped by human aspiration.

The view that people, in the absence of any clear objective values, contrive values for their own psychic health or social convenience, can even be found in ancient philosophy. The Greeks, for instance, distinguished between *physis* and *nomos*, that which was natural and that which was man-made. This did not refer to materials and artefacts but to laws and institutions, and especially to political forms. On the other hand, they were not too sure about values. Much was ascribed to the gods, but a great deal was also attributed to innate tendencies. Herodotus and particularly Thucydides have quite a lot to say about natural greed and aggressiveness. Later, intuitionist philosophers who were agnostic about the divine origins of values were happy to contrive their own 'virtues' such as 'beauty' or 'justice', by investing these qualities with an objectivity of their own. Such virtues were not thought of as having any metaphysical validity, but simply as embodying intrinsic properties which were valued for their own sake (Moore, 1947). The general recognition of these qualities gave them a kind of social authority. But why *these* qualities, which are not at all unusual, and not others, suggests at least the possibility of common values.

The objectification of values is also a feature of modern phenomenology. In this case, values are endowed with properties which are conducive to the realisation of social meaning. It is a move away from the essentialist stance towards a nominalist position which regards values as humanly constructed for social purposes. It is not so much that 'truth' is imposed upon everyday reality, but rather that it is seen to derive from that reality. Thus in the writings of Berger and Luckmann, religious values, for instance, are regarded as part of an all-embracing symbolic universe which provides a realm of ultimate meanings (Berger & Luckmann, 1967; Berger, 1967). They do not, like some neo-Marxists such as Louis Althusser, stress the relative autonomy of values, but maintain that values integrally reflect a reality which may have transcendental implications (Berger, 1970).

Whether values are innate or contrived, and if so *which* values are innate and which are contrived, has not been – and may never be – satisfactorily established. This is certainly the case with 'second-order' values of an aesthetic kind such as taste, etc., and may also be true of religious and moral values. In practice, however, by a process of unconscious assimilation (rather like Elias' cultural recycling) they do assume a kind of independent status. Values imply belief and belief involves commitment, and together they constitute the stuff of ideologies. Whether values are the springs of social action, or whether they are the rationalisation of the need for action is something which must now be examined. But we must bear in mind Habermas' reservation that 'a collective value system can never be achieved by means of enlightened discussion ... [i.e.] by consensus rationally arrived at, but only by summation and compromise ... values are, in principle, beyond discussion' (Habermas, 1974, p. 271).

The problem of relativism

If the question of the origination of values presents us with the most intractable problem in ethics, the question of relativism presents us with what is probably the most common problem. We have looked at this before (see the section on Emotivism in Chapter 4) but it is as well to make one or two further observations.

It is not at all unusual to hear of those who have been responsible for mass murder in some remote historical context referred to as 'children of their day', clearly implying, of course, that the Greeks or Romans or whoever, had quite different norms from our own and can therefore be excused for these thoughtless misdemeanours. This tendency to exculpate those who are not of our culture and who therefore 'couldn't have known better', is really a form of unconscious ethnocentrism that is quite common among social scientists – the very people who are quick to inveigh against ethnocentrism, given half a chance.

The more extreme forms of exculpation, however, are found among those who are actually willing to argue for the kind of cultural relativism which is prepared not only to condone what we would regard as barbarous acts but actually to pronounce them 'right' for the society concerned. This is particularly the case when the acts in question are judged to be irrational by our standards. We all know that modern societies have been guilty of the most heinous atrocities, sometimes on an unimaginable scale, but usually these acts have been seen to have their own perverted rationality. Some of the perpetrators, admittedly, had serious doubts but still went along with the system; many high-ranking German Army officers acceded to Hitler's proclaimed war of extermination against Russia in 1941-45 (see Correlli Barnett, 1990) despite their post-war declarations of moral reluctance. But when we return to those incidents that have taken place in far off times or far away places that we judge to be both cruel *and* essentially pointless and irrational, such as, say, Carthaginian child-sacrifice practices or Toltec/Aztec ritual bloodletting ostensibly to keep the cosmos in being (Carlton, 1990), are these things relative to their day and place, or are they to be regarded as reprehensible for all time?

There is, of course, something of relativism in all our thinking. It is not determined solely by pure reason – whatever we may mean by that – or by objective facts, but by our social background and psychological make-up, including those preferences and postulates which reflect our value system, however that is derived. But must this negate any suspicions we may have about the possibility of objective truth? We must naturally be very critical of the various assumptions on which it is possible for us to build different world views and we need to look seriously at the world views of other cultures and subject them also to critical analysis. This is perhaps the main task of philosophy, even if no philosophy is completely free from bias (Lewis, 1974, pp. 14-15). Just because we cannot see truth does not mean that there is no truth to be 'discovered'.

Excursus III. Comparative studies and cultural values: attitudes to virginity in tribal society

It may be that 'one cannot really explain a social fact of any complexity except by following its development through a social species' (Durkheim, 1964, p. 139). In other words, all human studies must be comparative if they are to have any real credibility. This must involve not only the comparison of different societies, but – as in the case of virginity – some consideration of a similar phenomenon in different *kinds* of society. Behind comparative studies generally there have been two generating factors: the explicit wish to understand and the implicit desire for change. It is this combination of cognitive and reformative aspirations which has informed much of the social research of recent years.

But there is also often a third element: the implicit assumption that by comparative investigation we can somehow uncover the 'natural order' of society, and get back to things as they were – and perhaps still ought to be. For example, there is a reluctance to see war as anything but a cultural invention, so attempts are made to get behind violence to uncover the pristine purity of the unsullied individual. By ignoring the trends of historical experience and concentrating on a few obscure pacifistic socie- ties, people are 'found' to be naturally non-aggressive. Similarly, it has been 'discovered' that people are, by nature, equal, and that social hier- archies are all part of an evil bourgeois conspiracy. The difficulty for those who hold such views or who have discerned such 'truths', is that when they do get back beyond the social order of conflict and criticism, of race and even gender, they find themselves confronted by a biological order which appears to endorse all these things; an order which favours the separation of the species, the distinctions of sex, and certainly the inequalities which many try so hard to ignore.

Such exercises are really a kind of well-intentioned reductionism – an attempt to reduce the complexities of everyday reality to some simple undifferentiated rule. Those who cannot easily accept that a social order should derive from the natural order must resort to some kind of alternative *imposed* order which may not accord with the inequalities and asymmetries suggested by the natural order, but will inevitably include its own particular anomalies and contradictions, as every order does.

One perennial problem about comparative studies is the task of deciding what is and what is not comparable. This issue turns on the question of whether it is more valid to compare societies themselves, or more useful to compare particular institutions or practices within those societies. To compare the social structures of, say, the United States and the Hottentots would be a somewhat fruitless exercise, but to compare their respective *family* structures might be rather more productive. The difficulty about comparing *whole* societies is that any statements that can eventually be made are likely to be very general and too inconclusive. It is usually much easier and more instructive to compare like institutions or practices in different societies. But it is important that these studies take due regard of the social settings, for if an institution or practice is isolated, as it were, for academic purposes, it inhibits understanding as to its real nature.

Comparative studies of human behaviour simply try to make 'true' general statements about the nature of society; in broad terms, they must try to answer three questions (Wells, 1970, pp. 12ff.):

(1) What is the range of variation shown by human society? This is an issue that might be assessed either statistically or impressionistically.

(2) What are the reasons for these variations? A question that can usually be answered only in the most tentative terms.

(3) What *common* principles lie behind existing social arrangements? Is it possible, for example, to detect any universal values underlying the complexities of human sexuality?

Any attempt to deal with these questions, particularly in the context of pre-industrial societies, is plagued by the problem of rationality. It may be that there is something in the structuralist argument that we all enjoy a shared reality; that whether we are primitives or sophisticates, we all possess the same basic thought structures. But – in one sense – this only complicates the problem. If we are so fundamentally alike, how are we to account for the kaleidoscopic variety of actual human behaviour? It seems obvious that over time behavioural patterns have developed according to varying as well as unvarying human needs. Pre-scientific peoples often *appear* to be so different from ourselves that they could almost be the products of a science-fiction imagination. Indeed, when writers of that genre want to 'create' an other-worldly culture, they often include some of the more bizarre ingredients from known historical societies to give us an eclectic but coherent alien world.

Are earlier peoples, then, really so different, and can we actually square their thinking with our own? Arguably, their fundamental needs and values were much the same, even if they were expressed in very different forms. These differences probably derive from the inverse relationships of two factors, namely, their necessarily limited appreciation of causality and their pervasive religiosity. Pre-scientific ideas are often baffling, and their convoluted reasoning sometimes eludes and even dismays us. We can understand the needs that generated the practices, and we can often fathom the values that informed the beliefs and rituals. But because their basic ideologies – their whole view of the world – was so far removed from ours, it is extremely difficult to discern why a particular need or value, such as survival, generated a particular *form* of response, such as, say, the Aztec practice of feeding human hearts to the sun.

How then does this relate to the question of virginity? To what extent does the non-rationality that characterises so much pre-scientific behaviour extend also to sexual practices? We have seen that the underlying concerns of earlier societies were much the same as ours, but that the explanations and coping-mechanisms were necessarily very different. Does this then apply to the sexual sphere? Curiously enough, not very much. Naturally, there was considerable confusion about the biochemical mechanisms underlying, say, reproduction, but this made little difference to actual *practices*. Perhaps the Tobrianders did think that women conceived because of the 'agitation' of sexual intercourse (Malinowski, 1932). Perhaps, too, we can hypothesise that the Central Bantu often had matrilineal systems because they were ignorant about the precise nature of the male role in procreation. But although this may have affected their modes of social organisation, it hardly seems to have impeded their actual sexual activities. As we shall see, attitudes to virginity reflected age-old usages which were sanctified by religion. Sex is not greatly influenced by a lack of cosmic awareness or by cognitive uncertainty. Understanding is not always a determinant of sexual behaviour.

However, it must be admitted that we know very little about sex in history. For simple societies, we have the traditional explorers' tales, and the almost mandatory condemnation by missionaries of practices that they considered undesirable. In more complex systems, there was a certain amount of legal comment together with the frequent disapproval of such practices as homosexuality and prostitution. But we rarely know what people actually *did* or really thought about such matters. What little we do know is not usually found in documentary form, but is expressed in certain kinds of art such as Indian Temple reliefs and classical Greek ceramics (Boardman & LaRocca, 1978). Some commentators seem to find this rather odd and just a little disappointing (Bullough, 1976, pp. 3ff.). But is this really so surprising? Pre-scientific peoples may have been very uncertain about the mechanisms of reproduction, but this hardly extended to the mechanics of sex. Surely the simple answer is best here? Sex has always been commonplace, and has a very limited range of expression. It was not *that* different from society to society; it was not *so* unusual or sensational that it had to excite comment. Perhaps people were not that curious about what others actually did because, in a sense, they knew already. Even in literate societies, it was not a subject that demanded documentation.

This is not to suggest that there was one overall perspective or one overriding orientation towards the question of virginity. There were exceptions and inconsistencies, certainly between societies, and often even within societies. So, for example, among the Burundi of East Africa, no sex relations were permitted for the young girls, but they were encouraged to masturbate and stretch their labia, presumably to prepare themselves for marriage. Apparently, they believed that men would not be attracted to them unless they had abnormally distorted labia. After marriage, they could only have sex with their husbands and privileged partners, and masturbation was prohibited (Bullough, 1976, p. 29). Similarly, virginity was esteemed among the South African Mpondo peoples, but it was regarded as a mark of hospitality if girls were loaned to strangers to be broken in (Roberts, 1977, p. 175). Polynesia presented a similar picture. In Tahiti, Captain Cook's sailors were surprised to find that people often copulated in public. In Hawaii, girls were promiscuous with visitors, although daughters of the nobility were much more modest. In Samoa too, girls could make love to strangers but not to other natives, and if a girl of the nobility was found to be a non-virgin before marriage, she could be put to death by her own father and brothers (Service, 1978).

In other societies, however, socialisation processes could be so organised that sex was regarded as a rather shameful activity which had to be merely tolerated by women. Among the Manus of New Guinea, women were encouraged to display asexual attitudes, and to view sexual activity with at least a show of indifference.

Generally speaking, in the pre-industrial world virginity was regarded as something to be prized and, therefore, something to be guarded. Fairly typical is early Peruvian society, where the rape of young girls could be punished by flogging and exile, and the rape of virgins by death unless the culprit agreed to marry his victim. For sexual offences, capital punishment was common. The rape of a married woman was punishable by death, as also was incest (although what constitutes close relations can be variously defined). Anal intercourse and bestiality were punishable by hanging, but even here much depended upon time and locality. The Mochica culture, famed for its erotic pottery, which had largely declined by the time of the Inca civilisation, i.e. from the 13th century AD, is said to have encouraged its temple virgins to confine their sexual activities to anal intercourse so that, technically, they still retained their value (Guerra, 1971). These views were not held by all other indigenous American peoples. The Caribs do not appear to have valued virginity except among the higher class girls who were virtually confined for two years before marriage. The central American Chibcha had similar ideas, and even regarded virgins as girls who were incapable of inspiring desire (Mantegazza, 1935, pp. 52-4). But it may be significant that stricter views on virginity were held by a number of relatively *developed* contemporaneous societies in Mexico. The Aztecs valued bridal virginity, and the Maya regarded the rape of a virgin as a capital offence, though if the man attempted but was unable to complete the act, he might be taken as a slave.

In these and other systems, virginity became a commodity which could be used for a variety of social and economic purposes. So among some tribal peoples in West Africa, it was traditional for a girl to be returned to her family, and the bride-price repaid, if she was not intact at marriage. But, by the same token, if a wrong accusation was made about a daughter's virginity, it was customary to demand the return of all or part of her dowry. To obviate the problem of having to arrange marriages for non-negotiable girls, some societies, for example in Polynesia, resorted to the expedient of celebrating betrothals when the bride and groom were little more than infants, so that consummation was postponed to a later date. Yet in the Caroline and the Mariana Islands, where promiscuity was normal before marriage, there was enforced chastity afterwards.

Proof of virginity was important, and bloodstained clothes might be demanded as evidence. In Samoa, a girl might actually be deflowered by hand by a chief, although in Arabia this was often done – more tactfully – by an older woman. In Egypt too, there is some evidence that the hymen might be deliberately cut prior to marriage. Less commonly, in both Cambodia and the Philippines, this might be done instead by a priest, as it was considered to be something of an obstacle to the husband. Traditionally, in Malabar, when the priests performed the same chore it was the virgins themselves who had to pay for their services.

Of course, defloration must not be confused with first intercourse. Many women are deflowered manually, as in some Australian Aborigine tribes; others deflower themselves – perhaps ritually, as among the early Romans. On the other hand, sometimes the privilege of *coital* defloration was given to someone other than the husband, as in some tribal groups in Gambia. Or it might be held that the girl was the property of the family unit and that she must be enjoyed for a night by their wedding guests before being handed over to the husband – a practice noted by Diodorus Siculus in the early Balearic Islands (ed. Oldfather, 1933). In Nubia, defloration was left for the husband, but it had to be done publicly, whereas in ancient Phoenicia it might even be the task of the husband's slave.

It can be seen from this that the entire question of female modesty is riddled with inconsistencies. For example, Marco Polo, the Venetian traveller and author, records that in 13th-century China some girls might be publicly prostituted by their mothers, but after marriage their chastity was highly regarded (Van Gulik, 1961). It is not unusual to find inconsistencies even within a particular culture area. There were North American Indian societies where girls were described as 'debauched' although their married women were said to be chaste (Chinooks), or where their speech was pronounced obscene although their *actions* were regarded as above reproach (Potowatami). Among yet others, women were renowned for their chastity (Apaches) even though this was viewed as exceptional (Underhill, 1971). Obviously, so much turns on the issue of perception and interpretation.

So despite the anomalies, the trends are reasonably clear. Girls were usually expected to be virgo intacta until marriage. Sometimes manipulation of the genitalia was encouraged, and in practice this may have constituted a form of masturbation. Sometimes stimulation of the clitoris might be allowed as a kind of didactic exercise – a learning operation preparatory to betrothal or marriage. This could take the form of deliberate dilation of the vulva, as among some Australian aborigine tribes, so as to permit easier intercourse (Ploss & Bartels, 1967, pp. 47ff.). In some circumstances, prostitution of orifices other than the vagina was both permitted and institutionalised. It was also not uncommon for girls to be deflowered artificially, either manually or with substitute phalluses, by themselves or others. But rupture of the hymen does not, on our definition, necessarily involve the loss of virginity, after all, it has even been known for girls to give birth to babies with their hymens still intact.

Actually, all these practices serve to reaffirm the importance of technical virginity in traditional societies. Some societies had serious strictures against unchastity in any form, others, as we have seen, had quite liberal attitudes and were not too vexed about matters of modesty. But whatever sexual norms were observed, the technical preservation of virginity was usually highly esteemed. Most societies had a ne plus ultra approach to adolescent sex. It was a question of so far and no further, and if this was disregarded, as, of course, it often was – the overriding consideration was to avoid pregnancy at all costs.

The desire – perhaps even the need – to ensure female chastity has resulted historically in all kinds of practices which, to the western mind, range from the strange to the positively bizarre. The cauterising of the clitoris and clitoridectomy, i.e. the excision of the clitoris, were believed to reduce or eliminate female sexual desire. Both are quite well attested in a number of societies, and clitoridectomy especially was well established among some Abyssinian groups, in Benin society, and among the Amazonian Jivaros where it was said to ensure the chastity of oversexed wives. Some societies obviously found the female sexual response a problem, but few would probably go as far as one 19th-century commentator who hypothesised that the prevalence of sodomy 'in warm countries where nudity is visible' is due to the fact that 'the woman is dishearteningly large in her organ ... and ... easy to be had' (Mantegazza, 1935, p. 90). In some extreme groups such as the 19th-century Russian Skopt sect it is reported that because they regarded sensual expressions of love as sinful and vain, they sometimes mutilated the genitals of both men and women, removing not only the clitoris but the nipples as well.

Not unknown, too, was the custom of infibulation where the female labia are clipped, stitched or 'fused' together in such a way that they adhere to cover the vagina. This was a painful but effective obstacle to sexual intercourse. In different forms, it was well established in a number of societies; partial infibulation of the anus was even known among boys in ancient Rome. In Nubia, it was sometimes used by African slave merchants to ensure the chastity of girls they wished to sell. Some traditions have claimed that there are sure signs – quite apart from the normal physical indications – which betray the girl who has lost her virginity and therefore destroyed her 'negotiability'. Most of these can confidently be consigned to the realms of superstition, as, for example, the idea that wreaths of roses only stay fresh on the brows of maidens, or that only virgins can restore an extinguished flame with their breath (Ploss & Bartels, 1967).

If a girl's virginity had been lost, there were ways in which it could be artificially 'restored', sometimes by the use of silk thread. Where further evidence was required, it could always be manufactured. A small piece of sponge or similar material soaked in blood – sometimes a pigeon's blood – was placed in the vagina to simulate the bleeding which sometimes attends perforation. On occasions this was done by respectable families in order to disguise their daughter's shame, and, of course, enhance her marriageability. But more frequently, it was a ploy of unscrupulous brothel owners. The Greek orator, Demosthenes – who admittedly was trying to make a good case – says of a particularly well known courtesan and madam named Neaira that she had seven slave 'daughters' whose virginity she sold several times over. Similarly, Mantegazza (1935, pp. 85ff.) claims to have known a Parisian call-girl who was 'deflowered' eighty-two times. This compares interestingly with Petronius' courtesan Quartilla (Satyricon) who could not remember ever having been a virgin. Unsullied maidens and 'doctored virgins' have always been in demand for a special clientele, but the privilege of defloration – either actual or assumed – usually comes at highly inflated prices.

The exceptions can easily blind us to the rule. Indeed, as we have already observed, it could be argued that they actually confirm the rule. In pre-scientific societies, virginity and chastity were usually qualities to be prized. They were normally part of the particular value-system, and were therefore upheld by the appropriate sanctions. It is here that we see that the role of religion in relation to sexual values is often ambiguous. Even sexually incongruent acts which in no way seem to support the values of virginity and chastity can be variously interpreted. For instance, where priests assume or are granted *ius primae noctis* (right of the first night), they are in effect confirming the cruciality of defloration. In this seemingly cynical act, they are really endorsing its importance. The value of virginity is reaffirmed while its destruction is legitimised. Even where religious institutions countenance prostitution, this effectively categorises certain forms of sexual activity in a way that indirectly helps to preserve the virginity or chastity of particular groups or classes of the female population. An ethos of sexual laxity throws these values into relief and confirms their social and moral status.

6

In What Sense Are We Morally Responsible?

We now have to consider one of the most intractable problems in philosophy which bedevils – directly or indirectly – ethical enquiry in particular and the social sciences in general, namely, the problem of how free we are to make moral choices.

Free will and determinism

Few people would deny that we live in a world of cause and effect. It would be difficult to see how science could proceed without making such an assumption. Causes are normally classified as either *necessary*, i.e. contributory causes, or *sufficient*, i.e. total causes. In the social sciences in particular we can rarely talk confidently about sufficient causes, but necessary causes can often be identified in relation to some event or condition. For example, if I ask myself why I decided to have muesli and toast for breakfast this morning, there could, hypothetically, be several possible answers. The decision might be related to what I had yesterday morning: did I want the same today or did I want a change? Perhaps I'm on a diet, and muesli and toast are required eating, or – not unusually – I'm pressed for time, and therefore I want something which takes little preparation and even less time to eat. But I like to tell myself that regardless of these antecedent and causal factors, I ate what I did because *I decided to*, and that nothing else ultimately determined my choice. But is that all there is to it? It can still be asked, why did I will what I willed when I willed it?

Determinism does not mean fatalism or *pre*-determinism. Determinism may be defined as 'the belief that everything that happens has a cause or causes, and could not have happened differently unless something in the cause or causes had also been different' (Carr, 1965, p. 93). In other words, all objects and/or events *must be* as they are (or will become) by virtue of the forces that necessitate them. Fatalism, by comparison, implies pre-ordination, some pre-conceived plan for each one of us. It suggests a fate or destiny which none of us can avoid, a 'que sera, sera' outlook that looks ahead with total resignation.

Experimentally, it is rarely possible in the social sciences to identify all the relevant preconditions which make for a particular effect. Our knowledge is always partial. Because human events are unique events, our knowledge, and therefore our capacity for judgement, is necessarily limited. The physical sciences work within certain assumptions, pre-eminently that of causality, and in everyday life the axiom that 'everything has a cause is a condition of our capacity to understand what is going on around us' (Carr, 1965, pp. 93-4). Free will does not have to imply that the idea of cause has no validity, but it does mean that regardless of the antecedents related to any act there is always the 'will' as an additional category of cause. This also helps to account for the accidental and fortuitous events that appear to change the course of our histories as these are presumably occasioned in some way by the wills of others. But perhaps these events impinge upon our experience in such a way that they *seem* accidental and fortuitous, and because we could not foresee them, their conjunction surprises us. Sometimes the outcome can seem unusual – even miraculous, such as the case of the man who escaped death in a massacre during the interwar Communist purges in Mongolia simply because his name was spelled wrongly on the proscription lists. At other times, it can be seen as incalculably tragic, as when, through a whole series of small accidental occurrences, Hitler was not killed as a result of a bomb-plot in July 1944, and the consequence was that the war went on for another year, the death camps flourished, and some two thousand or so people were executed because of their known or believed complicity in the plot itself.

At the macro level we might ask if there is a determined course, direction or plan to history. If so, we must also believe that there is some purpose and meaning in history which, at present, we are unable to fathom. Sir Karl Popper, for instance, insists that we should renounce any pretension to know the past 'as it was', and that the suggestion that there could possibly be some 'verdict on history' is intellectually untenable (Popper, 1966, vol. 2). So can the historian assume the pose of an overarching spectator, and presume to dispense praise and blame on people and empires, or is this an exercise in academic futility? History is now said to be partial and relative; there is no longer 'history', only histories which are incapable of any finality. Indeed, many Postmodernists would go further and insist that we can no longer trust history to give us anything like unvarnished 'truth' (Connor, 1989). Yet, having said this, it is difficult not to pass judgements on the inhumanity of the past and the ludicrous ambiguities of the present. At the same time, we can still acknowledge what undoubtedly passes for 'progress' in history in a fairly loose sense: we can say that given the 'nature' of humankind and what constitutes its 'basic needs' – two concepts which beg all sorts of pertinent questions – and the possible range of socio-economic solutions for the satisfaction of those needs, then human history must develop along reasonably predictable lines.

Some social science students find themselves in unfamiliar territory where history is involved; reading history often means wrestling with problems which they last encountered all too briefly at school (see Excursus IV). Life becomes even more difficult when they find that some forms of historical determinism have a metaphysical dimension. This can be found in texts ranging from the works of Plato to those of Toynbee and de Chardin in modern times. Arnold Toynbee, in particular, sees the meaning of history as a divine plan characterised by encounter and challenge, suffering and striving. He divides history into twenty-one civilisations (and several abortive ones), all of which have been overtaken by nemesis of one kind or another. Each decline is the same story – the society's failure in a crisis to convert an ideal into a singular opportunity. His theme seems to be that nothing fails like success. He hovers – like Plato – between an optimistic and pessimistic view of the future, hopefully toying with the possibility that one day humanity will find a spiritual solution to its age-old dilemmas. In this, Toynbee is substituting a this-wordly end-state for the other-wordly end-states advanced by so many religious systems (see Gardiner, 1959).

It can be argued that an analogous cause and effect process operates at the individual level. As we have seen, the conflicting arguments are often related to historical sequences and situations (e.g. Nagel, 1960), but it is also interesting to see how they are related to personal behaviour. Here too we have the free will/determinism paradox. Peter Berger has argued that 'an object or event that is its own cause lies outside the scientific universe of discourse. Yet freedom has precisely that character. For this reason no amount of scientific research will ever uncover a phenomenon that can be designated as free. Whatever may appear to be free within the subjective consciousness of the individual will find its place in the scientific scheme as a link in some chain of causation' (Berger, 1966, pp. 142-3). In other words, no matter what theoretical position we adopt the result is the same; unconsciously and emotionally, we act *as though* we are free. If we were not free, would we ever be aware of choice as a possibility? We all have to ask ourselves why we are as we are. We need to know whether our apparently voluntary actions are really the effects of a theoretically predictable conjunction of events or not. Are they the outcome of largely unrecognised historical antecedents? Are our characters what they are because of hereditary factors, or are they formed by past actions and experiences? Alternatively, they may be the result of our present circumstances and the external pressures acting upon us. So are we sociochemical automata or are we free, volitional beings? Detached scientific reasoning – perhaps with reluctance – endorses the determinist position, while our ultimate, direct experiences still cling to the idea that we possess free will.

On a Psychodynamic analysis, our conscious actions are determined by our unconscious, i.e. secret selves. As we have seen, this school maintains that our conscious thoughts are reflections – more or less sublimated – of the unconscious elements in our natures. To this extent, we are victims of forces that we cannot control. But if our thoughts are not free, and are really dictated by unconscious wish fulfilment, and our reasoning therefore becomes simply rationalising, this conclusion must also apply to psychoanalysis itself. This too is the mere rationalisation of the desire/wish to believe that human nature is of a certain kind and motivated in a certain way. It could, therefore, be argued that, as such, it has no relation to fact but simply reflects a certain condition in the psychoanalysts' unconscious minds. This is not to say that it is untrue, but to point out the meaninglessness of asking whether it is true or not. It follows from this that there is still great uncertainty on a Psychodynamic analysis about the areas in which we can be said to be either free or unfree (Joad, 1942).

So have we moral responsibility? It follows that if we are not free the responsibility for our actions is seriously in doubt. The argument, as frequently formulated, is that a necessary condition for holding a person responsible for an act is that the person had the capacity to act freely. Because if determinism is 'true', nobody ever acts freely, and therefore can never be blameworthy or punishable for their acts (Dworkin, 1970, p. 8). This presupposes that any individual could not have acted differently given the relevant causal antecedents. Acts are really the outworking of a complex of antecedents which make them predictable in principle.

The rather extreme determinist position is well put by Clarence Darrow who, at one time, was perhaps the most famous attorney in the United States: 'There is no such thing as a crime as the word is generally understood. I do not believe there is any sort of distinction between the real moral conditions of the people in and out of jail. One is just as good as the other. The people [in jail] can no more help being [there] than the people outside can avoid being outside. I do not believe people are in jail because they deserve to be. They are [there] simply because they cannot avoid it on account of circumstances which are entirely beyond their control and for which they are in no way responsible … (quoted by Dworkin, 1970, p. 1). Darrow is here arguing that even people condemned for heinous crimes are driven to do what they do by a combination of unfortuitous circumstances and inexplicable inner compulsions. It might, therefore, be profitable to look briefly at some particular crimes and examine the question of culpability.

Let us consider, first of all, the largely forgotten career of John Donald Merrett who, in his teens, quite inexplicably embarked on a career of fraud, forgery, blackmail and murder. He was born in New Zealand in 1908, and came to Britain with his mother while still a youth. He was exceptionally bright with a flair for languages, and coming from a well-to-do family was eventually enrolled at Edinburgh University but was more interested in being a student than actually studying. In March 1926 his mother was found by a maid bleeding from a bullet wound in the head. The maid had heard an explosion and had also heard the son shout out that his mother had shot herself. Mrs Merrett died in April, and, despite the suspicious nature of the circumstances, it was assumed that this was a case of suicide.

However, in November, the son was charged with forging his mother's cheques and with her murder. The defence was helped by no less a person that Sir Bernard Spilsbury, perhaps the most eminent pathologist of his day, the Scottish jury brought in a verdict of Not Proven, and Merrett merely received a one-year sentence for forgery. After his release, he inherited £50,000 – in those days, tantamount to a king's ransom – married a girl of 17 (despite being a inveterate womaniser) and changed his name to Chesney. He quickly got through the money, and then occupied himself with blackmail and fraud. Not uncharacteristically, he served with some distinction in the Royal Navy during the Second World War, and then, anxious for more lucrative adventures, he became involved in blackmarket dealings in post-war Germany. By 1954, these rackets were beginning to dry up, and in desperation, Merrett decided to rob his wife who was living with her mother in London at the time. He came back to England, renewed relations, got his wife drunk and arranged an 'accidental' drowning in the bath. Unfortunately, the murder was seen by his mother-in-law, and she too had to be killed. Merrett fled back to Germany and an international alert went out for him. This time he obviously felt that there was going to be no escape, and not long afterwards his body was found near Cologne – the matricide had settled for a bullet in his own head (Gaute & Odell, 1979).

It is probably a waste of time to speculate now on just why this obviously intelligent boy from a prosperous and caring family decided to embark on a life of crime. To suggest that it was simply greed is too facile, but this is the conclusion that most would probably settle for. The causal antecedents are untraced and probably untraceable, and it is tempting to see some cogency in Clarence Darrow's analysis. But if we do we are surely making do with something – anything – to fill the cognitive vacuum.

By comparison, we might consider the apparently growing problem of serial killers. A fairly typical case is that of Heinrich Pommerenke, who began his deadly career as a multiple murderer by molesting girls outside dance-halls at the age of 15. Soon afterwards, he embarked upon a series of rapes in Hamburg (1955-57), and then moved on to Austria where he is known to have attacked at least two girls in 1958. The following year, after leaving the cinema one evening, he accosted and raped an 18-year-old girl and then cut her throat. That summer, he killed again. Later, he took the train to Italy, and among the sleeping passengers, he found and molested a young girl student. She tried to escape, but he pushed her out of the train and, in his sexual desperation, pulled the communication cord. As the train slowed, he jumped after her, raped and then murdered her. Within a month, the 'beast of the Black Forest', as he was dubbed, claimed two more victims. He was finally arrested in 1960. He made a full confession, and was eventually charged with 10 murders (with rape), 20 cases of rape alone, and 35 assaults and burglaries, and was sentenced to a total of 140 years in prison.

In Pommerenke's case, there seems to be little doubt about the motivation. He claimed to have been inspired to commit these offences by watching sex films, though this hardly accounts for the killings. There does not appear to have been any overt sadistic element in the murders, in fact they all seem to have been rather rushed, with sexual gratification as the main motive, and murder as something of an afterthought (if it was to prevent identification, why did he not kill in the other rape incidents?). So here we have an instance of multiple murder which can – to all intents and purposes – be explained in sexual terms, but the question still remains, why should a young man resort to such extremes for sexual satisfaction? Are we to come down in favour of some kind of biological reductionism which treats such aberrations in deterministic genetic terms as a drive which could never have been changed? Or are we to think of such behaviour as merely an inclination – a proclivity – which ought to be subject to individual control?

This kind of phenomenon might be compared with the very unusual instances of seemingly motiveless crimes. Robert Lindner (see Hospers, 1961, p. 496) recounts the story of a young woman who opened the door of her apartment to a delivery man only to be murdered within minutes by this complete stranger. There was no attempted rape, no robbery, in fact no apparent motive at all. The police were baffled by this pointless and seemingly inexplicable killing, and in such circumstances were tempted to clutch at any half-reasonable explanatory straws. After further investigation it transpired that the delivery man had recently discovered why he had spent most of his life in care of one kind or another. He had formerly believed that his mother had loved him and had wanted to keep him, but had surrendered him to others out of sheer poverty. He then discovered that this was entirely untrue. Actually his mother was a prostitute who had found the infant an encumbrance, given her professional activities, and had got rid of him as soon as it could be suitably arranged. The man's memories were shattered; his love turned to disillusionment and hate. It happened, coincidentally, that the murdered woman was wearing a rather unusual ring which was very similar to the one worn by his mother. So it was hypothesised that at that tragic moment when she opened the door, he saw this woman as his mother and killed her.

This conjecture is a little far-fetched, but it was better than nothing. The murdered woman had become a substitute, a subject for symbolic revenge, and had unknowingly generated an all-consuming desire in the man to destroy an image that he had once cherished. Reason demands an explanation of some kind, and this was cautiously accepted when nothing better was forthcoming. The causal (determinative) chain had been reasonably hypothesised.

Rather different is the kind of case where there is really no doubt about the antecedent links, and where the clarity of the situation becomes the crucial factor in determining the degree of culpability of the offender. Some years ago in a Midlands industrial town in England there occurred a crime which falls neatly into this category. The proprietor of a small corner shop killed his wife in a rage by hitting her with an electric drill. It transpired that she had come home very late on the night of the murder and informed her husband that she was pregnant by another man and that she was going to leave him and the children. He knew that there was no possibility that the child was his because for some time he had been suffering bouts of impotence about which his wife had occasionally taunted him. She was younger than he, rather vivacious, and had decided that she was going to seek solace elsewhere – almost certainly not for the first time.

The irony of this case is that the post-mortem revealed that she was not pregnant at all, even though she obviously thought she was. Her confession was therefore unnecessary, but this together with the threat of desertion was enough to incite the fatal argument. So the causal chain was clear, the reasons for the crime were all too evident. The man, it was felt, had been gradually driven beyond the point of rational deliberation. This was seen as explanatory, and was regarded as the basis for a plea of diminished responsibility. He was found guilty but insane and incarcerated in an appropriate institution.

Obviously, there are some people, such as psychotics and psychopaths – however we define these terms – who do not seem to have the mental wherewithal to make 'normal' moral distinctions. But just how liberally are we to apply such terms? Is every offender – especially if the crime is incomprehensibly odious – ipso facto 'sick' and therefore not blameworthy? Are we prepared to argue that given the total circumstances no one can really be either praised or blamed for anything? Hospers points out (1961, pp. 504-21) that we must, of course, distinguish between compulsion and causation, between physical coercion and mental coercion, and then between different types of cause. We must also remember that the mind may constitute a particular category of cause. But, as we have already seen, to argue – as he does – that *our* decisions change the course of events, begs the question *why* we decide on this rather than that, why we make *this* choice rather than any other from a range of options.

Arthur Koestler summarises the position well when he writes that 'the aim of the historian, the psychologist, (and) the social scientist is to explain social behaviour by the interplay of cause and effect, by unravelling the conscious and unconscious forces behind the act ... Their aim is to trace and measure, not to judge. Nevertheless moral judgements seep into all our reactions and determine social behaviour, ... praise and blame ... whether justified or not scientifically, are essential to the functioning of society (Koestler, 1956, pp. 96-7, see also Carlton, 1994, pp. 167-77).

It really amounts to this: there is no completely satisfactory or final argument against determinism, so we must be determinists of some sort in order to live in a world governed by the 'forces' of cause and effect. But, at the same time, we must endorse some kind of volitionism to live with ourselves. Life would be intolerable if we believed that every word and every action was, in some indefinable way, pre-determined for us by our natures and the circumstances in which we find ourselves.

Excursus IV. Sociology and the study of history

It could be argued that sociology is part of the secular dogmata of industrialised systems. Its concerns are now almost entirely confined to theoretical analyses of the institutional and normative structures of modern societies. As a discipline, its interests are purportedly reformative as well as being disinterestedly academic. In the 'trade', there is a praiseworthy emphasis on relevance and an increasing predisposition towards the practicalities of policy and decision-making processes. It is absorbed by the problems that derive from industrialisation: the encroachments of the new technology and economic uncertainty; the expansion of the new colonialism and political instability; crime, terrorism and the anonymity of the urban situation – in short, the mounting pressures of living in the contemporary world. All these provide sociology with its current, rather formidable, field of enquiry.

The main concessions to the pre-industrial world are to be found in the fashionable studies of emergent societies where – with suitable ideological overtones – the birth pangs of transition anticipate the dynamics of industrialisation. Implicit in much sociological debate is the assumption that change, although not unequivocally good, is both necessary and preferable to the contemporary situation – whatever that happens to be. It is therefore regarded as the task of sociologists to supply the appropriate philosophical underpinnings for a new and better society.

While it must be conceded that the development of sociology as an academic discipline grew out of the need to interpret a rapidly changing world, it is a contention of this excursus that sociology has for too long been enmeshed in arguments about social change. Theories of social change proliferate, as does the literature to appraise them. Indeed, it might be argued – at one level – that sociology has become the mere documentation of change and its concomitant, the emergence of industrialised society. However, the fact that is particularly evidenced by the study of complex pre-industrial societies is that societies with a relatively unchanging social order are not only interesting in themselves, but are extremely important for any real understanding of social forms. Unchangingness has been the condition of societies for most of history, and craves the kind of analysis that has been largely overlooked by sociologists. How, for instance, are we to explain social longevity? How can we account for the fact that a society such as Ancient Egypt can retain its essential homogeneity for three thousand years? Perhaps Parsons has a point; social order *is* a problem. Unchangingness needs to be explained much more than change, and involves such issues as control, stability and value-consensus which have been the intellectual preoccupations of philosophers at least since Plato.

C. Wright Mills was surely right when he suggested that although history is the stuff of sociology, much sociology is still a-historical in its orientation (Mills, 1967). For too many sociologists, history effectively began with the industrial revolution. Before that there was a long and uncertain period of undifferentiated stasis, the details of which are either lacking or almost invariably prejudiced. History, as such, tends to be regarded as partial, relative and singularly untidy. Therefore any study which concerns itself with traditional societies may be seen as little more than an academic divertissement which, although unusual and even interesting, allows for few substantial conclusions. So the void remains. On the one hand, industrialised society is being suitably appraised; at the other extreme, simple societies are receiving their appropriate treatment. Indeed, the number of simple societies untouched by modern scholarship is now rapidly running out, and sceptics have observed that anthropologists have been reduced either to studies of quaintly anachronistic fishing villages in Western Ireland, or to the re-evaluation of the work of other anthropologists. By comparison, the work on complex pre-industrial systems is extremely slight.

Of course, there are some very notable exceptions: Max Weber's study of the agrarian economies and religious systems of ancient civilisations; Talcott Parsons' work on the typology and organisation of early societies; S.N. Eisenstadt's analyses of bureaucratic empires, and the studies of Gerhardt Lenski, Gideon Sjoberg and Michael Mann on pre-industrial social formations. These are but a few of a tiny minority of sociologists who have been complemented by a growing number of historians working in similar areas. One thinks of Perry Anderson and Crane Brinton, and pre-eminently M.I. Finley and Keith Hopkins, all of whom have strong sociological orientations. But all this cannot disguise the fact that complex pre-industrial systems are relatively uncharted territory for most social scientists.

The two main issues that confront the would-be sociologist of complex pre-industrial societies are, first, promotion and – dare one say it? – popularisation, and, secondly, the problem of method. The matter of promotion is really all bound up with the question of relevance. A not uncommon response of one's disciplinary peers is to query the value of the whole enterprise. In the face of already crowded courses, how can one find a meaningful place for the study of antique societies? Of course there is always the 'Option' – let the *students* choose – or it can be safely relegated to the odd introductory lecture of another course, or, failing this, there can be the occasional tantalising allusion to caste or slavery when dealing with stratification.

The issue is often further complicated by the academic deficiencies of the potential students for such courses. In the vast majority of cases, students' acquaintance with complex pre-industrial societies is almost non-existent. Their ancient history coverage – if any – at the secondary level will usually have been minimal. After a perfunctory nod in the direction of Early Man there is normally a hurried introduction to some of the more colourful aspects of the Classical World. Most self-respecting pedagogues hope to reach 1066 AD by the end of the first year; consequently the pupils effectively finish their tour of the pre-medieval world by the time they are twelve years old, and rarely return for a second visit. When and if they are eventually confronted with some 'facts' about pre-industrial societies, they often find them intriguing, even fascinating, but the material is so strange and unfamiliar that they tend to settle for safer and more 'appropriate' options.

In some senses, complex pre-industrial societies can seem like other worlds to the uninitiated. Indeed, in their more bizarre forms, as, say, in Ancient Egypt, they can appear so far removed from current experience that their study is only germane to a weird and esoteric minority. Yet at other levels, it can be seen that the value-systems that informed them were not so markedly different from our own. At certain levels, we can identify with the hopes and aspirations of pre-industrial man, but these were often expressed in ways which are unrecognisably foreign to the modern mind (Kemp, 1989).

The main problem, though, which vitiates the study of complex pre-industrial systems is that of method. This is a problem because there are all sorts of conceptual and practical difficulties in getting to grips with the social arrangements of past societies where evidence may be either lacking or ambiguous. What methods are applicable or, indeed, appropriate for the analysis of such societies? Normal scientific parameters present difficulties because documentation is often sparse, and the paucity of information – especially statistical data – naturally reduces the range of methodological possibilities. For instance, how can we sensibly address the question of whether, say, classical Athens was a slave-based society when we are not sure how many slaves there were, or even what proportion they comprised of the total population of the polis (Finley, 1983). In practice, all we can do with such quantitative questions is to extrapolate cautiously from a limited number of known historical instances and hope that we can arrive at a reasonable approximation (Hopkins, 1983). And this still does not take into account the disputed conceptual issue of exactly what slavery *was* in this type of society (Finley, 1964).

One way to proceed is by the well-tried use of models. Some theorists insist that 'we know a structure completely only if we can construct it, materially or intellectually' (de Jouvenel, 1967). That is to say, our knowledge of a structure is mediated by models which 'reproduce' the real world insofar as they enable us to make limited deductions about its forms and processes. But, having said that, models do have serious limitations. This is exemplified by Weber's ideal-type which is sometimes used in the analysis of pre-industrial systems. As Weber himself was well aware, use of the ideal-type is open to a whole battery of well-rehearsed reservations. By comparing the actual courses of events with the ideal-type, we are, in effect, ordering reality by isolating certain factors and identifying the differentiae. But the very fact that we can include or exclude the desired variables also means that we can reach the equally desired conclusions.

Problems of fallibility arise where the applicability of rational models is itself in doubt – taking rational to mean the logical correspondence between ends and means. Which kinds of construct are appropriate to the study of pre-industrial societies? Can we, for instance, relate modern Western models to these kinds of society? This problem is well exemplified by the models – and their underlying assumptions – which are found in modern economic theory. How can we apply this to societies where, in general terms, there was rudimentary technology, little capital formation, undeveloped banking systems, only embryonic entrepreneurial activity, and relatively small productive units?

Furthermore, the entire issue is exacerbated by the fact that in traditional societies aesthetic and religious values may complicate and even confound our understanding of social behaviour. How, for example, are we to explain the waking, washing and 'feeding' of idols in ancient Babylonia? More cogent still is the once pervasive practice of human sacrifice. Why use war captives as ritual fodder when they might be better employed building roads or temples or palace complexes or whatever? This must have occurred to the Meso-American cultures, especially the Aztecs who sacrificed on a gigantic scale, but it was largely disregarded (Fagan, 1983). Or why sacrifice the children of the privileged who one day would presumably have made up the warrior class, and then, like the Carthaginians, employ mercenaries to fight your wars (Warmington, 1960)? This was not mere caprice; economic need and political exigencies were regarded as secondary. These apparent irrationalities stemmed directly from the ritual imperatives which informed the system.

A study of complex pre-industrial societies offers sociologists both exemplifications and refutations of accepted theory, not least concerning certain aspects of 'class'. Some not uncommon tendencies towards stratificatory reductionism have to be qualified in the light of modern interpretations of traditional social arrangements. Take the issue of class and war. What are we to make of the Athenian practice of not using slaves in warfare? Of course, it could be argued that they were untrained and might even prove to be unreliable or dangerous if they were armed, but even a superficial reading shows that there was more to it than this. The ideology of warfare demanded that it be reserved for the more privileged groups. It wasn't a matter of simply exploiting the dispossessed. War was the pursuit of citizens, and sometimes resident aliens. To fight for one's *polis* was both a duty and an honour – a task which one could hardly leave to the lower orders of society (Garlan, 1975). Or let us take the related problem of 'class war'. It is disputable whether the term can be used meaningfully in the context of the Greek states if by 'class war' is meant a struggle to bring about some radical re-structuring of society. Certainly there was considerable conflict between the *aristoi* and the *demoi*, effectively the haves and have-nots, in many of the *poleis*. Fratricidal warfare was a favourite pastime of the Greeks, but even in Athens, arguably the most radically democratic of Greek states, this was not calculated to bring about the abolition of privilege and private property – and most definitely not the enfranchisement of all the members of that society. Citizenship was by birth, and then only for adult males. It was such a prized legal status that we find it reported that in 445 BC, during a distribution of grain, some 5,000 resident aliens (metics) who were found posing as citizens were struck off the city's register and sold into slavery. In the Slave Wars which plagued Rome, especially in the 1st century BC, there is likewise no evidence that the rebellious slaves wished to abolish slavery; they just did not want to be slaves themselves, and sometimes succeeded in making slaves of their erstwhile masters (Hopkins, 1978).

The study of complex pre-industrial societies can also serve as a salutary corrective to some current theories about the relationship between ideology and society. Ideology exerts important influences and shapes the course of human action in discernible ways, but just how and why is notoriously difficult to say. An idealist view that all ideologies are attributable to the primacy of ideas is not easily sustained. It is debatable whether ideas are produced in a vacuum; ideologies usually mirror the conditions in which people live, and there is often a suspicious coincidence between the particular ideology which is advocated or adopted and the interests which it reflects. On the other hand, it is equally – if not more – difficult to sustain the realist view that all values dissolve into ideology. This strips ideology of any independent meaning and consequence except as a *post-facto* attempt to disguise existing class interests. There is no fixed hierarchy of values which insists that men must always prefer, say, economic advantage to social esteem. And all this is, of course, conditioned by what is considered dominant or determinant in any given situation (Hall, 1977).

It has been argued that sociologists should adopt a purely nomothetic approach to historical studies because sociology is primarily interested in the general and recurrent rather than the unique and particular (Bierstedt, 1959). There may even be a certain impatience with the historian who is preoccupied with 'facts' and patently fascinated by the details of surviving documentary and archaeological evidence. Obviously, 'without texts, there is no history'. And some selection of these materials is an essential prerequisite of historical method. However, we ought not to become the slaves of materials that come into our hands by chance, as this may inadvertently exaggerate or minimise the significance of particular societies (Grant, 1952, pp. 8ff.). Furthermore, it is still possible for the sociologist to make valuable deductions about the nature of those societies even where the evidence is limited or actually 'oblique'. This has been done with great ingenuity, for example, by the historian M.I. Finley. Using sociological techniques, he has made a fascinating study of Homeric society based on the narratives of the *Odyssey* and the *Iliad* (Finley, 1962). It is, therefore, not only sometimes possible to reconstruct earlier societies from restricted source materials, it is also possible to deduce certain principles of practice and organisation using related forms of analysis (Sjoberg, 1965). Political theory, economic theory, and even race theory (Snowden, 1983) have all been employed to advantage in this respect. The application of theory detects the significant differences *and* highlights the interesting uniformities in human society. And if it is some kind of philosophy of history we are looking for, such formulations are only possible when the broad sweep of pre-industrial history is taken into consideration.

The cautionary words of the late C. Wright Mills concerning both historians and sociologists are still relevant here (Mills, 1967). He maintained that some historians are mere compilers of alleged fact and spend most of their time just grubbing for details. He insisted that many of their speculations are inflated fragments of knowledge which are often unlocated in the larger world. But much depends upon the historians in question. It would seem that more and more are now giving as much time to interpretation as they are to bland description. And more are prepared to test socio-economic theories in historical situations (Sutherland, 1985). Complementarily, some sociologists have come to realise that it is not enough simply to sketch in the historical background as a preamble to their current studies. They have found that history is required to explain not only why something *has* existed but also why it has *persisted* over time. Of course, historians and sociologists still like to score off each other, especially when it is a question of validating a particular theory or supporting a favoured ideology. But mercifully the days of Spencerian procrusteanism are largely past. Each is beginning to learn from the other. This is why such theorists as Norbert Elias and Michel Foucault are to be applauded even if they do not always handle their historical materials with complete confidence, or, indeed, in Foucault's case, with less than complete trust (Macl.Currie, 1986). They have at least appreciated the need for a historical perspective, and demonstrated that it can be usefully interiorised by sociological ideas. But historical facts – as far as we can discern them – are still important. A historical particular may yet be enough to refute the sociological generalisation.

Despite all this, the value of the historical perspective is still often questioned. There are those who doubt that we can derive anything really useful from the examination of early societies. And this is demonstrated by their patent neglect. Robert Walpole once suggested that the only thing that we learn from history is that no one ever learns anything from history, but in this case it was not so much a criticism of the study of history, as a scepticism that men will ever take the lessons of history to heart. There are, of course, innumerable culs-de-sac in history; it is impossible to discern any clear or coherent pattern in the kaleidoscope of events. There appear to be no inviolable rules, merely the repeated and fumbling attempts of societies to decide what the rules should be. All we really know is sequence – 'just one damned thing after another'. But this does not mean that it is all a valueless enterprise. Lord Acton once maintained that the prize of history was an understanding of modern times, and he was simply reiterating Confucius' observation in the 6th century BC that men studied the past with a view to their self-improvement.

There may seem to be something quaint and vainly idealistic about such notions. Some critics have gone so far as to suggest that modern technological society is so different from anything in the past that traditional values really have a very doubtful value in the present scheme of things (Gellner, 1963). But are the *basic* values of society *so* different, and have people really changed or are they likely to change *that* much? Even a cursory look at earlier societies does not leave much room for optimism. Perhaps we should deplore the traduction of the traditional because history may actually fortify us against the future by giving us a clearer idea of the present (Grant, 1952).

Duty, desire and moral absolutism

We have discussed various aspects of moral relativism in some detail, so it is appropriate – indeed, necessary – that we now consider the claims of those who take quite a different theoretical stance: who seriously question anything that smacks of emotive subjectivism, and who are particularly opposed to relativism. In this respect, it would be particularly instructive to look at the work of Immanuel Kant (1724-1804) who represents the anti-emotivist stance *par excellence.*

Kant is regarded by some as the father of modern philosophy. He is certainly one of the most important thinkers of this or any other age, and despite the fact that he has been disparaged by some academics (e.g. Bertrand Russell, 1948), and others have found him very difficult to read, he is generally respected by fellow philosophers (e.g. Korner, 1964). Henry Aiken even goes so far as to suggest that he had one of the most daring and original minds in the whole history of human thought. It is probably not an exaggeration to suggest that before Kant, it was generally assumed that human perceptions of the external world conformed to the nature of things. Kant tried to show that the external world as *we* know it conforms to the nature of *our* perceptions, and he contended that we see things not as they are, but as *we* are (Aiken, 1957).

Kant was a man of modest beginnings. He was the son of a Königsberg saddler of Scottish descent. He went to Königsberg university at 16, remained there for six years and continued as an unsalaried lecturer for many more. At 46 he became a professor, but he did not produce his *Critique of Pure Reason* until he was 57, followed seven years later by his magnum opus on ethics, the *Critique of Practical Reason*. He enjoyed no obvious advantages; he was in no sense a man of means like Descartes, nor did he have useful aristocratic connections like Bacon, so he had little opportunity to travel abroad and meet foreign savants. He was physically unimpressive, being barely five feet tall and slightly deformed in the chest and one shoulder. He was also undeniably eccentric and lived a life of extreme simplicity, rising summer and winter at 5.00 am, and taking only one formal meal a day with friends – which was often more like a seminar – followed by the ritual of a walk around the square at precisely the same time every day. He began his lectures at 7.00 am, and it is said that his teaching resembled preaching, mainly because of his habit of forsaking his manuscript and devoting the last ten minutes of a lecture to moral applications. Little wonder that Königsberg tended to regard him as a kind of prophet.

Kant tackled the problem of appearance and reality by maintaining that there are two different worlds of analysis, that of things-in-themselves (noumena) which we strive to know but which are only dimly perceived, and things-as-they-seem (phenomena), i.e. the things that are real for us and which can be empirically validated. He asked how sensations are organised, and what these sensations 'meant'; and he came to the conclusion that the human mind is not just a passive mirror which reflects the distorted patterns of things-in-themselves (as Plato), but rather that it is an active agency which itself 'composes the raw material of sense experience into a world of conceptualised phenomena' (Aiken, 1957, p. 33). In other words, he is hypothesising that we 'manufacture' and develop the conceptual apparatus which is appropriate for our ordering of the external world.

For our purposes, it is most useful to ask what it was that Kant was trying to do for ethics. And it is his approach to understanding and conceptualisation that gives us the clue. He was trying to construct a system of ethics which would permit the kind of moral statement that is both within and without experience. A statement that was *within* experience in that it could be experientially validated, and *without* experience insofar as it was not subject to experience and particularly that it was not subordinate to emotions and personal inclination. In effect, he was trying to reconcile subjectivist and consensus orientations to ethics. He thought he could do this by constructing moral propositions which would command universal respect and were not relativistic but invariable, in short, a form of moral *law*. This, at least, was his intention, and it could be argued that his intentions and his methods ultimately proved more interesting than his results. So it is important to see what he set out to do, the novelty of his approach and the logical consistency of his arguments, and some of the far-reaching implications of his system.

He attempted (a) *to define the nature of goodness and the good person*. He concluded that 'goodness' does not consist in being high-born or handsome, wealthy or intelligent. In fact, he dismissed the criteria that most people use. 'Goodness' is neither will-power nor self-discipline nor any form of stoical fortitude. Why? For the simple reason that a person may use these qualities for evil ends. He also argued that striving for the betterment of society, agitating for social reform, or preoccupying oneself with all manner of good works may be quite worthless because a person may serve such ostensibly good causes for unworthy motives. With what appears to be disarming simplicity, Kant then goes on to maintain that there is nothing absolutely good except *good will*. But what is the good will? How does Kant define it? Well, he says, it is not a good disposition – this may be an advantage, but it is hardly commendable as a virtue because it is merely acting in accordance with one's nature. Furthermore, he insists that goodness should not be seen as abstinence of some kind. If I say I have never been drunk, indeed that I have always been a total abstainer – which happens to be true – it really tells you very little about me. Alcohol has no temptation for me, so I don't have to struggle against some pernicious vice. It merely informs you about something I don't do – it tells you nothing about what I *do* do. Perhaps I just like to know when I'm enjoying myself.

For Kant, then, to do good for the sake of goodness is the foundation of the moral law. He is not suggesting that altruism can be safely combined with self-interest. After all, goodness may not pay any obvious material dividends. To have a good will towards others, and really want the best for them – something which is often notoriously difficult to desire – is, for Kant, the only true altruism.

He attempted (b) *to divorce ethics from inclination*. Kant fully recognised that we are bio-chemical organisms with instinctual patterns of behaviour. All the more reason, he postulated, why values could not rest on uncertain foundations and why morality could not be made subject to facile individual whims. Morality – to do good – Kant insisted, was *duty*. He appreciated – in anticipation of Freud – the irrational elements in our natures, the tendencies that are sometimes difficult to control. For these reasons he argued for the primacy of duty over inclination.

Does this mean, therefore, that duty is above desire? Should duty always come first? Well, it can mean this but it need not. Ewing, for instance, gives the simple example of a parent who is more highly regarded if he/she cares for a child out of love and not merely because of family obligation or social expectation (Ewing, 1957). Neither does it mean that we *must* take the more difficult course just because it is more virtuous. Indeed, Kant recognised that sometimes duty and desire may happily coincide. After all, few pregnant girls would want their boyfriends to marry them just out of a sense of duty; it is far better if their sense of obligation coincides with what they would really like to do. Of course, a sense of duty is something that often has to be cultivated – people are not always sensitively aware of their obligations, and even when they are, they may not know how to fulfil them. The golden rule, that we should love our neighbour as ourselves, is very like Kant's injunction never to treat people as means, but always as ends. Neither is very easy to observe conscientiously; they are both above inclination. Naturally, we cannot make ourselves care for some people; we cannot love to order. But this is not what we are being asked to do. What is being enjoined is that we treat others *as though* we loved and respected them: to *try to* treat them in the same way as we would treat our friends. There is little virtue in being nice to those we care for, although, in practice, it is those we care for that we are often most impatient with simply because we do care for them. It is certainly an indication of good will if we can treat those whom we may actively dislike without discrimination.

Kant attempted (c) *to shift the emphasis from the consequences of actions to their motives*. We have seen that the Utilitarians with their stress on happiness as the end of human behaviour might be tempted to justify the means whereby this is achieved. Kant, on the other hand, argued that motives were more important than consequences (Murphy, 1970). This is laudable in intent, but must be seriously qualified in practice. There are circumstances in which the motive is good but the consequences are bad. The history of religious persecution, for instance, is littered with examples of callous repression for what were ostensibly good reasons. Or there are the circumstances where the motive that is advanced may, in fact, be ulterior. If a man lies to his wife about his adultery, he may reason that he is doing this so as not to hurt her, and in order to keep the marriage intact. But is he really doing it to spare her feelings or his? And then there are the situations where the motive and the consequences are virtually inseparable, as when, say, a person lies to a terminally ill relative about the nature of his or her disease.

There may, of course, be no such thing as a pure motive. All motives are mixed and even confused. It is said that by 1916 the soldiers on the Western Front did not really know why they were there – if, indeed, they ever knew (Wolff, 1958). They were just there because they were there. Sometimes one motive may predominate over the others, yet often it is impossible to identify any unadulterated motive behind most actions. But motives are extremely important and insofar as we can we should try to discern the motives behind the action. We saw with Utilitarianism that the consequences and ends of human action are inadequate criteria upon which to base moral decision-making because they are not – indeed, cannot – be fully within our power either to predict or to control.

Kant also attempted (d) *to anchor ethics to constraint of an objective kind*. He argued that judgements were practical imperatives, and that moral reasoning is not necessarily addressed to the resolution of intellectual doubts but to the removal of irresolutions of the will. His view was that, more often than not, most of us know what we should or should not be doing, but fail in the determination to do it. He suggested that these judgements were of two kinds. The first kind are *those that arise from conflicts of desire*, for which Kant advanced the concept of the HYPO-

THETICAL IMPERATIVE. This simply tells us what we must do if we wish to satisfy a particular inclination. So if, say, we wish to pursue an academic career, we must first subject ourselves to the discipline of obtaining a good degree. This is quite straightforward, and could not possibly raise any serious argument. But the second kind of judgement is rather more contentious, namely *that which arises from conflicts of natural desire and duty*. Here we are back to inclination versus the claims of obligation. In this situation, Kant advances his famous CATEGORICAL IMPERATIVE, which demands that we perform the 'right' act regardless of inclination. It is rarely a question of academic debate or intellectual doubt. In this case, Kant puts forward one of his most telling arguments in favour of the residual morality of the human species, maintaining that we are all conscious of things we either ought or ought not to do, but that the actual response differs with different individuals and with different cultures – although there does seem to be a kind of Lowest Common Denominator morality throughout the world. But this is not what primarily concerns Kant. What he stresses is that it is not necessarily particular features of morality that are universal but morality *itself*. It is the universal *sense of constraint* that matters. People may feel this constraint about different things, but they all feel a sense of constraint about *something*. It is the sense of obligation that is universal. Naturalist explanations for the origins of moral obligation are not entirely convincing. 'I want'/'I desire'/'I wish', etc. are understandable, but why 'I ought ...'?

Essentially, Kant (e) *attempted to universalise ethics*. We saw earlier that he was very opposed to Emotivism; he was convinced that the kind of relativism that relied upon individual feelings was not a very sure foundation for morality. Thus he insisted that we can only have a moral law if we are prepared to *universalise our maxims*. Here he is really saying something which we first heard in infancy when, having been caught out in some stupid misdemeanour, we were asked 'What if everyone did it?'. At the time we probably vaguely entertained the thought that not everyone does do it – at least, not all at the same time. But it was – and still is – a salutary reminder that we had acted foolishly. Perhaps we should be prepared only to act in such a way that our maxims can hold good as universal laws even if, in some cases, this could lead to bad reasons for morality.

As Kant put it, the moral law is a criterion for testing, not a premise for deducing principles of conduct which claim to be right (Broad, 1962, pp. 122-3). Kant suggested that we should ask ourselves the question, 'What if everyone acted as I propose to act now?', and gave the example of suicide, which would be self-defeating for the species and the particular individuals concerned. He also raised the question of lying. If all people lied, the virtue of veracity would disappear. Communication would fail for lack of meaning – a situation which could now be developing in response to modern advertising techniques. Do we believe even half of what we see and hear in the media when we know that someone's commercial interests are being served? Truth-telling is still officially the social 'rule', but none of us needs reminding how frequently it is infringed. It has become almost a convention now for people to break the rule by consent ('Can I speak to Mr Jones, please?' – significant hesitation – 'No, I'm sorry, Mr Jones is not in.' Yet everyone knows what this means. You know, they know you know, and you know that they know you know…). We have effectively made a new rule to cover infringements of the earlier and underlying rule. It's almost like inventing a new kind of truth.

Immoral conduct, therefore, for Kant, meant making exceptions in favour of oneself. Yet doing this is an implicit recognition of a rule, because breaking rules indirectly confirms their validity. This raises some awkward questions. Kant's example of lying, for instance, is a little unfortunate because it needs to be highly qualified. Can any deviations be allowed and in what circumstances can they be allowed? A spy in war-time may lie to his captors not to save his own life but to protect his friends. Can this be excused? Does lying include *all* types of lies, or a particular type of lie in a particular context? When confronted by the prospect of lying, are we expected to universalise our maxims on the basis that all lying is wrong, or are we supposed to universalise in terms of what we would wish others to do in these particular circumstances? On the other hand, is it a cop-out to extricate oneself from the dilemma by saying that no rules can be kept in all circumstances, and that what we are really required to do is to recognise that truth-telling is *ideally* good? Many 'deviations' of whatever kind can work if they remain small-scale deviations, otherwise they are self-defeating in that they no longer have the appeal of being deviations.

Lastly, (f) Kant *attempted, in the moral sense, to reconcile the free world with a lawful world*. The idea of a law is the key to a correct understanding of what he meant by the imperative – the principle which is valid without exception. Yet this too must be complemented by a correct understanding of freedom. He insisted that unless the moral will is free either to do or not to do what the moral law prescribes, morality itself is an illusion. So we are back to the two worlds of analysis. As phenomenal selves we conceive ourselves as physical organisms, and our behaviour is subject to natural causes. In this spatio-temporal sense, we cannot really conceive ourselves as free, we are determined by the natural, physical laws that govern our existence. But at the same time, we are also possessed of a noumenal self which, for Kant, seems analogous to the idea of an immortal soul. And he suggests that it is not necessary to suppose that the forces of cause and effect operate beyond the spatio-temporal domain. He is therefore saying that we are subject to determinism, yet, in a very important sense, that we also have free will, because we have to believe the will is free in order to give reality to the moral life. Indeed, Kant goes further, suggesting that we belong to a moral realm which is not subject to the phenomenal order, the natural world of space and time, and that such metaphysical assumptions about the moral order are entirely compatible with the rules of scientific enquiry.

Kant, then, is stressing the existence of an inner, inviolable self which is free to will no matter what external constraints are imposed. He sees us as members of a moral universe which is part of an immutable divine order. He acknowledges that the traditional theological 'props' for that order were misconceived and that such an order could only be ultimately validated in moral terms. The consistency of his general argument can thus be summarised as a logical sequence: we all have a universal sense of ought/ought not and this constitutes the essence of moral constraint. Ought implies *can* – the obligation plus the freedom to act, because moral constraint implies moral capacity, and moral capacity implies moral freedom. Therefore *can* implies *must* because moral freedom implies moral responsibility.

Ethics as a discipline develops as we pass beyond the stage where we are governed by traditional codes. A moral sense can be said to be present when these rules are internalised in such a way that we see them as part of our 'natures', and then to the point where we begin to think critically in terms of general *principles* which hold good for us despite the challenges posed by everyday existence. But can such principles ever be regarded as objective? It is here that we may think it valuable to take the possibility of universals seriously: the universal nature of the moral sense and the universal distribution of so many moral ideas which give some validity to the notion of moral objectivity.

Morality and the problem of therapy

The social sciences are essentially theoretical disciplines, but they can have certain practical applications. This is particularly evident in Psychology, whose therapeutic capacities are worth investigating because although they are among the most disputed aspects of the discipline, they are also among its most potentially rewarding features.

All therapy is in some way related to *conflict*, which, in turn, is usually related to *goals*, and these are conditioned by *values*. Conflict is generally categorised as either intrapsychic (individual) or intergroup, i.e. external to the individual but necessarily impinging upon his/her behaviour. Personal problems can obviously have social repercussions such as, say, the need for personal esteem which in certain sub-cultures is expressed in delinquency. Complementarily, social problems can have personal effects, such as business worries that generate seemingly intractable sexual problems (Carlton, 1980). Therapy, of course, is directed towards the modification of behaviour by a variety of techniques which are calculated to alter responses and reactions either by *reflective* (thoughtful) or *reflexive* (instinctual) means. A great deal of therapy is therefore taken up with learning or re-learning the appropriate social responses.

We can look at conflict under a number of different headings:

(1) *Conflict involving goal-ambiguity*

Here we are thinking of the situation where the goal or objective in question has both a positive *and* a negative incentive value. Take the very common problem of what to do about aged parents and grandparents when they can no longer easily look after themselves. Often – and perhaps questionably – it is thought undesirable to have them living with their own children or grandchildren. Perhaps there is no room for such an arrangement anyway; and perhaps they need special nursing care: this can all lead to further problems, and so it is often decided, despite possible enormous expense, to house them in a retirement home where it is hoped that they will receive the best of attention, and where – in some cases – they can be conveniently forgotten except for the occasional obligatory visit. For the more sensitive advocates there are often twinges of conscience because while there is an undoubted sense of relief that the aged relative has been settled, there is also a heightened sense of guilt about the way it has been done. The ambiguity lies in the opposing incentive values of the action.

(2) *Conflict involving goal-incongruity*

This is the situation where objectives are seemingly irreconcilable. We can think of circumstances that are not that unusual where a youth from a working-class home hopes one day to achieve professional status and in order to do so applies to become an undergraduate student. His parents, however, expect him to go out to work and pay for his keep rather than give him money, and they may therefore refuse to make any contribution towards his grant. Eventually a situation develops which may actually threaten family relations. How then is this student going to satisfy his own aspirations *and* please his parents at the same time?

(3) *Conflict involving goal-indecision*

This speaks for itself. Take the very common instance of students who are not at all sure if they have made the correct subject-choice. Higher Education can be a delaying mechanism – a matter of putting off the evil day. Students often don't know what they want to do, and if they do, they are not certain how best to do it, or whether to settle for second-best. Changing direction does not present serious difficulties in their first term, or maybe even in their first year. But after that it becomes a frustrating problem. They are too far from the beginning to go back, and just about far enough from the end not to see it through. This is the dilemma. They decide to go on, but there's no enthusiasm any more. From then on they are just serving their time.

These situations involve means-ends problems characterised by value-uncertainty, and all are vitiated by *ambivalence* insofar as they involve incompatible responses. Uncertainty can lead to the indecisiveness that psychologists call *behavioural vacillation*, and sometimes to *behavioural arrest*, the situation where any decision seems to be impossible, or even to *procrastination*, the unwillingness or inability to make any decision at all. It is always possible to decide to make no decision.

In some instances, this means falling back to the status quo ante, which itself constitutes a kind of decision. In other instances, e.g. in the case of subject/vocational choices, some decision *has* to be made; the critical question concerns the *bases* on which such choices are made.

What about *intergroup* conflict? How are such resolutions made, or, at least, what kind of analysis is useful for a therapeutic approach? While we are on the subject of education, let us look at the problem of unruly class behaviour at the Secondary level, a matter with which we are all presumably familiar. First, we must *define the problem*, although this is not always as simple as it appears. Is the difficulty with the teacher, the teaching environment, or with the pupils themselves? If it is the teacher, is it one of method or manner? If it is the mode of instruction, is it the content of the material or – as can easily happen – the way that content is structured, or is it the actual presentation of the material in lessons? If this can be established, the remedy may not be very far away. This might necessitate an *avoidance solution*, that is removing certain disruptive pupils from the class, or even reassigning the teacher to other duties, possibly 'easier' classes or administrative tasks, providing the timetable will allow this. In Higher Education, this could mean being relegated to a more supernumerary role on courses, or actually being given leave to take a higher degree just to get the teacher away from the institution. A much more questionable expedient is the *confrontation solution*. This involves actually exacerbating the problem and thus heightening the tension by giving the teacher more difficult classes to take. Ultimately, of course, unruly behaviour is the behaviour of the pupils; they are the ones who, in the end, must bear the blame, but their responsibility is minimised if both class teaching and class management are at fault. It may therefore be somewhat heartless, but nevertheless effective, if the teacher is confronted with even more traumatic conditions in terms of both subject-matter and pupils. This leads to a crisis, not unusually resulting in early retirement. (I knew of one poor woman who did this, and afterwards a small book was found in her desk entitled *How to Survive the Classroom*.) This solution may seem morally indefensible, but headteachers and education authorities are usually pragmatic people, and the 'solution' often works.

If we step up a gear, and think of Higher Education departments where there is a conflict between staff and the Head of Department, we may find that the *intrapsychic* response mirrors the intergroup problem. The individual here may also try to solve his/her problems by the techniques of confrontation and/or avoidance. The trouble – whatever the cause – may well begin with open disputation (confrontation) and then proceed to isolation (avoidance) with each side refusing to negotiate with the other – a situation which can sometimes continue for months. (I recently heard of a Social Sciences professor at one of our most prestigious universities who died of a heart attack after prolonged difficulties with his staff. A link cannot be established causally, but it is certainly conceivable that stress was a contributory factor in his death.)

Where the conflict is not one of goals but a *conflict of motives*, the incentives towards any particular action or goal my be multiple and therefore demand – and often produce – a similar incompatibility of responses. This could be illustrated from many walks of life – politics, industrial management, etc. – but let us stay with education and consider the situation of an employee who, for various reasons, has become a liability to the institution and an embarrassment to his colleagues and students. (I have known this happen for a variety of reasons, ranging from abysmal teaching to persistent sexual harassment.) There may be serious attempts to 'remove' such a person. Usually it is hoped that this will happen as painlessly as possible by encouraging that person to seek employment elsewhere. But in Higher Education that is much easier said than done, not least because among professionals there is an inevitable conflict of motives. As members of the same Union they are under an obligation to support a fellow employee's cause while, at the same time, recognising the employer's case. Also, if one of their colleagues can be removed with reasonable ease, so can they. It's all a matter of precedent. By protecting another's interests, regardless of their own personal and professional values, they are indirectly protecting their own.

So when it comes to doing anything about our own problems or those of others, we first have to ask ourselves about motives, why we do or don't do anything. And this is where we must make that oft-mentioned important distinction between reasoning and rationalising. *Reasoning* about a situation is an intellectual exercise based upon clearly articulated analytical principles. But *rationalising* often means making excuses for ourselves which we entertain with varying degrees of conviction. Psychology texts often mention the phenomenon of 'bystander indifference', that is, those situations in which a person is in difficulties – in danger of drowning, say, or being mugged or whatever – and onlookers who witness these incidents make a host of excuses as to why they did absolutely nothing about them. This sort of thing raises the problem of *conflicting explanations*, which is sometimes called cognitive dissonance. This term, popularised by the psychologist Leon Festinger (1962), denotes the state of mind which is said to exist when people find that they have a severe conflict between their beliefs and the factual evidence which appears to contradict them. They find this mental state intolerable and usually either change their beliefs or distort the awkward facts. For example, a person who smokes is persistently confronted by the fact the smoking causes – directly or indi-rectly – a host of diseases, and in the UK alone kills 300 people every day. That person has either got to listen to the facts and give up the habit, or try to persuade himself that it's all right, and that it will not happen to him.

Closely allied to this is the *problem of conflicting rationalities*, where a subject holds two views at the same time – but knows that both cannot be right. Let's take the example of a person who is alcohol-dependent. He tells himself that he is a rational person, he worries about his condition, about the mounting evidence for heart disease, liver disease, etc. He thinks perhaps he should cut down on his consumption. Tension and anxiety increase, and he may drink more to combat these, and so a downward spiral develops if the problem is not resolved.

By various forms of therapy it is sometimes possible to change behav-iour, but in many actual cases it is not uncommon for a person to distort his perceptions about his own situation. If, for instance, a person feels that he has failed in some way, he is probably more likely to experience dissonance if he recognises this failure as something of his own making, but less likely to experience it if he rationalises the situation by attributing the blame to somebody else or some unavoidable external circumstances.

Therapy can take very many forms depending upon the particular school concerned:

(1) *Psychoanalytical therapy* is primarily engaged in seeking the *causes* of current abnormal behaviour which are often attributed to traumas in infancy. Sometimes such techniques yield interesting results, but the causes of these behaviours may prove to be ultimately undetectable. Techniques of association and transference are commonly used in order to facilitate recollection and recognition which are regarded as necessary precursors to restoration. It is still debatable whether the explanations offered for such behaviours really derive from the subjects' revelations or whether they are imposed by over-enthusiastic analysts.

(2) *Behaviour therapy*: we have noted already that Behaviourists, unlike the Psychoanalysts, concentrate on alleviating *symptoms* rather than seeking causes. Behaviour therapy comes in four main types:

(a) *Aversion therapy*, which may be conducted with the aid of hypnosis, shock treatment and even emetics, and is common in the treatment of drug-dependency.

(b) *Satiation therapy*, where the patient is exposed to 're-lived' experi-ences of his/her maladaptive behaviour to the extent that they lose their attraction. The technique known as 'flooding' may be used, whereby patients are played tapes of themselves when confronted with a variety of challenging situations, and it is hoped that these will enable them to face their fears, anxieties, or whatever, in the future. For example, some cardio-thoracic departments which once relied solely on 'relaxation' tapes are now showing heart by-pass patients videos of the operation (or, in some cases, part of the operation). This can be done prospectively or as part of the programme of post-operative therapy. Paradoxically, it is calculated to increase fear but reduce anxiety. It is hoped that patients will be so affected that they will do their best to obey instructions about diet, exercise, etc., so that the problem does not recur.

(c) *Assertive-response therapy* usually entails role-playing in which patients assert 'authority' in a number of pre-arranged situations. Its weaknesses are obvious. If the situations are contrived, they are usually *known* to be contrived. It is all very artificial, and there can be no guarantee that patients are going to behave similarly in *real* situations.

(d) *Redirection therapy* is a variant which is aimed at re-educating patients to make new and improved responses. It is sometimes used in sex-therapy, when, say, an impotent male is treated to the attentions of a willing, attractive, female. (It's quite amazing how many volunteers some sex therapists can muster.) But even if this encounter is successful, there is no guarantee that it can be repeated with the patient's normal partner who has obviously done nothing for him in the past, and who may even have contributed – perhaps unwittingly – to his present condition.

(3) *Humanistic therapy* (which includes Encounter Groups, Growth Movements, etc.) distrusts unconscious or biological determination, and instead stresses *willed action* as the route to potential self-improvement. The emphasis is on positive attributes and human capabilities. It can take the form of mutual exploration to discover deep-seated fears and hostilities which inhibit healthy relations, and this kind of communal catharsis is given full vent in group therapy, particularly by the Minnesota Method which has had some success especially with those who are drug-dependent. It attempts to deal with rejection by a process of self-criticism. The problem with these ritual explorations is that they can generate as much resentment as they alleviate. 'Revelations' can be a source of anxiety when, later on, subjects regret their confidences. It is all very well to emphasise potential and improvement, but it can be dangerous to tell people that they are capable of what they are not, and – with self-health groups – to suggest that they are responsible for their own condition. This is highly disputable and in many cases cruel and insensitive. Frequently disease is attributed to patients' 'stress', an ill-defined and little understood factor which they often cannot reduce without incurring yet more reinforced anxiety. And this is often compounded by the misleading implication that they can, by prescribed techniques of diet, meditation and so forth, effectively cure themselves. Some 'experts' talk as though we can all be liberated from the tyranny of our physiologies, and take charge of our own lives, but there has to be a limit to this kind of freedom. The environment is replete with viral and bacterial enemies that are only waiting for a suitable opportunity

to challenge our natural immunities and our sometimes vain attempts at self-conditioning.

Excursus V. Morality, guilt and obsession

The phenomena that we designate as obsessional behaviour are coming in for a considerable amount of re-appraisal at present (note, for example, Daniel Wegner's article in *Psychology Today*, June 1989). Particularly significant are the facts that (a) a number of famous historical figures (Darwin, Bunyan, Samuel Johnson, etc.) and well-known personalities (e.g. Woody Allen) are said to have been afflicted by such problems; and (b) that the prevalence of this 'condition' – one hesitates to use the term 'disease' – is much more widespread than originally supposed. One authority estimates that it affects 1 to 2% of the population (Toates, 1990). It is worth noting too that there is some consensus among specialists that it is a condition that tends to affect particularly intelligent, creative individuals. This is not an invariable rule. But the evidence is clear that there is a higher incidence among those that tend to be extraordinarily fastidious and perfectionist – and productive – in their work and routines.

The point of this Excursus, however, is not to survey the territory or to summarise the findings, but rather to question the general conclusions of some of the literature. The criticism is not about diagnosis – insofar as this is possible in our present state of knowledge – but more about suggested treatments which seem, at best, to be highly dubious.

For simplicity, obsessional experience can be divided into *compulsive behaviour*, i.e. activities that assume the status of rituals which have to be completed (e.g. excessive hand washing) before subjects can achieve any peace of mind, and *obsessive thoughts* – the subject of this discussion – unwanted but persistent images that plague subjects, and which they seem unable to dismiss or eradicate. Such thoughts do not normally result in any outward manifestations, although in their extreme depression some subjects are known to inflict physical injury on themselves or on their surroundings, or perhaps – in their frustration – on other people. Most commonly the injury is self-inflicted either as a form of punishment or as a means of temporary distraction from the thoughts themselves.

This condition may develop over a period of years or it may begin quite suddenly, perhaps triggered by some disturbing experience – a film, a news item – almost anything can do it. More likely it is untraced and seemingly untraceable. In the early stages, subjects feel ashamed and try to hide the symptoms from others. They may develop the habit of absenting themselves periodically – without explanation – from other people. Bouts of seeming inattention and a proneness to talk to themselves are symptomatic, and may generate suspicions of growing eccentricity. Those that care for them become deeply concerned, and eventually the subjects are no longer able to conceal the nature of the problem.

Subjects appear to be powerless to deal with their thoughts; the more they try to suppress them the more insistent they seem to become. The more they tell themselves that they are rational human beings who ought to be able to control these things, the more they are really reaffirming the weakness of their position. They wake in the morning telling themselves that today is going to be different, but in the very act of doing so the thoughts intrude – almost as though they were waiting for this very moment to renew the siege. Every resolution seems to confirm their infirmity and their incapacity to improve their own condition.

How are we to account for this? Well, we must first of all admit that we have no adequate explanation – in fact, not even an entirely convincing hypothesis. Wegner tries bravely with a tentative 'loop' analogy of reinforcement. He maintains that with each occasion, indeed, with each act of resistance, the problem is fed back and amplified in 'the mental analogue of a cycle that produces squeals in a poorly adjusted address system'. He advocates an end to suppression, 'the thought you suppress can wind up haunting you – simply think the unthinkable and gain control'. In other words, thoughts reinforce thoughts in such a way that a syndrome is created from which there seems to be no escape (Carlton, 1980). Suppression generates reinforcements, so don't suppress thoughts any longer – recognise and admit them, and they will eventually disappear, or, at least, trouble you no longer.

The 'loop' analogy is only an analogy; it is hardly a theory – we are a long way from that – or even a convincing hypothesis, but it is a useful insight into what is taking place in the mentality of the subject. What we have here is really a legacy of Freudianism combined – perhaps a little uneasily – with modern behavioural techniques; this is a strange but not unusual combination (Marks, 1978) and deserves one or two critical observations.

In the study of obsessional phenomena it is easy to confuse irrational behaviour with *non*-rational behaviour. Irrational behaviour is, in many ways, analogous to earlier ideas about sympathetic magic. The belief that ritual A will affect situation B is found, for instance, in certain forms of witchcraft. Similarly, the obsessional person may think that if he fails to clean his teeth three times before breakfast there will be an earthquake in Peru. This is an extreme example; usually the results of the thoughts/rituals are believed to affect matters much nearer home. Relatively innocent behaviour takes on a contingent quality, though, needless to say, no connection can be demonstrated between the thoughts/rituals themselves and the incidents – often of a harmful nature – which they are supposed to have caused.

Non-rational behaviour is quite different. Here the subject's thoughts/actions can be seen to have an *in*direct effect on particular situations. If we take seemingly nonsensical war dances as an example, we find that in many tribal societies the ostensible purpose of the ritual –

their manifest function – was often to render the warrior impervious to the enemy and ensure success in battle. The actual or latent function of the rituals was to 'psych' the warriors in preparation for the fray – what Malinowski called the 'confidence theory' of magic. In other words, some apparently non-rational acts have a certain rational quality. Primitive practices sometimes echo the non-rational but not irrational behaviour of the obsessed, especially if they are intensely moral or religious persons – and it is this moral dimension that is discounted by much of the literature. The obsessional subject may act in ways which are analogous to primitives. In his attempts to counter or rectify his own harmful or unwanted thoughts, he may 'construct' a whole armoury of alternative thoughts with which to neutralise the impressions and images that he regards as evil. This attempt to interpose an illusionary shield between the unwanted thought and the image which may accompany it has been described as 'beating the devil to the punch'. The subject tries to distinguish between the thought – unbidden and unwanted – and what he actually *means* by what he thinks, and then – to make it even more convoluted – what he would *like to mean* by what he thinks. Of course, it is all fantasy, but then so is the obsession itself. It is fantasy and counter-fantasy; a war of good and evil.

Not all obsessions are about eating, or making sure the doors are all locked or putting the cat out at night. Many are accompanied by very acute mental pain. This is why the moral/religious issue should never be ignored. There is some evidence to support the view that people with strong moral and/or religious ideas are particularly prone to such obsessions. For them, unwanted thoughts are frequently regarded as sinful or even positively evil, and this necessarily involves questions of guilt. Those who suffer in this way are often quite unable to face up to the thoughts, and this is why they deny certain orders of reality and indulge in counter-fantasies which they hope will anticipate the pernicious nature of the obsession.

In a way, it is somewhat reminiscent of the ancient Egyptian belief that the Sun-god, Re, travels across the sky every day in his ship of millions-of-years, and at night defeats Apophis – the ruler of darkness – and rises triumphant at dawn. But there is always another night and another struggle. Often the obsessive experience takes on a meta-quality in that the subjects cannot even bear to think about thinking. The half-formed, unarticulated thought then becomes an ever-present fear; subjects forever feel that they could be plunged into an abyss of guilt from which there is no forgiveness. For such people repetition of the thoughts generates such grave uncertainties that they begin to doubt their own moral integrity. Are they basically good people beset by wicked thoughts, or fundamentally wicked people trying to be good? It is almost as though they had created a malevolent alter ego who urges them to think *this* and imagine *that* – they are caught up in a vortex of moral ambiguity which leaves them clinging precariously to their sanity.

For such persons techniques such as flooding and exposure – advocated especially by behaviourists – could prove disastrous. To think the unthinkable is to think the unforgivable. And from this there is no return. Curiously – and contra-Freud – cases have been reported in which the subject *only* experiences unwanted thoughts with the 'conscious mind'; there is little evidence of them in the dream state. What – one may ask – has happened to the murky world of the unconscious whose insinuations are supposed to catch us unawares? It is as though the fundamental Freudian schema has been turned upside down.

Guilt – or the sense of guilt – can be destructive. People can be so burdened by shame and regret that they are no longer able to contemplate their futures with any confidence. Hence the reactions of the power-of-positive-thinking school of humanistic psychologists such as Maslow and Carl Rogers. But maybe guilt has a place; perhaps it needs to be reinstated in the vocabulary of psychology. Could it not signal the beginning of a new approach to moral health? The psychodynamic theorists do give it due recognition but make the common mistake of thinking that it is patently irrational because it is assumed to be based on erroneous premises. Nothing of course could be further from the truth for those for whom the moral – perhaps spiritual – dimension is paramount.

How Can the Study of Values Be Applied?

There is no area of social life that is not underpinned by value assumptions. Often these are explicit and are intellectualised as beliefs, ideologies and moralities, but sometimes they are implicit and largely unrecognised even though they interiorise the everyday world in unperceived ways. So having looked at some of the theoretical issues relating to the character and appropriation of values, it might be profitable to see in what ways our discussion can give us a better idea of some of the issues posed by modern society. In no sense can we claim that these studies are going to solve anything: but they might give us a clearer insight into the nature of some contemporary problems and even help us to appreciate that analysis must precede amelioration.

This section could thus be useful in class and seminar groups. The arguments are meant to be provocative as well as informative, and are intended to stimulate discussions and raise questions about current issues.

Aggression and violence

At the outset, we should perhaps distinguish between aggression and violence. Aggression should be seen as something that is potentially true of all of us; it is the more general term and subsumes such kindred attitudes as competitiveness and assertiveness. It can, of course, be symbolic and verbal as well as physical. Violence is patently more extreme, and denotes the attempt to dominate or harm others by hurting them or possibly their property.

To judge by stories in the media, we are living in an increasingly aggressive society. On closer investigation, however, such a charge may not be warranted or, at least, should be treated with some reserve. Everything, of course, depends on where we draw the baseline. Statistics before the 19th century are rather uncertain, but we do know that medieval muggings were by no means rare. Today, it is certainly true that crimes of all kinds have reached disturbing levels. Crimes against property are still more worrying *numerically* than crimes against the person, but violent crime such as assault, rape, and especially murder understandably claim much more attention. The British Home Office statistics which are published every year are not exactly encouraging. They seem to indicate a trend towards increasing violence, but these figures have to be interpreted with care. Crimes of violence in the UK have doubled in the last twenty years, although they still only account for about 5% of all known offences, with the most violent crimes, i.e. robbery with violence, rape and murder, accounting for about a third of one per cent.

Insofar as types of crimes are reflected in the prison population, we can say, broadly, that most prisoners are working class, male and young (i.e. aged between 17 and 40). Middle-class crime is now beginning to attract more attention from the police and the courts. Nearly two-thirds of convicted male prisoners have committed crimes against property, and about a fifth have committed violence against other people. Approximately one in twenty-five is there for sexual offences.

As we all know, with crime, so much depends on reportage, and on the public's attitude towards crime and criminals. There are certain indefinable fashions in crime and crime reportage: a few years ago it was mugging, now it is car theft and ram raids. Murder, on the other hand, is always in fashion, and retains a fairly steady rate from year to year, with the chances of being killed by an unknown person rather low compared with the danger of a lethal assault from a friend or member of the family. The particularly worrying trend is that murder by shooting has – like violent crime generally – doubled in the last twenty years. The figures for rape and sexual assault are also interesting. There now seem to be fewer inhibitions about reporting this kind of attack. It may be that any reluctance women have in reporting rape and sexual assault is not just due to embarrassment, but because – unlike with property that has been damaged or stolen – there can be *no effective restitution* of the 'goods' or for the crime. And to complicate matters, there are still serious problems about defining the exact nature of the crime, as evidenced by the William Kennedy Smith trial in the USA in 1991, where the issue of 'date rape' hampered the prosecution's case.

What we do have today is some indication that resorting to violence may be more precipitate than it was, say, earlier in the century. The evidence for this is not entirely reliable, and is, in fact, largely anecdotal, but the stories are numerous enough to suggest that perhaps more people actually court violence, and are certainly more prepared to use violence and not argument to settle disputes. This was reflected in a light-hearted cartoon depicting a party scene with guests looking on at a scowling man standing menacingly over a dazed figure on the floor who is being addressed by a woman saying apologetically, 'You must excuse Henry, he has no verbal skills.'

What is causing a great deal of concern to the authorities is the increasing preparedness of people to use violence in the course of crime and also in confrontations with the police. In the UK in the past ten years,

26 officers have been murdered, and over a thirty-year period since 1960, the numbers have doubled with each decade. In 1990, an average of 50 officers a day were assaulted. Once such assaults were quite rare, and the murders of policemen even rarer; from 1940 to 1965, murders of police officers averaged only one a year. One possible contributory cause is that since the abolition of capital punishment in 1965, violence has become almost *de rigueur* for certain professional criminals (*Sunday Times*, 22 December 1991).

There is some evidence too that violence is associated with television. It is not so much that it is directly encouraged, despite the countless scenes of mayhem and slaughter, but that it is unwittingly *legitimised* by TV. This does not happen overtly, but on some viewers, especially children, the effects are subtle and pervasive. A great deal of research is going on in this area, but so far the conclusions are still somewhat tentative and guarded. Yet the anxieties still persist. One wonders if young children always appreciate what is real and what isn't. Can they, for instance, discern the difference between the horror of war as depicted in newscasts, the simulated violence of films, and the bizarre antics of the oft-criticised Tom and Jerry cartoons in which the characters are regularly burned, flattened or skinned, but are always back to normal by the next episode? On the other hand, it is well-known that the razor-sharp Freddie has become something of a cult figure among older children for whom he now continues his pathological pursuits on video. The commentator, Roy Ridgeway, maintains that it is not so much *what* frightens children, as the fact that nothing much frightens them.

Again it is interesting to ask to what extent this seemingly insatiable desire for an apparently unvarying diet of – albeit vicarious – sex and violence is something that is learned or something which is innate, and how much actual violence is the result of emulation. One particularly perplexing if rare phenomenon is that of mindless 'copy-cat' crimes. The killings by Richard Speck in Chicago and Charles Whitman at the University of Texas were followed – coincidentally? – by a rash of other shootings. When NBC showed a film entitled *Doomsday Flight* about a mad bomber who threatened an airline, it was followed by five bomb threats within 24 hours, but *only* five, so most people were obviously unaffected. The problem here is to know whether such incidents or programmes really generate violence or whether future events are subsequently attributed to them.

The public response to media violence has been surprising. The Docherty and Morrison study found that in the UK only two respondents in ten blamed TV for the increase in sexual immorality, and only one in ten blamed TV for the increase in violence. Does this indicate considered judgments, or does it suggest an imperceptible erosion of standards? The key factors seem to be:

(1) The amount of violence witnessed.

(2) The quality of violence witnessed, i.e. whether it is gratuitous or otherwise.

(3) The personal qualities of the aggressor. (Note, for example, the sympathetic treatment evident in the 'Death Wish' films in which the hero wages a ceaseless vigilante-style crusade against criminals whom the police seem powerless to touch.)

(4) The justifiability of the aggression. (Note the 'Equaliser' series on TV, in which violence is always used in what is portrayed as a good cause.)

(5) The extremely important but often unassessable 'qualities' and disposition of the viewer.

Concern about these issues has given rise to three main hypotheses:

(1) The *Catharsis hypothesis*, which posits that the impact of the media – especially TV – may actually be beneficial in that it allows for the welcome release of pent-up emotions. But it has to be asked how such a 'safety-valve' hypothesis is to be validated. How do we measure tension release? No one can ever know what any individual *would have been like* if he/she had not read that paper or seen those programmes on TV.

(2) The *Modelling hypothesis* suggests that children in particular model their behaviour on certain TV stereotypes of the Rambo variety, and therefore become retrogressively more violent. The experiments of Albert Bandura are often cited, in which children were shown films depicting scenes of violence, after which they were given toys which they proceeded to abuse. Whether this really tells us much is not certain. Many children use their teddy bears as punch bags, and think nothing of twisting their arms or pulling out their eyes, but they are a little more hesitant about doing the same to other children. I think we must assume that even quite young children know the difference between toys and humans.

(3) The *Catalyst hypothesis* is really a compromise view. Some – and some *only* – are affected by what they see and read. Some are influenced and some obviously are not. TV, in particular, is therefore regarded as a catalyst for a few only for whom – for reasons we do not fully understand – it acts as a trigger for certain latent aggressive urges.

There are several generally recognised *theories of aggression*: these fall into four main types, and in some ways constitute a reiteration of the teaching of those well-established 'schools' that we have already considered. At the most fundamental there are *physiological theories* of aggression. They argue that brain damage, or an excess of testosterone (male hormone), undue electrical stimulation, etc., can all cause people to act aggressively. There is some very suspect research which even attributes aggressiveness in female children to the fact that male hormone was administered to their pregnant mothers (Michael, 1968). What does this actually tell us? Is aggression such a singular male preserve? True, most violent acts are committed by men, but to what extent is this conditioned by greater muscular strength and particular circumstances? Is aggression really a matter of chemicals or culture? Can chemicals alone account for individual differences? And can chemicals really determine the specific forms that aggression takes?

Instinct theories emphasise possible in-built, innate tendencies toward aggression. Freud even argued for an unspecified human proclivity towards self-destruction – the Thanatos (i.e. death) instinct – and he contended that under certain conditions this becomes re-directed towards others. He also hypothesised that if we did not release these suppressed emotions from time to time, they might lead to various forms of debilitating neuroses. He suggested that these emotions could possibly be canalised in sport or find expression in other relatively harmless ways. Similarly, Konrad Lorenz maintained that aggression is part of the fighting instinct which has been developed over time in order that we might survive. Paradoxically, this instinct to harm and kill, either to defend ourselves against others or to acquire something *from* others, is seen to be related to the mating instinct in that reproduction is facilitated by the union of those who are either strong enough or cunning enough to survive.

These are either pessimistic or realistic theories of human behaviour – depending upon one's point of view – which have a great deal of evidential support from nature and from history. They imply that our aggressive instincts may be subject to control by cultural conditioning of the higher brain centres, but that they will never be eradicated entirely.

Aggression-frustration theories, which are particularly associated with Leonard Berkowitz and his school (Berkowitz, 1962), suggest that aggression is evinced when we are irritated in some way by other people or thwarted by adverse social circumstances. These external conditions are said to generate feelings of animosity and vengefulness that are often difficult to tame. Such ideas have more than a hint of plausibility, but there are one or two points that should be noted. These theories seem to stem from a desire to see human nature in a particular light; some theories – especially those of a more humanistic persuasion – like to think that personal behaviour can be conveniently attributed to some external source, and that if we could so organise our lives that all these offending obstacles were removed, then there would be a full flowering of human potential. We are thus urged to change the educational system, alter political arrangements, give people the 'right environment', abolish the family, or whatever, and all will be well. This has a familiar ring: people are not to blame – merely their circumstances. But optimistic as these views are, they still have to admit the presence of aggressive drives that are activated in particular ways. There is no evidence that aggression would disappear if we could take away or neutralise those things which annoy us. Indeed, it is the overcoming of such difficulties that may actually aid our personal development.

What are rather elaborately called *Cognitive (neo-Associationist) theories* are really refined versions of the aggression-frustration approach. They maintain that people encounter – or are likely to encounter – certain adverse situations that they would like to avoid. The negative effect of these unwelcome experiences generates feelings of anger and irritation which can lead to flight or fight (aggression) and this, in turn, produces unpleasant memories and associations which can then lead to further aggression. Generally speaking, the former criticisms apply but, additionally, there is the faint implication – no more – that really flight is behaviourally preferable to fight; that to avoid aggression is the morally superior option. This has to be arguable, and must depend on a complex of pre-conditions, though it is undoubtedly true that in some circumstances to walk away from a fight takes more courage than to start it, especially if others are there to witness the incident and treat it with ridicule.

Learning theories really elaborate similar well-tried themes, and maintain that people learn aggression in the ways that they learn anything else, and adapt by imitation and reinforced experiences. Aggression is therefore not regarded as being in any way innate except in the sense that we must all have the *capacity* for aggression. But again we have problems. There are notable exceptions to these theories, and they leave so many questions unanswered. Where and how do people learn to be aggressive? And exactly what kind of aggression is it? Is it copied in general ways or in specific terms? I think of the well brought up young Somerset cricketer who no doubt learned something of aggression among his school friends. He murdered both his parents, apparently out of exasperation, tipped their bodies over a cliff, and went off unconcernedly to meet his girl-friend in London. Did he learn *this* at Public School? Furthermore, learning theories cannot easily account for the behavioural ambiguity of certain early experiences. For instance, while it is known that children who are treated harshly may grow up to treat their own children in a similar way, it is also known that children who witness cruelty to animals are so repelled that they never treat animals cruelly themselves.

It seems reasonable to assume that some combination of theories is most appropriate. No one theory accounts for every eventuality or contingency. At the micro level, we see that individuals are all obviously capable of aggression and respond to different sets of circumstances in different ways. The same is true at the macro level. Some societies, especially small tribal societies such as the Pueblo Indians of New Mexico, were known, in general, to be a non-violent people. But other simple societies, such as, say, the Kwakiutl of British Columbia, which were also relatively small-scale, displayed considerable aggression. Such tendencies cannot simply derive from genetic factors alone; some environmental/learning process must be involved which conditions sensitivity to certain types of stimulus, which, in turn, influences the form of response that is generated. Aggression is obviously most likely in the face of aggression, or where a process of de-individuation is taking place and people are losing their personal or collective identity. It is significant that even the Pueblos did not maintain their passivity under the encroachments of the Spaniards.

We live in a world of institutionalised aggression which is often canalised – and sanitised – as sport or commercial, industrial or even educational competition. Yet important as the economic dimension patently is, nothing is more fearful – and seemingly ineradicable – than the threat or actuality of war. It is still perhaps the greatest evil that besets mankind. Since the Second World War, which alone claimed over 20 million dead, there have been over a hundred other conflicts of one kind or another which, in all, have accounted for about as many deaths again.

A number of reasons has been adduced for the incidence of war, none of which – yet again – is adequate by itself. War can be seen as an *economic necessity*, a method of obtaining riches, land, slaves and women, what Stanislav Andreski (1968) calls 'ophelimites' (desired things). It can be an act of *revenge*, but the initial aggression will probably have been motivated by something else, as in the case of the famous (fictional?) expedition of the Myceneans to Troy which was ostensibly about revenge but which was possibly mainly about trading rivalry. War is also about *prowess*, especially so in the days of individual valorous combat as found among the medieval knights, for whom the show of courage was seen as evidence of true manliness. Similarly, war is about *heroism and status*, nowhere better displayed than among certain North American Indian tribes and particularly the Aztecs of Mexico. It can also be regarded as a *mark of nationhood*. Both Mussolini and Hitler took the view that war tests a nation's mettle; that a people that cannot fight does not deserve to survive. And, not least of all, war can be waged for *ideological motives*, to propagate a particular religion or belief-system. It must be said though that sometimes ideology is hopelessly confused with other, more materialistic, motives, and often actually disguises them. In short, aggression has been – and is – so persistent and widespread that it becomes virtually impossible not to think in terms of human infirmity. Experience and learning may give *form* to aggression, and account for specific aggressive *acts*, but they still do not explain aggression *itself*.

Deviance, drugs and decriminalisation

There is probably no topic in the social sciences – and certainly in sociology – which commands so much attention is as deviance. Together with criminological studies generally, it comprises some of the most popular courses in social science degrees. And yet the term deviance is not that easy to define. Before we try to do so, and before we look at some of its theoretical and practical applications, perhaps we should remind ourselves briefly of the three main theoretical orientations in sociology – consensus, conflict and interactionist – which are reiterated ad nauseum in the introductory texts, since they are particularly pertinent to the question of deviance.

The consensus perspective assumes that there is – or should be – agreement on fundamentals such as norms and values, if not on actual practices and procedures. Consensualists stress the implicit harmony in society and argue that it is patently obvious that if this basic agreement did not exist, neither could society exist. So if, for instance, most people were not fundamentally honest, social intercourse and everyday commerce could not continue, and even general communication might become impossible. Consensualists are therefore keen to emphasise the essential functionality of society and its institutions. They 'see' society as an interlocking system of interdependent institutions and practices which have evolved to ensure societal viability and – presumably – historical longevity. These have been developed in ways that best suit the society in question, the assumption being that on the whole things run better *this* way; if this were not so, it would have developed different institutions and practices. Therefore if anything is to change, it should be gradual and cautious. And because society is viewed as a coherent structure, it follows that it can therefore be studied scientifically and analytically, and it is further assumed that the whole is supported by these common value-ideas which give it not only cohesion but a specific identity. The consensualist perspective can thus be said to be clearly holistic, positivistic and conservative in its orientations.

The consensualist perspective is normally contrasted with the conflict perspective, even though, in some ways, they are not as far apart as they are often said to be (see Lipset, 1976, pp. 172ff.). Conflict theorists assume that *tension* is the natural state of things, whether we are thinking in cosmological, geophysical or social terms. Society may *appear* to be stable, but in reality what we are witnessing is the uneasy tension of forces which can – and often does – break down in social disruption of one kind of another. This perspective is frequently associated with Marxism, and is applied at every level, from the nation state to the nuclear family. Underlying tension is therefore seen in an elemental sense, and there is often the additional – and somewhat radical – assumption that this is not necessarily to human detriment, but may be both necessary and desirable as a precursor to human betterment.

The third perspective, interactionism – which is of much more concern to us here – is a reaction against consensus and conflict theories which are alike in that they both advance *general* explanations about the nature of society, whereas interactionism is more concerned with small-scale transactions of social action in 'negotiable' situations. It has individualistic orientations in that actors are seen as 'victims' of societies' definitions and categorisations. For example, homosexuality is regarded as deviant only because society by some sort of understood consensus has decided that it is. Theoretically, this means that it can be re-negotiated, though this will necessarily entail the gradual re-education of society. One can appreciate how this approach can readily lend itself to such kindred ideas as labelling and social stigmatisation of various kinds.

All these perspectives have something to tell us. All are useful in different ways, especially as the bases for a variety of research methodologies. None should be discarded out of hand just because it does not have the right kind of radical or reactionary image. There is a sense in which any statement about society implies consensus. Society could not exist without some sort of agreement about norms, values and procedures. An anarchic society is a contradiction in terms. Even in primitive societies there was some general consensus – albeit uncoded – about practice and organisation. In modern societies, with all their disagreements and conflicts, there is a general level of consensus. There has to be, otherwise society could not continue. Conflict, even revolution, may be one way of securing reform, but there has to come a point where some degree of unity is achieved. Without stability, life becomes unendurable. We have only to think for a moment about the 'Dark Age' periods in the histories of a number of societies, including our own, which were characterised by invasion and fratricidal wars. All have been marked by cultural retardation, economic uncertainty and political instability. Conflict can never be permanent conflict. Even where the balance is precarious, some kind of equilibrium *has* to be established. No matter how uncertain that equilibrium is, it always *is* established eventually for practical social purposes. Interestingly, the Marxist dilemma about whether social change should be evolutionary or revolutionary is – in one sense – misconceived. If one looks at the problem on an extended time-scale, it could be said that *all* change is evolutionary; revolutions are mere ripples on the surface of time.

Whatever sociological perspective we use, there are several theoretical problems with what we broadly call deviance. At the most basic level, how are we to define it? Should it, for instance, be defined in terms of a *deviation from the norm*? But then there is more than one kind of norm. Do we mean *statistical norms*? (The term deviance was first popularised by statisticians.) In that case, if we find among a certain social group, say, members of a religious sect, that divorce is only 1:100 marriages when the statistical norm in the UK is approximately 1:3, we can refer to this as deviant behaviour. However, in general, we tend not to use the term deviant in this way. Then should we confine the use of the term to *behavioural norms*? But then what exactly is behavioural normality? This obviously varies from society to society, and interpretations will differ within any *one* society. So if someone wishes to argue that homosexuality is not normal, he will be right in the statistical sense, but whether he is right in a quite different behavioural sense is now a subject of keen debate.

Deviance, of course, cannot exist without consensus. Deviation, by definition, implies that there is some kind of majority agreement about the 'rules'. First of all, it involves the idea that rules of conduct are *necessary*. These can be *imposed* rules which are considered mandatory, such as legal restrictions, or *implied* rules of an informal kind such as being fair, truthful and so forth. But no society exists without them. Every society has – indeed, *has* to have – codes of some authority to enforce these rules where necessary, although, in practice, approval and disapproval have been particularly effective in checking possible abuses and ensuring some measures of compliance or conformity with the rules.

Deviance not only implies that rules are necessary, it also implies that norms of conduct are *recognised*. This, in turn, involves certain assumptions about rationality. It suggests some evaluation of what is considered right and wrong, desirable and undesirable in society, and – more to the point – how and why such categorisations are made. Do they derive 'naturally' – the consensus view? Or are they structurally determined – the conflict view? If deviance, then, is really about breaking the rules, ignoring or contravening the (possibly uncodified) norms, why does this happen? Is there a physiological factor, an X/Y chromosomal imbalance which affects human behaviour? Some still harbour the somewhat discredited idea that there is some correlation between personality and body formation (see the work of Sheldon on personality types). Or is deviant behaviour perhaps due to faulty socialisation – or lack of necessary discipline and suitable parental guidance? Not least of all, how are the rules made? How do norms come to be norms, and how do they come to be readily accepted by some and rejected by others? And are there no such things as good or bad, only rules that make them so? These are matters we have already considered in other contexts. There are no certain answers, but, as we have seen, there are useful theoretical insights which will, at least, help us to understand the problem better.

The conflict view would have us believe that deviance is a structural inevitability. It presupposes that society is always in a state of tension – always on the brink of disruption or even dissolution. This is held to have certain advantages, particularly that of constant re-evaluation which, theoretically, can – or should – lead to change and reform. Ostensibly, this was the subject of Mao-Tse-Tung's Cultural Revolution in China, an attempt to engender a sense (or process) of perpetual revolution through constant questioning, and the persecution and humiliation of those – especially intellectuals – who were not following the 'ways of truth'. But, as seemed obvious to many observers at the time, it all had little to do with re-evaluation and much more to do with the consolidation of power. All questioning was supposed to lead back to the same answer – the inherent superiority of the Communist status quo.

According to the conflict view, deviance – and, in the narrower sense, crime itself – results from inherent structural inequalities, economic and social deprivation, etc., and will only be reduced, perhaps even eliminated, when these injustices have been remedied. Superficially attractive as this thesis is, it is actually riddled with all kinds of inconsistencies. There are situations where, for example, high unemployment co-exists with low levels of crime, others where there is considerable affluence alongside high levels of deviance, as, for example, in the middle-class drug culture in the USA. And this is quite apart from the acknowledged weaknesses of deprivation theories generally which can be constructed to cover any and every situation.

As an example, let's look at the ethnic dimension and crime in the USA – a subject which often raises academic blood pressure. The crime statistics here are really quite horrifying. There is a murder about every 22 minutes, a rape every 6 minutes, a theft of some kind about every 8 seconds. Violent crime (i.e. murder, rape, aggravated assault, etc.) has increased approximately 60% in the last twenty years. So the general trends are worrying, especially the increase in apparently motiveless murder. Discounting the more sensational serial killings that have so far been detected, we find that about a third of all murders are committed by someone unknown to the victim. These trends may well be partly related to the greater accessibility of handguns, and to the growing popularity of violence on film, TV and video, but is it also connected with deprivation of some kind? What then of the ethnic element? Blacks constitute about 12% of the general population, but nearly half of the prison population. Is the problem 'race', per se? Interestingly, something like 83% of assaults and about 70% of robberies and rapes are *same-race* crimes. This has significant behavioural implications: if crime is about 'race' and not primarily about economic and status factors, why isn't there more black-versus-white or white-versus-black crime? Blacks are thus in more danger from other blacks, and whites from other whites, than they are from each other (note, for example, the mafia-like black factions who are warring with each other for control of the heroin trade in Detroit). Murder is now the leading cause of death among black males between 24 and 34 years of age. This rate is eight to nine times higher than the rate for white males in the same age group, who are more likely to die from car or motor-cycle accidents.

American negroes are a minority amidst a dominant white culture, but a culture that is nevertheless rapidly becoming a *common* culture of a highly heterogeneous society. Is crime therefore a reaction to a structural situation, or, perhaps more accurately, a transitional situation? Is it a form of escape or disengagement from intolerable circumstances? Is it possibly a short-cut to the privileges and assurances of wealth in a status-conscious society? Or is it all of these things? And what, therefore, of the deviant behaviour of the non-economically deprived? Are we to interpret this as a form of exhilarating diversion in a *satiated* society?

Frightening as crime figures and trends are in the USA and in so many other societies, when compared with the total population they still only represent a minority. The vast majority still observe the rules without which society would not be possible. Humans naturally seem to organise themselves this way – perhaps, after all, they *are* rule-observing animals. The cruder type of conflict view really constitutes a kind of *displacement*, a shifting of the blame from A to B. As such it is really only a half-truth. Its inadequacy lies in the fact that it is essentially reductionist in that it tries to explain complex situations and motivations in terms of particular crucial variables.

What then about deviance as a social construct? The interactionist view is that rules are related to actors' meanings. Therefore, society manufactures deviance by labelling certain acts as desirable and undesirable. In the interests of tradition and conformity, rules are simply contrived for purposes of social control. The essential interactionist position is that nothing may be wrong, it is only legislation and untutored opinion that make it so. All acts are therefore negotiable on specific bases. The 'logic' of this approach is that if we re-classify, say, homosexuality as normal this would do away with all sorts of problems and, at the same time, welcome back into the legitimate social fold many who have been stigmatised and ostracised for too long. Yet how one re-classifies the general tenor of orthodox opinion is anybody's guess. It's a little like saying that if we eradicate marriage as a social practice we could then eliminate the expense, the hassle and the trauma of divorce. But how will society cope with the upheaval for partners and possibly children that marriage's inevitable substitute, separation, will undoubtedly cause?

This much vexed issue of de-classification and re-classification is particularly relevant to drugs and the drug-culture, especially the 'soft-drug', cannabis, though some would extend the argument to LSD and certain designer drugs, and even to heroin and cocaine. The implication is that the drug-experience is a form of self-expression and self-realisation that should not be proscribed by the rules. The argument is that some or all of these drugs should be decriminalised in order to bring the practice out into the open and hopefully *reduce* drug consumption and particularly the criminal activities associated with it. What does not seem to have been carefully worked out by the cannabis decriminalisation advocates is just how private cultivation could be controlled, how distribution could be supervised, and how the spread could be limited. And this leaves out of account the ominous possibility of people graduating to more dangerous drugs.

The world trade in what are classified as illegal drugs is estimated at about £400 billion a year; the profits from cocaine alone probably account for something in excess of a quarter of this. It is contended by some (e.g. Coleman, 1989) that this illegal problem should become part of the *legal* drug problem along with alcohol and tobacco which kill infinitely more people than the present illegal drugs. So far, so good. But it is difficult to see just what transferring them from one category to another will do, especially as the world is not doing that well with its present legal drug problem, largely because of the huge revenues that drugs generate. It may well be that decriminalisation would make drugs cheaper and more freely available. This might consequently reduce some of the crime that often accompanies drug activities, from large-scale crime associated with the control of the markets to the small-scale pimping, prostitution and theft which are sometimes necessary to finance the habit.

But what will decriminalisation do for the problem of creating new addicts? And how can it possibly help to stem the significant spread of HIV-AIDS which is now closely correlated with the sharing of infected needles? The experiment in unofficial needle-exchange carried out in Liverpool where police closed a blind eye to what was going on is still inconclusive as an anti-drug/anti HIV-AIDS measure. And in Zurich, where addicts customarily congregated in a park to 'share' and presumably trade, the authorities have decided to re-think their policy of issuing free needles; the same thing has recently happened in liberal Amsterdam, and for much the same reasons. The Netherlands is noted for its 'normalisation' policies and recuperative programmes which tend to favour the addict, yet the traffic in drugs was not reduced, the numbers of clients increased, and the presence of these people offended the sense of public decency to the extent that the authorities were forced to do something about it.

Among sympathisers there are often pleas to see things from the addict's perspective, to consider what is in the interests of the drug user (Engelsman, 1989), but some of the governments who were well-known for their relaxed attitudes to drugs are obviously now wondering if a more repressive stance is called for. Indeed, a strict policy in relation to both dealers *and* users now operating in Sweden has had remarkably promising results. An 'easy' policy on drugs will almost certainly increase the legal problem; it is not likely to decrease the numbers of the dependent, especially with those drugs which are known to be highly addictive. What, for example, will decriminalisation do for those whose drug-dependency has been transmitted to their children? In 1991 it was estimated that some 375,000 babies were infected in the womb by one or another of the illicit drugs, the most common of which is cocaine, particularly in the highly addictive form of 'crack'. Foetuses suffer damage when the oxygen supply to the womb is reduced as a result of the mother taking the drug. Apparently, many of the children require special education, and when this is available, as in the USA, it is about three times as costly as ordinary education. It is said that the problem is increasing at such a rate that New York alone will spend in excess of £500 million in the next ten years on education for these children (*Sunday Times*, 8 March 1992). The mothers concerned almost invariably live in urban ghettos in near hopeless socio-economic situations. Many purist Marxists are quick to condemn such economic conditions as the outcome of exploitative capitalism, but also condemn the victims who they feel should be changing society, not disengaging from it. Yet are they right in assuming that if social conditions were improved the drug problem would inevitably be reduced?

To summarise: the consensus approach is criticised because it is said to be conservative and conformist, although this is open to debate, as many of the recent neo-functionalist texts clearly show. The conflict approach also has its weaknesses, but then both the consensus and conflict views are only *perspectives*, just ways of looking at things which are useful some of the time. The interactionist view, on the other hand, could be categorised as a non-system in that it appears simply to consist of a loose net of ideas based on a kind of situational logic. It is salutary in the sense that it enjoins us to look again at given 'verities' – institutions, policies, and particularly values – and to re-examine the social definitions that have been constructed by our culture. But it also makes the often unwarranted (and mistaken?) assumption that the traditional and the usual are somehow suspect and therefore ripe for serious modification. Surely that which is customary and venerated usually deserves some respect? Traditional policies and practices have evolved over long periods, and therefore merit careful, not hasty, evaluation. The rules we have are there to ensure some measure of stability, because without stability – as so many modern states demonstrate – there is nothing. Social systems that are in perpetual ferment allow for little constructive action. Social order is the vital prerequisite and perhaps also the guarantee of that action.

Race and ethnic relations

In this most contentious of issues, we must inevitably begin with the problem of terminology. Which terms are appropriate, and, what is more important, which terms are *accurate*? Initially, it is necessary to distinguish between racialism and racism (Carlton, 1990). In everyday speech these terms tend to be used interchangeably. Not everyone would make this distinction, and some would use the same terms differently, but it is certainly useful to separate them in practice. Racialism seems to date from the indefinite past. We do not know of a time when some human groups did not differentiate between themselves and others on some basis or another. This might be held to justify – if, indeed, any justification was ever contemplated – such things as killing, rape, enslavement, etc. Racism, on the other hand, is a relatively modern phenomenon. It is the intellectualised conviction that some peoples are *inherently* superior or inferior to others and that no matter how much education and technology are introduced, the 'inferior' will never rise significantly above their present cultural level.

To some extent, the theoretical issue is vitiated by semantic disputation. What terminology is suitable for both academic and general purposes? Some, for instance, seem to prefer the term 'ethnic' to 'racial', so how can these be distinguished? Ethnocentrism is often used to express a preference for one's own people based on *cultural* factors and may not be directly related to race as it is popularly conceived. Historically, all sorts of people have unquestioningly assumed that their culture and their group values, indeed, their general way of life, is superior to that of others, in, say, artistic, intellectual and political achievement. This may not be without some justification although it may have little or nothing to do with race as such. Similarly, we should not confuse colour with race although here again in popular usage, the two terms tend to be employed interchangeably. Race does not necessarily imply colour, but some find that young students who are not too well aware of the Holocaust are inclined to think in these terms.

Insofar as we do identify or associate race with colour, what terms are we to employ? How much depends upon the particular social context in question? Must terminology be tempered to particular audiences? Some terms are undoubtedly offensive to some – for most people the word 'nigger' doesn't go down well no matter how it is used. Some even object to the term 'negro', and yet, etymologically, it is a purely neutral word. In South Africa, negroes will often refer to themselves as 'blacks', yet in the West this is often construed as denigratory, and terms such as 'Afro-Caribbean' are preferred. The terms 'coloured' (sometimes reserved for Asians) and 'non-coloured' are also used, but they really make semantic nonsense because we are all coloured in one way or another. The most ridiculous position, which is adopted by some well-meaning people, is that of insisting that one should be defined as one *wishes* to be defined. This is sometimes taken by those with a seemingly clear Marxist orientation. But – on my reading at least – this is something Marx would never have endorsed because he insisted that it was one's *objective* relationships that mattered. A person may wish to identify with the cause of blacks, Asians, the working-class, displaced persons, or whatever, but this is just a subjective aspiration. I remember a student who called herself black when she was actually a Turkish-Cypriot. We cannot make ourselves what we are not, no matter how sincere our intentions. If one isn't one just isn't.

The differences between races are relative, not absolute. We all belong to our human family, but it has to be recognised that the differences *do* exist. The task of the natural scientist is to ask *how* and *why*, while the task of the social scientist is to try to explain why these differences have become significant for *social* purposes. The physiological factors are extremely complex. Blood-groups, for instance, do appear to follow broad geographical lines; so we find, for example, that Group O is common among American Indians while Group A is extremely rare. Susceptibility to certain kinds of disease such as intestinal ulcers is common among Group O Europeans, and Group A people are more likely to develop intestinal cancers – both of which may be due largely to dietary factors, though this is not certain. We are still not sure how to account for certain mutational changes. There may just be the possibility that some take place in response to social conditions, although this has been seriously questioned. There is an even more bizarre possibility that there can be inherited acquired characteristics: this is very much a minority view, but it is still being debated.

Trying to trace the effects of selection in controlling differential rates of fertility, reproduction and survival among specific genetic combinations is almost beyond us, especially when taking patterns of migration into consideration, but we are reasonably confident that some of these changes must take place in response to *environmental conditions* (Darlington, 1969). For instance, the incidence of sun-burn and particularly skin cancer (melanoma) which has more than doubled in the last ten years or so in Europe, is not nearly so high among dark-skinned people who have more melanin which absorbs harmful ultra-violet rays. But in high lands and in areas of seasonal cloudiness, white skin has advantages, especially in winter, as it permits maximum irradiation of vitamin D which is absorbed directly into the bloodstream. It would not, however, be wise to attribute everything to environmental conditions, especially when it comes to group formation. Many peoples, such as the Maya in the rainforests of Guatemala and the Incas in the uplands of Peru, have settled in the most unconducive surroundings but have still developed high civilisations. The environment presents humans with many possibilities, some of which are uninviting and severely circumscribed. It therefore imposes limits on development in any particular area, although, as far as the future goes, we cannot pronounce on these limits because the accelerating advance of science and technology liberates us, to an appreciable extent, from the constraints of our 'natural' living conditions. And they also enable us to see the potentialities that exist in restricted environments – witness the Israeli experiments in cultivation in the inhospitable Sinai desert. Such factors impinge on the issue of race insofar as they may modify our understanding and appreciation of differential cultural development.

When it comes to modern group formation as we find it among immigrants in the UK, and particularly too in Germany and France, it is not difficult to see why people come together as they do. They form groups in response to the need to express a common identity, in a recognition of common interests, and often in an attempt to maintain their ethnic culture. Yet if these are the sole reasons, why then have they left their homelands? Often it is to secure better political rights and more conducive economic conditions, even where these have brought their own problems. They often have to confront and combat discrimination and various forms of prejudice for which there is no legal remedy. Furthermore, there are the difficulties that Muslims and Hindus especially encounter with their children and the increasing conflict with Western norms, particularly in relation to education, sex and marriage.

The whole issue is probably better seen in in-group/out-group terms rather than in racial terms. But when is an in-group an in-group, and an out-group an out-group? As with prejudice, it can work both ways. Each group can be equally intolerant of the other, especially where there is a cultural mismatch. We are all well aware of the ungenerous treatment some out-groups can receive even where they constitute the majority of the population. Yet where they are minorities they can be vociferous – even objectionably so – in the pursuit of their respective interests. We can see this where Muslim, more specifically Pakistani, agitation for schools to observe their particular dietary rules has not won them too many friends, and some of the *anti*-racist organisations, as distinct from those advocating *non*-racism, who insist that race is the primary experience, have often shown themselves to be as prejudiced as those they condemn.

One of the main difficulties with the minority/majority approach is that majorities and minorities can vary with the social context in question. If we take the Northern Ireland conflict, we can appreciate that Catholics are a minority which, in view of reproduction rates, could soon become a majority. But in the overall setting of the whole island they are already a very clear majority. Better still, if we look at the Arab-Israeli situation – which, in purely racial terms, is a tragic conflict between brother Semites – we think of the Arabs as a persecuted minority whereas in the context of the Middle East they are an overwhelming majority with enough wealth and land to spare to solve the Palestinian issue if they wished. The obvious truth is that they have used the Palestinian problem to justify their antagonism to Israel. When Palestinians have sought refuge elsewhere they have even met hostility from their Muslim neighbours who have often been willing to send them money, but who do not want them in appreciable numbers inside their borders. Syria has kept them in place in Lebanon which had its own share of problems when it looked as though they were making a bid for control. The Kuwaitis encouraged them, but disillusioned with their disloyalty in the Gulf War they have resorted to persecution. And in Jordan they were crushed unmercifully by King Hussein when they threatened to take control of the country.

Another besetting problem about race – which is not greatly aired – is that it is sometimes exploited for ulterior political purposes. In a recent Commonwealth Games, for example, it was intriguing to witness the deviousness of some of the participant nations. However good the anti-apartheid cause, the issue was undoubtedly used for a little political muscle-flexing by those who threatened to boycott the Games, although many of them were receiving aid from the UK, and some were even trading with South Africa. It is highly arguable whether sport should have been made the victim in this kind of dispute. It was not as though these states were the last word in democratic organisation. Until recently, India was dynastically controlled and was brutally suppressing some of her own minorities. Many, like Zimbabwe, were one-party states, and not a few had serious internal problems of their own which involved corruption (e.g. Nigeria), violence (e.g. Uganda, Kenya) and – if some reports are to be believed about non-Commonwealth states in Africa – genocide (Burundi). Britain too has been guilty of similar hypocrisy over such matters as banning rugby and cricket tours. Players – rightly or wrongly – have been made to pay the price for disregarding Government policy, when that same Government did not extend its restrictions to *all* sports, and conveniently omitted to mention its multi-million-pound investments in South Africa.

In thinking about race it is important to bear in mind the cognitive and affective as well as the behavioural aspects of the problem. Thus we must distinguish between *beliefs* which are related to values, *opinions* which are less clearly defined, and which may be held or proffered in contradistinction to convictions, and *attitudes* which normally connote a response that may or may not imply some behavioural intention. Attitudes are formed by observation, example and exposure, although education and inculcation can generate negative as well as positive responses. Attitude formation is something we have yet to learn a great deal about. We are not at all sure, for instance, what determines *flexibility* – a willingness to change, and *obduracy* – an unwillingness or apparent inability to change. Both are particularly pertinent to the question of race, and both tend to be associated with Liberalism and Conservatism respectively. Here we encounter the problem of stereotypical thinking in which complex configurations of assumed traits are attributed to particular groups. Negroes may be seen as idle, morally lax and capable of only limited mental development; Jews intolerant, mean and prone to sharp practices, etc. There may be some vague, vestigial truth behind some of these highly generalised suppositions, but whatever it is is rarely considered contextually or weighed against the overall situation. It is all too easy to extrapolate from particular instances to races in general, and to ignore historical antecedents, e.g. that medieval Jews were largely forced into the deplored activity of money-lending because other, legitimate professions were denied them. Even exposure to other races and cultures is an uncertain remedy (Piliavin et al., 1981); (think of the kittens who are reared companionably with white mice, but who will still attack brown mice). Exposure can sometimes turn novelty into hostility. This is most likely where there is a rapid increase in an immigrant population, as has happened in the UK and parts of Europe. One is reminded of critical mass theories in physics which hold that beyond an optimum point the properties of substances begin to change. In social settings this point is often not knowable, but beyond it attitudes appear to alter – and not always for the best.

Racial attitudes are understandably related to socio-economic circumstances. Not infrequently poor whites are more antagonistic to blacks and Asians than those of the more prosperous middle classes. They do not always see them as fellow members of the working class, but rather as rivals in an underclass who are there to undercut them and take their jobs. Middle-class whites who are far removed from the conflict at the base of the social hierarchy can therefore afford to adopt liberal attitudes. They do not feel threatened by the presence of blacks and Asians, whereas poor whites who are only on the next rung of the social ladder are sometimes afraid that their livelihoods and living areas will be adversely affected. So although official policy may be directed towards integration and assimilation, individual actions may well run counter to the rules. But ambivalence may prevail, e.g. where the official policy is directed against non-whites, the actions of some individual whites such as alleviating hunger may contravene official policy (Turner, 1976).

In the USA, racial attitudes have been categorised as *dominative* where prejudices are acted out as discriminating behaviour either inside or outside the law; as *ambivalent* where there are these mixed feelings of sympathy and hostility; as *aversive* where prejudice is subtle, where there are professions of liberalism without any actual social interaction (Kovel, 1970). Surveys in the USA suggest that although the colour prejudice situation has improved considerably in recent years (Deaux & Wrightsman, 1984), there is, in some quarters, evidence of symbolic racism where whites object to 'unfair' advances in black causes (e.g. education) which they see as blatant examples of positive discrimination (Maconahay & Hough, 1976). Outside the USA, one can see variants of this, for example, the protests of high caste Indian medical students who have objected to special places being reserved in medical schools in favour of members of the scheduled caste (previously, the 'outcastes').

There is, of course, no *one* cause of prejudice and discrimination, but for simplicity of analysis, we might consider the following factors which inevitably overlap:

(1) *Historical factors*

In so many situations we find that there is a gross misunderstanding of the nature of the case. The Greeks and the Romans, although quite tolerant of non-whites – of whom Greeks in particular had relatively little experience – never really understood either the culture or the religion of the Jews. Not that they would have acted *that* much differently towards them if they had. Anyone who seriously questioned the authority of their overlords, much less threatened them, was marked down for 'treatment'. Jews could sometimes prove difficult to control, especially when alien armies tried in any way to suppress their religious practices. Resistance, especially toward some of the Hellenistic kings, particularly the pathological Antiochus Epiphanes (d. 164), or to some of the later Roman Emperors, met with the harshest of measures. Just before the capture of Jerusalem in AD 70, the Roman conqueror, Titus, who was soon to be Emperor, was crucifying up to 300 Jews a day outside the city walls as a punishment and as a form of deterrent to other would-be rebels.

Where suppression has been eased there is often a legacy of distrust and suspicion. This is most evident after decolonisation when the newly-enfranchised peoples cannot forget or forgive their previous subservient status vis-à-vis their former masters. This has been particularly notable in such states as Kenya, Uganda and Tanzania, where Africanisation policies have favoured neither the whites who have decided to stay, nor the Asians who – in many cases – had been imported by the whites to work on various capital projects such as railways, etc. In Uganda, for instance, Asian immigrants constituted a high proportion of the lower middle class trading fraternity, and aroused the jealousy of the native Ugandans who saw them as economic rivals.

(2) *Politico-economic factors*

We have already seen that these are often much more important than race, although they are often mistaken for racial issues. Indeed, the problem of interpretation vitiates so many conflict situations. The 'troubles' in Northern Ireland are frequently seen in religious terms, as is also – to some extent – the conflict in Sri Lanka between the Singhalese and the Tamils. They are manifestly not religious in origin or purpose, although religion is incidental in both situations, and is sometimes used to justify certain hostile attitudes. The basic problem is one of *power*: who controls what and how? Similar difficulties arise in relation to colour. Some of the most intransigent problems in the modern world may be considered to be broadly ethnic in type, but they are certainly not about colour as such. The problems in Indonesia, Fiji, where imported Indian workers are in continual dispute with native Fijians, and the tribal groups in Burundi, Nigeria, Uganda and South Africa are all essentially about power and advantage, but are deceptively *expressed* in racial terms. Sometimes there are situations where the political and the economic have to be separated. Consider the influx of mainly poor East European Jews to the West in the late 19th century which aroused economic jealousy, but where there was no significant political dimension.

(3) *Socio-cultural factors*

This is a catch-all category which includes such multifarious factors as population and differential rates of reproduction. When one ethnic group is literally out-breeding another, or where a minority group is multiplying a great deal faster than the host society, problems are almost bound to arise. This category must also include the matter of cultural disparities. The 'traditional' one-parent family set-ups among West Indian immigrants, for example, did not always endear them to their white neighbours who, especially in the 1960s and 1970s, did not take that kindly to such heterodox arrangements. One large-scale survey has shown that while only 6.7% of white children, and a very low 1.3% of Asian children were born to unmarried mothers, more than a quarter of those from an Afro-Caribbean background – where there is also a high incidence of marital breakdown – were born to unmarried women (*Sunday Times*, 9 June 1985).

Other cultural differences, such as dietary habits, dress, leisure activities and language/accent/argot, though relatively minor, can all occasion suspicion and dislike among those who are unaccustomed to them, and who take the view that 'if they want to live here they should be like us'. Perhaps some of these attitudes are unwittingly perpetuated by media images. Though normally very much against the racially bigoted, the media may actually generate bias among the indigenous population by appearing to indulge in a little positive discrimination from time to time. Special minority magazines and programmes, in particular, may actually reinforce prejudicial attitudes rather than reduce them.

It could be that all these 'factors' rely more on description than explanation. They say more about the *conditions* in which prejudice arises and discrimination is expressed than about the root causes of the problem. Arguably, the real causes are buried in the personality. Freudians might contend that we all have tendencies towards *transference* (of guilt) and towards *scapegoating* – in other words, blaming others for the inadequacies and faults that we see in ourselves. Learning theories, on the other hand, might detect the causes in faulty education and training, in responses to the wrong signals (or wrong responses to the right signals?). But interesting as these psychological approaches may be, they still do not really tell us why these psychological proclivities (defects?) should take these particular forms. Prejudice is often notoriously ignorant and inconsistently directed. Jews, for instance, have been seen as too exclusive *and* too intrusive, as capitalistic *and* subversively communistic, even within the same societies. Whatever may be deep-seated and perhaps unanalysable in our psyches, one cannot help but feel that social factors determine the *focus* of prejudice, and that racial values are often rationalised according to one's interests, despite the nature of the evidence. Ultimately these issues raise questions of meaning and legitimacy; fundamentally, we are yet again talking about perception and cognition. The race issue can be essentialised in terms of divergent and perhaps irreversible rationalities.

The ecological dilemma

Living, as we do, in an age of truly impressive technological advance, we can readily appreciate the growing intensity of concern over our physical environment. Modifications to living conditions – notably in the West – have not only been swift, they are still rapidly accelerating. In virtually every sphere of activity almost unimaginable changes have taken place: transport, communications, medicine, etc. Everywhere science seems to be outstripping those areas of learning we broadly call the human sciences – if, indeed, they *are* sciences. It is doubtful if we have made that much progress in the arts, though that depends on how the term progress is defined. The corollary of this rapid scientific and industrial advance has been serious concern as to whether these changes can be justly called progress at all.

There are two main strands of thought about this; there are those who welcome the changes, and fail to see any long-term problems about the future. They agree that we have difficulties, but do not see that any of our problems are insuperable. Where difficulties do exist, they feel that eventually science will come to the rescue. But does this mean the 'uncritical acceptance of the blessings of economic growth with the comforting corollaries that technology will find a way around any difficulties that may arise and that adaptable humankind will come to accept – even like – conditions of crowding, regimentation ... that are now distasteful to us?' (Fisher, 1972, p. viii). Then there are those who are diametrically opposed to this, and take the view that the planet faces an immediate crisis which even now it may be too late to resolve. Few thinking people can ignore the fact that there are problems, but is science the villain of the piece, as the environmentalists insist, or is science really our only salvation? Some extremists even deplore the very idea that science, as we understand it, ever materialised. But surely the idyllic notion of a return to the past can be no more than an Arcadian dream. How many really want a world without its modern amenities?

Economic growth was once regarded as a universal panacea which would solve all our most pressing problems. With the 1960s this comforting notion began to be challenged. Embryonic environmentalist movements grew up in the 1970s, consisting – as Sterling Brubaker puts it – of 'diverse strains ... a blend of the holders of traditional anti-materialist, conservationist and naturalist views together with neo-Malthusians, ecological pessimists, elements of the consumer-protectionist movement, action-oriented youth, and air-breathing citizens' (Brubaker, 1972, p. 24). Yet it can hardly be said any longer that these people had 'plenty of vitality but no unifying doctrine'. They are now fairly unanimous about what is wrong even if they are not all clear about the possible solutions.

Primarily, there is the problem of population (considered in a separate section) which has roughly doubled in the last forty years to its present 5 billion, and is estimated to reach about 7 billion by the end of the century. At this rate, assuming resource adequacy and environmental tolerances, by the year 2600 there will be standing room only on the planet. The ecosystem generally is felt to be under threat. In 1990, Worldwatch commented on the related issues of global warming, pollution and the depletion of the ozone layer. They estimate that a fifth of the world's population is breathing contaminated air which may cause as many as 50,000 deaths in the USA every year, a situation that is hardly helped by the 400 million cars on the planet. The depletion in the protective ozone layer – about which there is still some uncertainty – may account for the increasing incidence of skin cancer of which there could be as many as 600,000 cases a year (*Sunday Times*, 1 March 1992). If the international scientific consensus is right, the increase in carbon dioxide in the atmosphere and the subsequent generation of a 'greenhouse effect' will have devastating consequences for the next century. Friends of the Earth argue that this is coming about largely because of deforestation. They say that some 45% of the world's rainforests has been destroyed in the last 30 years, and about 1.8% of the remaining forest disappears every year (Porritt, 1990). This, in turn, contributes to soil erosion. It is estimated that some 17 million hectares of forest are lost every year, and that 6 million hectares of new desert are formed in the same period through poor management and changing patterns in the climate. It is believed too that the water shortage throughout the globe is affecting the livelihoods of innumerable people; water consumption has probably doubled during this century, again a factor that is aggravated by population growth and Western lifestyles.

Environmental degradation, then, can no longer be a peripheral preoccupation. On a worldwide scale, it may be that millions of lives are at stake. Small policy adjustments are not enough. The current view of those concerned is that something radical and comprehensive needs to be done immediately. These global conditions, aggravated by soil erosion, deforestation and over-grazing, are affecting the Third World most of all. It is here that incomes – already pitifully small for the majority of the population – fell most dramatically; in Nigeria, for example, by almost 30%. The poverty experienced by so many in these developing countries which comprise something in the order of one sixth of the world's population is almost unimaginable in the West. Of these, about one fifth is hungry to the point of near starvation and at least another fifth is seriously malnourished. Britain has proposed that the richer nations should try to relieve the government-to-government debts of the 26 states who are on the World Bank's list of Severely Indebted Low Income Countries. Their total debt is around 116 billion dollars (about the same as Brazil's national debt). The idea is that their debts should be cut by two-thirds, absolving them from interest payments for five years, and extending repayment periods to 25 years. The poorest countries have been paying something in the order of 25% of their trade earnings to debt repayments and would actually pay twice this if they wanted to cover all the debt that was outstanding. Approximately ten billion dollars is paid by Africa every year in respect of debts. With investments failing and incomes falling, many Africans are worse off now than they were 30 years ago (*Guardian*, Environment, 12 July 1991).

These difficulties extend even to those countries where formerly there were high hopes of successful development. Indonesia is a good example of this. In 1988, the World Resources Institute at Washington D.C. reviewed the case of Indonesia, which, in theory, had developed one of the world's healthiest economies. Between 1971 and 1984, its gross domestic product had grown at the impressive rate of 7.1% a year, but all this was bought at the cost of a serious depletion in its natural resources. From 1970 onwards it began to lose its rainforests, and from the early 1980s its oil reserves shrank by the equivalent of ten billion dollars a year. The cost of soil erosion alone in terms of lost productivity is estimated to have amounted to an average of 484 million dollars a year (*Guardian*, ibid.).

The plight of these Third World peoples now looks like being shared by many in Eastern Europe who are the victims of hurried ideologically-inspired industrialisation. The difficulties are formidable. Forty years of centralised economic planning, which promised so much, has come to nothing. The almost obsessive concentration on heavy industry – largely to the neglect of everything else, especially the human cost – has led to the daunting problems they now face (*Guardian*, 19 January 1990). It is estimated that in Czechoslovakia some 70% of rivers are polluted and 50% of the forests are dying or damaged. And while 2% of Czech investment is used for various environmental projects, a combination of inefficient bureaucracy and insufficient technology is seriously hampering progress. The situation in Poland is even worse, in fact it is now thought to be the most polluted country in Europe. In certain areas, sulphur dioxide deposits exceed 100 tonnes per square kilometre, and heavy metals are found in the vegetables in these polluted locations. In the Krakow district alone about 60% of produce is said to be unfit for consumption. Little wonder that life expectancy is significantly lower and infant mortality significantly higher in these areas. Certain ecological measures are being taken, but money and resources are scarce, even though help has been offered by the World Bank, Sweden, Holland and Germany for specific projects. Things were no better in East Germany, where in 1988 it was reported that 37% of the forests were dying, and perhaps another 50% adversely affected. Some 66% of the rivers have been polluted by noxious emissions from power stations which, as yet, are not subject to very stringent controls. Many of these rather outdated stations are said to run at only about 26% efficiency compared with, say, 60% in Japan. Water is a key factor too in Bulgaria where it is thought that if present practices continue, the Black Sea will be 'dead' within ten years. In neighbouring Romania, only 15% of river water is reported as being fit to drink, although the country's sulphur dioxide emissions are some of the lowest in Europe. This contrasts markedly with Hungary where emissions are a major problem. All these countries are beginning to tackle the problems but are facing seemingly insuperable problems of money, resources and – to some extent – know-how.

Humans are not the only ones to suffer. There are countless life forms on the planet, of which only about a million and half have been identified. Uncertain too is the number that are now apparently condemned to extinction, possibly as many as 50,000 species a year. Each is a unique and irreplaceable entity. This does not mean that every one is indispensable, but, as far as we can understand, they appear to comprise a huge and unimaginably complex eco-system which is necessary to sustain the viability of the planet. The threat is not to any particular types of species – a wide diversity of creatures is disappearing from lakes, forests and islands, indeed, wildlands everywhere. To give just one example, the otter, once common in the British Isles, is now struggling to survive. There has been a loss of habitat with the clearing of the river banks, but most of all there is the pollution of the rivers which has gradually reduced the otter population in England by over 90% in the last thirty years. The poisons cause liver lesions and damage to the immune system; some deformities have been observed, as well as serious damage to the female reproductive system (*Sunday Times*, 23 February 1992). Amphibians are affected, and so are reptiles such as turtles, many of which are extremely rare. Wild cats and bears are rapidly declining in numbers, largely through human exploitation, and it is said that some two thirds of the world's 150 species of primates will soon be lost. Many West European countries report that their mammals are threatened; in Australia, some 50% of mammals are likely to become extinct. One of the worst cases is that of the African elephant. Ivory exports were banned by the UN Convention on International Trade in Endangered Species in 1989 after poachers had reduced the African elephant population by half. In some states, both rebels and security forces are known to be partly responsible. It is reported that in Mozambique, where the national parks are now like ecological deserts, some 50,000 elephants have died during the civil wars. In Zambia, in one park alone, the herds have been reduced by 80%. And similar stories are told of Zimbabwe, which considers itself a role model for wildlife preservation (*Sunday Times*, ibid.). Indiscriminate snaring and killing together with deforestation have also contributed to an incalculable decline in the bird population, which affects perhaps as many as 75% of the world's birds. Fish too are endangered, especially in the freshwater lakes, and even invertebrates are not immune (*Guardian*, Environment, 3 January 1992).

This sorry saga of gloom and despondency doesn't end here. We now have a Worldwatch report on the growing problem of nuclear waste. We all welcome the general lessening of tension between the West and what was once known as the Eastern bloc, but one by-product of the astronomically expensive arms race has been the build-up of vast stocks of radioactive waste. Nobody is now quite sure what to do about all this spent fuel. Only very recently has it come to public notice that despite protestations to the contrary the Russians have been dumping nuclear waste in the Kara Sea for the last twenty years. This 'burial ground', some way to the north-east of the port of Murmansk, is now causing considerable concern on the mainland, and is regarded as very dangerous for northern Europe if, as suspected, seepage is affecting the food chain.

A typical reactor discharges about 30 tons of waste a year. There are several hundred reactors in operation producing some 5% of the world's energy. The mathematics of pollution should therefore be simple but for the fact that this is liable to double by the end of the century. The really serious process of dealing with this unwanted irradiated fuel will not begin until early in the next century; until that time much of it is being kept in 'storage' pending a decision on its final disposal. At least this is a great deal better than the early days when in some countries it was simply thrown into the nearest river. Disused mines are now a favoured type of storage area, and with so many mines going out of operation Britain has become a centre for the lucrative business of nuclear 'reprocessing'. But with plutonium-239 – a principal component of nuclear bombs – having a half-life of 24,000 years, it had better be laid to rest in a very secure vault.

How is all this to be tackled, and how is it going to be paid for? There is an agenda for hope that includes both theoretical and practical measures to alleviate the situation. But to some extent they sound like a counsel of perfection. We know that more aid should be given to the poorest nations, but we also know that there are serious problems about distribution. In Sudan, for example, much of the aid from the West has been 'requisitioned' to feed not the people, but the military forces that claim priority. But perhaps we should be prepared to give even though we are more or less certain that only a *fraction* of what we give will find its way to those for whom it was intended. A better trading environment would also help. Not only is more labour-intensive agricultural growth required, but cash crop produce must not be inhibited by unnecessary protectionism in overseas markets. Debt, as we have seen, accounts for a very high percentage of all export earnings – perhaps as much as 20% – so some kind of debt relief would be of enormous value to the developing countries. We also have what is, apart from population, the very singular problem of war. This diverts resources away from development. More often than not, it is said to be for 'liberation', although it is often highly doubtful whether the ordinary people are much better off with one regime than another.

Yet, having said all this about the need to help the Third World, we mustn't confuse growth with development. The West has exported the idea of increased GNP as a world-wide panacea. Wider markets and larger profits are seen as *the* answer. The desirability of economic growth and its benefits is regarded as a self-evident, universal good. But is it based on wants or on needs? We are all aware that some governments, and especially revolutionaries, often seek rapid, utopian 'solutions' to their problems, yet although the needs are urgent, perhaps a little more emphasis on piecemeal social engineering might save a lot of unnecessary suffering.

Money, by itself, can be one of the main sources of the problem. Easy access to cash has often led to extravagance of the most imprudent kind. One notorious example is the Brazilian dam project at Balbina which has been plagued by controversy and corruption from the beginning. It cost a billion dollars and was one of some 1,600 mega-projects launched in the Third World during the Cold War 1970s at a total cost of over a trillion dollars. From the beginning its 'economics were dubious and the environmental damage it caused staggering'. It has been dubbed 'a monument to institutional insanity'. In this and other cases, 'commercial bankers [have] lent without due diligence ... [and] Third World leaders, unrestrained by the laws, legislative rules, and ballot boxes that give a populace control over its government's expenditures, borrowed for their own personal benefit ...' (Patricia Adams, *Guardian*, 3 January 1992). Development must be – to use the current buzz-word – 'sustainable'. Growth, attractive as it may be, has *quantitive* implications; it means more – especially more consumer goods, whereas development should be seen in *qualitative* terms – not so much more, as *better*. The goal is all-round, continued improvement which is, as far as possible, conducive to the environment. It should not be production for production's sake which, as Illich suggests, has transformed the earth into a junkyard by creating waste (Illich, 1991). He argues that for too long economists have entertained the naive assumption that the economy is like a machine that simply generates value, whereas it is actually creating 'disvalue'. Production should be for the enrichment of all. But can this be achieved?

There is little doubt that many countries are now serious about environmental concerns. Advisory organisations have now been set up all over the world, and they seem to be unanimous in their conclusions that radical changes of policy are required if we are to avoid total disaster. Some reports have gone further and have argued that it is primarily the developed countries that are responsible for all this, and that – in one way or another – they are still controlling the purse strings, and therefore the forms and rates of development in the Third World. The implication is that their motivations are essentially exploitative and that they are really pursuing a policy of re-colonisation by new methods.

This does tend to discount the fact that with all their faults, the developed countries are places where people live longer, are better housed, better fed, better educated and better medicated, and that these are just the things the Third World both needs and desires. And who can blame them? True, it is a situation that is ripe for exploitation. So many developing nations have not got a very attractive array of goods to sell; others are small, virtually one-commodity economies such as Cuba that have been either very much tied to limited outlets (e.g. Cuba's sugar exports to Russia) or are at the mercy of the market – neither of which is an enviable situation. It is hardly surprising, therefore, that being unable easily to develop or to diversify, so many poor countries take the short-cut of borrowing to get what they want, or of entering an aid-based patron-client relationship with a powerful state in order to secure the necessary benefits – a situation from which they find it very difficult to extricate themselves. So despite the drawbacks, the Third World must depend both on the largesse and on the fair-mindedness of the developed countries in the short term, in the hope that in the longer term they will be able to sustain their own viable economies – assuming, of course, that the environment can stand it, and that by that time we are not all defeated by overproduction and the debris of rampant industrialisation.

There is, however, a salutary coda to all this – a question we must ask if we are to be fair to the argument. In this discussion so far there has been an explicit attack on human irresponsibility regarding the environment, and the implicit assumption that all we need to do is to get nearer to nature, because nature knows best.

How accurate is this? If there were no humans on the planet, would nature achieve its own balance? Presumably, yes, but it would be a very different kind of balance. And if, one day, we humans destroy ourselves – not an impossible scenario – what then? Arguably we will have left the planet to other life-forms: to grossly mutated weeds and rats, and those bacteria which are thought to be immune to radiation. The disillusioning truth is that the harm we can do to the environment is well-matched by all the harm that the environment does to us. We have only to think of all those 'alien' life forms which bring suffering and death to the wary and unwary alike. The Earth is not a paradise. It is replete with dangers from diseases which we know were here long before the advent of man. Now we need to work on the problems so that we can more nearly adapt ourselves to the planet, and the planet to our human requirements. But science must take considerable care along the way; its motivations and values must be more divorced from political and commercial considerations. We are only going to survive when the proper concern of mankind becomes mankind.

The problem of population

Arguably, population is the most pressing problem in the world today. This would probably be agreed by environmentalists and non-environmentalists alike. Those who take an extreme 'back-to-nature' position appear to do so on the tacit understanding that what nature requires should be the ultimate guide to our behaviour. In effect, they are imputing some kind of purpose to nature. It is doubtful that very many people take this extreme position, although many environmentalists seem to be not that far from it. Most would take a more moderate view and argue that reproduction must be geared to existing resources. But even these divide into those whose primary concern is to restrict population (e.g. Population Concern, an offshoot of the Family Planning Association) and those who put much more stress on the environment, arguing that given the enormous profligacy of nature, there is still enough food and energy in the world for everyone if only they were properly produced and fairly distributed. But how persuasive is this view when the arithmetic of exponential growth demands that humankind must exercise urgent restraint over reproduction? In 1830 – only yesterday in historical terms – the population of the planet was about one billion. It then took almost 100 years (1927) to reach two billion, 33 years (1960) to reach three billion, only 14 years (1974) to reach four billion, and just 13 years (1987) to reach five billion. In the early 1990s it stands at about five and a half billion, and by the end of the century it will certainly be well over six, and possibly close to seven billion. Multiplication of this kind obviously cannot go on.

Reproduction is the first requirement for the success of the species, and there is a certain irony in the fact that 'as man escapes predator and pathogen and achieves great reproductive success he must deliberately limit his numbers' (Brubaker, 1972, p. 203). Something must certainly be done – and done quickly. The traditional rationales for high birth rates – family survival and security, or national needs in terms of increased numbers of soldiery – are no longer as compelling as they once were. There are 90 million more births than deaths every year; 255,000 new humans to feed every day, the vast majority of whom (about 94%) will be born in the developing countries where poverty is most acute. There was a post-World War II surge in the birth rate in the USA and Britain. Generally birth rates in the developed countries have declined in what is sometimes termed the post-industrial period, when 'the relationship between fecundity and prosperity was too close to be ignored' (Brubaker, 1972, p. 204).

It is the population problem which vitiates and exacerbates the entire ecological debate. One may have some reservations about the dire prognostications of the Friends of the Earth and similar likeminded groups, but Jonathan Porritt is surely right when he says that even if the earth's life-support systems turn out to be more resilient than anticipated, and even if new technologies do enable us to meet human needs by distributing wealth more equitably, and even if our leaders find the political will to make things work, 'those standard population projections spell untold misery for millions of people, and the steady elimination of ecological diversity across the entire planet ... all [this] work could be simply swept away by the rising tide of humanity' (Porritt, 1990, p. 181).

At the present time at least a billion people live in degrading squalor. They are – in the main – unhealthy, uneducated and ill housed, and their poverty is such that eventually many become numbed and even brutalised by lives spent in a social ethos of neglect and desperation. The plethora of plans and projects dreamed up by well-intentioned officials and environmentalists has really done little for them. Billions have been spent on development schemes but all to little avail, partly because the task is becoming increasingly formidable, and partly because of the general inefficiencies which vitiate so many aid programmes. Aid agencies and their governments all too often 'lurch from fad to development fad' and are even said to try to hide their failures behind 'a smokescreen of jargon and acronyms, endless meetings and unfathomable hocus-pocus' (*Guardian*, Worldwatch, 3 January 1992). Even the UN's food and agriculture organisation (FAO) has been accused of promoting policies which mainly benefit the rich and the powerful at the expense of the poor. The FAO employs some 6,000 people and spends £343 million a year to raise nutritional levels and living standards and eliminate hunger, but its critics contend that actually it is creating the conditions for more starvation. This, they claim, is happening because the FAO has simply become 'a front organisation for multi-nationals, dam-builders and agro-chemical firms to promote expensive, high-tech agriculture that boosts yields but benefits only a rich elite while it devastates the environment' (*Guardian*, Environment, 26 April 1991). It is said that poor farmers are made landless and that they gravitate to the towns and just add to the swelling numbers of urban poor. Warranted or not, such accusations express a prevailing concern that not enough is reaching those who really need it. But is it all the fault of the agencies? What happens when help *is* sent? A not untypical example is that of Sudan. In the recent past it was reported that the warehouses of Port Sudan were packed to the rafters with supplies of food, and that each day more and more was arriving from the West. Few could complain about the generous scale of international relief, although there is actually nothing like enough food to meet all the country's needs. But that is hardly to be expected. So there were ominous murmurings because Sudan's huge potential for feeding itself had not been met, and this was in part attributed to years of underinvestment and mismanagement. There is little doubt that, other than the drought, the key complicating factor has been the civil war. One writer speaks of 'political and diplomatic shenanigans ... [and] bloody-mindedness on both sides' (John Vidal, *Guardian*, 'Waiting for the wave of death', 26 April 1991). The war has been responsible for hundreds of thousands of deaths and massive destruction, and has been an enormous drain on the country's limited finances. Meanwhile, no one is even prepared to guess at the prospective mortality rate. In 1984 and 1985, in a similar crisis, 200,000 people died. This famine was studied intensively and many lessons have been learned, but it has proved to be almost beyond the people's capacity to put them into operation. Transportation, agreed policies about allocation and actual distribution are all problems, combined with the inability of the rural populations, swelled by refugees, to do more than try to satisfy their immediate needs. At the moment, the tendency is to wait until the crisis arrives instead of setting in train the necessary policies and provisions for the next anticipated emergency (Maxwell, 1991).

What are the facts behind these disturbing images of starvation? What is it like for those who have to suffer? The hungry are prepared to tackle any wild food that is only barely edible, even shrivelled blades of grass. On such bare diets, children can become seriously malnourished within a week, especially if no milk is available. Indeed, without liquids they are likely to die in a few days. And yet, worldwide, 1.2 billion people lack water that is safe to drink. Such people naturally want to stay in their home areas if at all possible, but, in desperation, will trek to wherever food can be found, often to relief camps where they find others as weak as themselves living in squalid, near-hopeless conditions. They lose their body fat, and lack of the right nutrients causes the breakdown of muscle tissue and an eventual state of complete debilitation. At this stage, disease is likely to set in, particularly kwashiorkor, which results from protein deficiency; and this will very soon lead to death. The process could take months, but often only weeks depending on the original state of the person in question. Life expectancy in such areas is predictably low by Western standards. In Sudan it is perhaps as high as 50 years, but in Ethiopia, similarly prone to famine, as low as 41 years. Very many die in infancy – in Mozambique, for instance, about 375 per thousand before the age of five; this is hardly surprising when one considers that worldwide about one in three children are undernourished, owing to a pernicious combination of extreme poverty and ignorance (about one billion adults cannot read or write, and some 100 million children of primary age are not at school). Health education is in short supply in so many of these areas. Compare these figures with Britain where only about 11 per thousand die in infancy.

Disease is the ever present danger. Every year nearly 3 million children die from diseases that could be averted by immunisation. So much disease in the Third World is preventable; measles, for example, for which there is a vaccine, kills 10 million people a year, mainly children. We know how to treat tuberculosis, yet it still kills 1-3 million people a year. This high incidence of 'traditional' diseases is exacerbated in some areas by the prevalence of HIV infection which in attacking the immune system makes the contraction of other diseases – particularly TB – more likely. The only snag is that AIDS – terrible as it is – tends to distract the world's attention away from many other infections that have a higher incidence and, in absolute terms, i.e. in number of deaths, are equally lethal.

With some diseases there have been notable successes: smallpox is a case in point; more recently, leprosy of which there were perhaps 20 million cases in the 1970s has now had its numbers halved, and it is hoped that it will be eradicated early in the next century. On the other hand, there are many diseases which are not responding to preventative measures as well as we would like. In fact some, such as malaria and cholera, are reaching epidemic proportions in areas where living conditions help them to spread. Cholera claimed 16,000 people in 1991 out of some half a million who had contracted the disease. In one epidemic in Peru that year, 250 people were dying every day. The government there has set aside a contingency fund in case it returns; at present it is ravaging other parts of South America and Africa. Cholera is caused by a bacterium which latches onto the wall of the gut and shrivels victims by dehydration. It came to Britain in 1831 and killed 60,000 people, but by strenuous and concerted efforts by the health authorities, it was eradicated by 1893. Such schemes are barely, if at all, possible in many parts of the Third World where access to clean water is severely limited, though a great deal more could be done even with limited facilities. Poverty obviously governs what can and cannot be done. So much works against the people; In 1990-91, because of the cholera epidemic, Peru lost about 400 million dollars from a slump in exports and tourism – some of which might have been used to promote better living conditions and greater health awareness.

Treatment and control of malaria have become more difficult since the development of insecticide-resistant strains of mosquitos and drug-resistant strains of the illness itself. It is estimated that over 260 million people are infected, with clinical cases reaching 107 million annually, of whom 1-2 million die. New drugs are being developed, but there are certainly not enough resources to treat all those at present infected, and WHO experts think that in future the incidence of malaria may increase by 5% a year. The other main debilitating diseases which are also often fatal are likewise spread by enemies in the natural world: bilharzia from infected larvae of water-snails (perhaps 200,000 deaths a year); filariasis, another parasitic disease this time caused by worms and their larvae which is spread by a variety of blood-sucking insects including mosquitos; try-panosomiasis (sleeping sickness) spread by tsetse flies in Africa and blood-sucking bugs in South America that feed on infected animals, which is difficult to cure because its symptoms are not always easily discernible. The list doesn't end here, but enough has been said to indicate the scale of the problem, and to demonstrate that nature is not always a friendly ally.

If further exemplification were needed, one could point to those insidious diseases which affect humans indirectly by attacking the vegetation which they need to survive. Cassava, for instance, is a staple food of Africa that is particularly susceptible to pests and diseases, especially the devastating mosaic virus which scientists are doing their best to contain. Work at the University of Zimbabwe is already producing impressive results, but even so it is impossible to combat all the problems of the cassava. Drought, as such, cannot be prevented, only some of its effects. Attempts can be made to try to improve its storage properties, for it deteriorates in 1-3 days if not quickly processed into flour; and to increase its food value, for its protein content is very low; and to reduce its cyanide content, which can become dangerous if the plant is not properly processed (Walgate, 1990).

Another of the major dangers in the Third World is pregnancy. This is meant in two senses: first, in terms of the reproductive rate, and secondly, because of the complications that can arise in childbirth and unsafe abortion. As we have seen, the world's population is growing faster than earlier predictions indicated. The critical factor here is obviously that of family planning. The dissemination of knowledge of contraceptive techniques and availability of contraceptive aids is now one of the most urgent tasks facing family planning agencies who are still battling against prejudice and superstition in many areas. The figure for current contraceptive use worldwide is about 470 million couples or around 46% of couples in the reproductive age range. Figures have to be approximate, but it is estimated that regional figures are 15% in Africa, 50% in Asia and 56% in Latin America (Population Concern). The overall figure is influenced by the success of China's rigorous family planning programme. If this is excluded, contraceptive use in the remainder of the developing world is only about 30%. According to the United Nations projections, the worldwide figure needs to be somewhere in the region of 70% by the year 2000 before we can say that population is anything like under control. Needless to say, this is a seemingly impossible task.

In some regions, childbearing begins as early as 12-13 years, and 15-16 years is common. In some cultures too polygyny is well established, and families are often large despite the fact that 20-45% of deaths among women between 15-49 years arise from pregnancy-related causes. This may be compared with less than 1% in the UK, USA and much of Europe. There is, in fact, no bigger difference in terms of health between the rich and poor countries than maternal death and illness. The ratio of infant mortality is about 1:13, while maternal death can range from 1:21 in Africa and 1:73 in parts of South America. According to WHO, of the half a million women who die annually from pregnancy-related causes, about 99% are in the Third World. This is often the result of repeated childbearing, and the real figures may be considerably higher than reported. And the problem does not stop there; for every maternal death there are several pregnancy-related illnesses which may contribute to various kinds of permanent disability.

With so many natural hazards, one would think it the sheerest lunacy to add to them. It may be irrational and is often unnecessary, but, as we all know, this is just what humans do. There is little that influences the mortality and morbidity rates more than war. Urban areas are often badly affected – even devastated – but usually it is the rural populations that are harmed most of all. Rural economies decline from the effects of conflict and neglect. Cultivated areas are drastically reduced through loss of tools, seeds, and wholesale depopulation. Grain reserves are used up or are confiscated by warring factions, the people go hungry, and then disease takes its toll. All these things combine in a self-reinforcing syndrome. The UN classifies about 40 million people in Africa as 'food-insecure', and about half of these have been affected by war, many of them as refugees and displaced persons. Mozambique, for instance, has about 4 million internally displaced persons, and possibly another million in neighbouring states. Angola is in a similar plight, although the numbers are not so large. Many of those who have become homeless because of wars long past, in Nigeria and Uganda, for instance, are still not settled, and continue to lead an uncertain and impoverished existence.

War plays havoc with commercial enterprise; traders are often unwilling to travel in such treacherous conditions. More importantly, it also has a very serious effect on health services; veterinary, vaccination and pest control services are often curtailed, and the work of charitable agencies in trying to bring help to the people is frequently hampered by the warring armies. In addition, there are the positive measures taken by the factions in laying mines in some areas, in discouraging cultivation that might help their enemies, and attacking those villagers that they feel are unsympathetic to their cause. Not least of all, there is the sheer expense of the wars. Spending scarce resources on military hardware has run up huge debts in countries which can least afford them. The drain on foreign currency is enormous, especially as a proportion of GNP, and extra foreign currency is often not forthcoming, as outsiders are loath to risk high investments in war-torn states.

Few observers deny the need for family limitation of some kind. What is clear is that we cannot possibly go on as we are. The plight of the hungry and diseased makes it imperative that some urgent measures are taken to control the world's burgeoning population. Nature and human need are patently at variance here. Nature flourishes on numbers, but then it has to in order to make up for its 'deficiencies'; nature may be prolific, but it also has its casualties. If, then, we are going to restrict our numbers, how is this to be done? It is surely not enough to give Third World villages a few condoms and tell them to go away and use them. They need to know *why*. And if they cannot be convinced of the global implications, then appeals must be made to their self-interest. But suppose none of this works either quickly enough or extensively enough – should more radical measures be taken with abortion and sterilisation on demand? Should other states take their cue from China and enforce family limitation? And if so, on what bases should restrictions be made? Should the same criteria apply to all; if reproduction is to be rationed, is it to be done on an egalitarian basis, or should there be some form of eugenics programme based on selective breeding? If so, who is going to make the choices? And can this ever mean the elimination of the 'unworthy', the mentally retarded, the hopelessly deformed and disabled, the racially undesirable, or simply those with low IQs who fail to meet certain pre-determined standards?

The problems are endless, and perhaps intractable. Democratic society has always shunned compulsion in these matters. Many pre-industrial societies – even the sophisticated Greeks and Romans – were prepared to practice infanticide and, much less commonly, geronticide to solve their population problems. But in modern societies there has usually been an implicit assumption that individual decisions about family size would normally be compatible with social requirements. Maybe this is no longer the case. Perhaps, in view of the urgency of the situation, more extreme policies will eventually have to be adopted with appropriate sanctions for non-compliance. The possibilities are open – *and* ominous. It savours of an unwelcome 'Brave New World'. But what else can we do? We must face the realistic scenario of what is likely if we do nothing. According to just about all informed opinion, the countdown to demographic disaster has already begun.

The economics of health

In 1991, the UK government published its long-awaited report entitled 'The Health of the Nation'. This is basically a consultative document that outlines objectives and strategies for the coming decade. It is concerned to identify and address the main health issues, and stresses its commitment to:

(1) Health promotion, treatment and rehabilitation. It reiterates that good health is determined by a range of influences, genetic inheritance *and* physical and social factors.

(2) The prevention of avoidable disease and premature death, which it relates largely to life-style. There is a strong emphasis on re-education, especially concerning smoking, alcohol consumption and diet, all of which involve the wide dissemination of information. And while recognising that health does not necessarily equal fitness (note, for example, the premature deaths of certain fitness enthusiasts such as Jim Fix, the doyen of the jogging cult), it lays considerable emphasis on regular exercise.

(3) Ensuring that health services are available to all without prejudice or discrimination.

(4) Making certain that the system is correctly administered and monitored.

(5) The formulation of policies that will convert the rhetoric into reality.

(6) Ensuring that the system makes the best use of available (by implication, *limited*) resources.

It is clearly pointed out that there are competing demands for expenditure by Government, and that it is therefore necessary to assess the effectiveness – in terms of health 'gains' – of particular services and practices.

It all sounds fine, but because we are really talking here about inexhaustible need, the conclusion is inescapable that if we continue to run the system on less than adequate resources, hard decisions will have to be made, and someone is going to suffer. What kind of a price, then, can we put on human life? With the stupendous costs involved in running the NHS, and with more expensive technology, how can we meet the bill? With medical and surgical 'breakthroughs' being announced almost by the week (though often not to bear fruit for several years) there are rising expectations of health care that are not easy to satisfy. At what point do we have to admit that modern health care programmes – good as they are – are either insufficient or otherwise too ambitious? How much can the nation afford? And on what bases are these necessary – but difficult – decisions about economies to be made?

First of all, there is the fairly straightforward problem of measuring costs. For example, a baby born with spina bifida 30 years ago would most probably have died. Now it might be saved after several operations, but this will entail the use of scarce resources that might have been employed elsewhere. Would – or could – they have been used to better effect? Or take the case of patients who need kidney dialysis. The machines at the district hospitals may well have been donated by a local charity – so many are – but what of the technicians and trained nurses to operate them? It is possible for some patients to have treatment at home if the right training and facilities can be made available. But as far as the hospitals are concerned, whole wards have to be closed down for want of suitable staff. Is this the best use of scarce resources? A bone marrow transplant costs about £12,000. Is it therefore worth undertaking, given the economics of the situation? All other things being equal, it almost certainly should because, in economic terms only, it could cost up to £125,000 to nurse a dying untreated patient.

Before we complain too loudly about how difficult things are in the UK, it is worth reminding ourselves that in developing countries the situation is unimaginably worse. In parts of Africa, for instance, it can cost as much as 40% of the total health budget just to equip *one* hospital to something like Western standards. Meanwhile 85% of the population get virtually nothing – a factor that is greatly exacerbating the AIDS problem. This imbalance can be seen even in South Africa, one of the most privileged states in terms of health provision. Here we have the anomaly of a medical service that was so advanced that it was able to carry out the first heart transplant operations, while in many parts of the country there was only one doctor per 50,000 of the native population.

Costs have soared, both for personnel and for the increasingly sophisticated technology such as scanners which currently cost about £1.25 million each (although orders will probably be accepted once half a million is available). A good example of the complex nature of the problem is the debate concerning cancer screening. The current National Breast Screening programme tested 100,000 women in its first year. In that period 733 cancers were found, that is 7.3 per thousand, which is only slightly above expectation (6.6 per thousand). Breast cancer affects about one woman in twelve (some authorities suggest as many as 1:10), and it was assumed that screening would probably save up to 30% of deaths, but it might actually save only 6-7%. One main problem with these tests is that they tend to concentrate on the most-at-risk categories, many of whom fail to respond to the call for screening anyway. They have restricted the tests mainly to middle age ranges, yet a disturbing number of cancers have shown up in younger and especially older women. But costs and practicality factors have precluded screening everyone.

Or again, take the question of cervical cancer screening, which is another highly problematical area. Screening is becoming more popular, but – in general – the results are so disappointing that questions are being asked about its cost effectiveness. Cervical smears taken at surgeries and hospitals are difficult to cost. Of every 1,000 women tested in the UK only about 7 are abnormal, and most of the 4,000 or so women each year whose abnormalities have developed to cervical cancer have never been tested. A breakdown of the economies of cancer prevention (1990) shows that it costs:

£100,000 to £200,000 for every life saved by a cervical smear.

£39,000 for every life saved by the National Breast Screening programme.

Only £534 for every curable malignant melanoma detected at skin cancer clinics.

These figures give more than just a pause for thought; among other things, they raise questions about what we mean by a 'life saved': at what point can we be confident of such a statement? And it is also worth asking about those other cancers which can often only be tested for at a prohibitive cost.

These economic issues are difficult to disentangle from the moral questions involved. How are the critical decisions to be made? One school of thought argues for the adoption of a QALY (Quality Adjusted Life Years) system in which decisions are taken on the basis of life expectancy. At least 10 further years of life at 'maximum quality' = 1 QALY, so if, for example, we compare heart transplant patients (each transplant costing perhaps £100,000) with leukaemia patients, we arrive at the equation: One (uncertain?) transplant patient = 10 leukaemia patients with an anticipated 10 years of poor quality life. How should we then choose to spend the money? The idea of stressing *quality* as well as quantity of life has to be worth consideration, but how do we assess quality, what exactly are the criteria? How, in certain cases, can we balance physical mobility against mental agility? The measures are so arbitrary that it begins to sound like a quasi-scientific guessing game.

To elaborate on this theme a little more. Let us look at the matter of coronary heart disease, which is the biggest killer of men (1:3) in the Western world (women are catching up, but we are not quite sure why). In fact, coronary and other forms of arterial disease probably now account for about half of all known deaths.

(1) It takes many forms, valve problems, arrhythmia, but mainly arteriosclerosis.

(2) It is not confined to the old: tests on the bodies of American servicemen who had died in the Korean war showed that many already had the beginnings of coronary disease, although similar signs were notably absent in the Koreans. The 1988-89 Regional Heart Study in the UK even showed early symptoms of hypertension in a number of young children. Both *appear* to point to the possibility of diet as a critical factor.

(3) It undoubtedly has an hereditary dimension; the best way not to get it is to have healthy parents.

(4) There may be an environmental dimension, i.e. a socio-economic

factor; there is certainly some disparity between the North and the healthier South.

(5) Some evidence – disputed by a recent Finnish study (*Sunday Times*, 22 December 1991) – indicates life-style as a factor: smoking, drinking (?), diet (saturated fats, cholesterol) and especially lack of regular exercise.

(6) Some heart disease may not present as pain (angina) but only as breathlessness which many mistakenly interpret as just being 'out of condition'. (It is worth noting that, strictly speaking, angina does not exist – the word simply means the pain that comes from the restriction of the arteries. Some people erroneously think of it as 'the disease' when actually the disease is arteriosclerosis which is potentially fatal.)

On what basis, then, is it decided who will live and who will die, given that a by-pass with hospitalisation might cost as much as £10,000? Various criteria are used. Potential usefulness to the community is certainly one important factor, as also is age – in certain areas, coronary by-pass operations are not likely to be given to those over 65. And where this does not obtain, it is not that unusual to wait up to two years for a by-pass – such is the pressure on staff and beds. It is estimated that if all adults of 24-69 years were screened for heart disease, the current cost would be about £44 million and would save an estimated 8,216 lives. If, on the other hand, only *men* with a history of heart problems were thoroughly screened (exercise tests etc.), less money would go further; for only £7 million or so an estimated 1,419 lives would be saved.

The question of *who* makes the critical decisions will become more acute if the voluntary euthanasia advocates have their way. This seems unlikely in the present climate of opinion in the UK, but it could come via the European Community if enough people are found to follow Holland's example. The spectre of the Nazi euthanasia programme for those designated 'unfit' is still with us, and many are convinced that even voluntary schemes are open to all kinds of manipulation and abuse. Should life be terminated even if it is done with the acquiescence of the patient? Under what circumstances? And who makes the final decisions – the professionals, the family, or both? And who actually administers the fatal injection? It is well known that non-institutionalised euthanasia already takes place especially in hospitals in cases of terminal illness. If the disease doesn't kill fairly swiftly, the pain-relieving drugs will. The practice is rarely admitted openly, but it is known to occur, often with the unquestioning connivance of the patient's close relatives. Perhaps this is how it should be. The system seems to work quite well this way with matters unspoken and understood. If euthanasia were to be institutionalised and therefore ritualised, all those awkward questions we have posed would have to be answered. Many therefore think that, on balance, things should probably stay as they are.

A further question that must be asked is what *kinds* of treatment are to be regarded as 'legitimate' for a National Health Service for which we are all paying? Should any kind of alternative medicine be included? This can range from the highly suspect black box diagnosis, homeopathy, etc., for which there seem to be no rational scientific bases, to fringe techniques such as acupuncture which is accorded some credence by some orthodox practitioners. Can the NHS afford to be experimental in this way? And what about cosmetic surgery? The removal of unsightly scars and disfiguring birth-marks would probably be seen as both physically necessary and psychologically therapeutic, but can we say the same about age-defying face-lifts and breast-enhancing silicone implants which are suspect anyway?

There is too the controversial public-versus-private medicine issue. Private medicine is becoming increasingly expensive, and health insurance is becoming something of a cut-throat industry among the companies concerned. Costs have rocketed, and companies are beginning to quibble about the kinds of claims they will accept. They are also fussy about applicants, and they will not pay out on any complications that may arise from a previous condition, say on persons who have declared operations for cancer or heart disease. And given that serious illness occurs with advancing years, the companies want more and more money from those who are least able to pay. Little wonder that one of the largest health insurance companies lost 100,000 customers in 1990-91 (admittedly, largely through withdrawal of firms hit by recession) and was short to the tune of some £63 million.

We must ask if private medicine is a form of queue-jumping. And can this be justified in moral terms? Is the 'compromise' strategy of private consultations followed by public treatment, possibly in hospital, a legitimate ploy? Intending patients may rationalise their actions in terms of 'freedom', and argue that if they want to forego, say, a new car, or an expensive holiday, and use the money for an operation, it is their choice. Advocates of private medicine also maintain that it takes some pressure off an already overtaxed NHS. But surely this only works if private medicine is carried on exclusively in private hospitals, and if it is also assumed that there is a surplus of medical staff for *both* types of institution. And this must beg the question of what is meant by a surplus. There is some evidence that too many professionals are being trained who are still without work. Should we encourage professional migration – train people to work abroad? Should, say, overseas students (e.g. Asian doctors) return home where presumably their qualifications and skills are most sorely needed?

How do consultants and doctors explain *their* divided loyalties? Some declare that their first allegiance is to the NHS but then adjust their schedules to fit in private work. Recently it was reported than an eminent consultant at a London teaching hospital on a salary of £30,000 a year was actually earning £250,000 a year. There were few official checks on his time, and his outpatients nearly always saw his registrars. Others – certainly in relation to urgent operations – openly admit that they 'can't do it any quicker if you pay' and seem to have little truck with the private sector. The NHS hospital administrators, on the other hand, are not that averse to private patients, and sometimes positively welcome them. At £200 a night and on cripplingly tight budgets, can we blame them?

Prevention, treatment and rehabilitation are all making demands upon the Exchequer. The average cost of the NHS in 1990 was about £350 per person. Much depends on the age-category of the patient, since the cost increases tremendously with advancing years:

16-64 years:	£ 190
65-75 years:	£ 570
over 75 years:	£1,470

We can see that there are all sorts of unanswered – perhaps unanswerable – questions about health policy. How are decisions arrived at, given that every decision, even if ostensibly economic, involves value considerations? Can we make reasonable predictions about life expectancy – a critical question in relation to health insurance? How can we assess 'quality of life' – the QALY issue? This utilitarian approach has to be flawed in that quality means different things to different people. It is reasonable to anticipate new and revolutionary medical breakthroughs in the not too distant future, but until that time, the basic question is *how much* is the nation really prepared to pay for?

Sex as liberation

There is a common supposition that Western society is currently undergoing a 'sexual revolution'. This is said to be evidenced by a liberalisation of attitudes and practices in sexual behaviour, and is underpinned by an increasing mastery of medical technology especially in relation to contraception and sterilisation.

This discussion questions the validity of this thesis at four different levels:

(1) It points to the lack of clarity of much of the evidence which both indicates tendencies towards more responsible sex as well as more casual sex. Some studies, e.g. campus-based studies, are seen as atypical, and the proliferation of romantic fiction appears to support an 'ideological' return to traditional mores.

(2) It indicates the ambiguity of the trends: are we experiencing sexual revolution or merely sexual evolution?

(3) It takes issue with some of the *values* implicit in the thesis, and asks

whether medical statistics indicate the desirability of radical change, especially with the increasing incidence of sexually transmitted diseases.

(4) It shows that when current trends are set against a broad historical backcloth, there is little that is really new in actual sexual *behaviour* in modern society.

The question of values – sexual or otherwise – presents perennial problems. The age-old argument as to whether values are universal or relative to specific societies is largely resolved if we adopt a means-ends explanation. The means or *expression* of the value may well be relative, although the value itself – the end or goal – is universal. It therefore comes as no surprise to find that cross-cultural studies of moral values in the UK, Taiwan, Israel, Turkey, Mexico, Jamaica and the USA indicate a basic commonality of orientation. In fact, it is argued that children in these societies pass through very similar stages of value development, and that these sequences reflect the value development patterns in societies themselves (see Calderone in Gordon & Libby, 1976).

This analysis of development suggests that the first, or *pre-conventional* stage, is that in which people are responsive to cultural rules and norms, but these are interpreted hedonistically and instrumentally in terms of rewards and punishments and the exchange of favours. An important feature of this stage is the identification of those who enunciate the rules and those who are required to implement them. The second, *conventional* stage, is characterised by interpersonal concordance. The maintenance of group values is seen as important and there is clear recognition of authority and social order, but the primary sanction is that of public approbation – a conformity to stereotypes of what the 'majority want' or what is 'natural'. In the third, or *post-conventional*, stage which follows (corresponding to adolescence in the child), there is a more marked utilitarian emphasis. But although consensus is important, there is a search for meanings outside traditional authority. The movement is towards logicality and consistency, looking for the reconciliation of moral needs according to self-chosen principles.

Laudable as it sounds, this kind of scheme begs two particular questions. The first concerns the matter of *imposition*. Does this analysis really derive from the contemporary studies of the societies cited, or is it simply a neat model into which moral development can be conveniently slotted? The last stage, in particular, has such utopian overtones that one wonders if it arises *from* experience or whether it is an aspiration *about* experience. In short, are we here dealing with substantive matters, or are we still in the realm of normative constructs which are only oblique representations of reality? Do we simply see here the kind of humanistic development one might wish to see? The second question concerns the matter of *extrapolation*. It is arguable whether this scheme really represents the developmental sequence of moral maturation in individual human beings, and it is positively contentious if we are to suppose that it can then be extended to society itself. If we try to do this, we are faced with the age-old dilemma of moral progress and how – if it exists – it can be satisfactorily related to social structure. This is a formidable task. Only with considerable caution can it be said that any patterns have ever been discerned or connections between the variables established.

To those whose concern centres on sexual behaviour, the question of values is particularly relevant. It is generally accepted that Western society has been going through a period of unprecedented change in the last century, notably since the 1870s with the introduction of more sophisticated contraceptive techniques. Impressionistically, this has had a liberalising impact on sexual attitudes and practices. It is contended that something approaching a secularisation of sexual values has taken place. Sex has not only become demystified, it has also become de-ethicised – divested of its moral trappings and subjected to humanistic critical scrutiny. It is said that we are moving from a moralistic approach to sexual values to a more causalistic appreciation of what sex means in the modern world (Davies, 1975). Moralism tends to be preoccupied with morality, per se. It stresses moral laws and moral authority, and is primarily concerned with the personal *intention* of the actor, and may also seek religious validations for what are regarded as traditional verities. Causalism, on the other hand, is more relativistic, more 'factual' in its approach to sexual matters. It takes the view that particular problems merit particular solutions, and is therefore naturalistic and pragmatic about sex. In effect, it is a kind of modified utilitarianism, laudably concerned with the reduction of short-term pain in order to promote, in this case, short-term happiness. And, paradoxically, equally concerned with both the consequences of action *and* the actor's personal *motivations* – always a problem for classical utilitarianism. This distinction between moralism and causalism is similar to that made between moralism and factualism (Wilson, 1961). Each school defends its beliefs in different ways. The moralist resorts to religion or codes or conscience, the factualist to social expediency and what is held to work in actual situations.

Evidence of a shift not only of attitudes but also of behaviour is not simply impressionistic. It is there for all to see, especially in the media where reiterated themes become self-fulfilling prophecies. But the manifestations of change are not confined to popular presentation. Even the clamorous demands of magazines such as *Cosmopolitan* ('If you want sex, *say* so, it's time to take the sexual initiative', January 1980) do not exhaust its concerns. The change in moral attitudes and sexual behaviour has been the subject of numerous studies, and is now well-documented in the relevant journals. By the early 1980s, at the more trivial Opinion Poll level, similar trends appeared. One survey (*Sunday Times*, 2 March 1980) indicated that the public thought that British society, although more knowledgeable, had become less moral and less tolerant. It suggested a decline in both ethics and etiquette. People were said to be less kind and polite as well as less honest; with more open-mindedness, people were regarded as more selfish and aggressive. There are often considerable divergencies between the received moral wisdom and survey findings on the issue of sexual morality and certainly these have become more marked in the last decade. There appears now to be no dramatic difference between the mores of sexual practice and those concerned with the representation of sex in the media. Women were once far more opposed than men to pornography and open display, and nudity was found to be offensive as was also the use of obscene language. But although there is some reactionary feeling, the evidence suggests that these trends are changing.

Polls are often somewhat suspect, but they do try to provide an ordered numerical picture of public opinion. A well-conducted poll samples a carefully selected cross-section of the population to reach a mixture of ages, sexes and classes. It can therefore indicate a range of different emotions and beliefs and reduce these to something which is reasonably coherent, and much more reliable than personal anecdote. What it cannot do is to tell us the sort of people we really are; it can only indicate the sort of people we *think* we have become. Indeed, what we are given in so many surveys and studies of a more serious nature is largely description rather than explanation. Few would dispute that changes, which may be genuinely important, are taking place, but this still leaves us with the problem of how to account for them. As so often happens in social research, the intentions are frequently more impressive than the conclusions.

It is necessary, therefore, to take a look at *what* is happening even if we cannot always say why, and try to assess its significance. Are we experiencing a period of mere sexual relaxation, or are we undergoing a fundamental sexual revolution? Some modern commentators write as though we are on the threshold of a unique era of sexual enlightenment and practice. Sex is seen as a virtual panacea for the world's ills, and the source of final liberation. Just how persuasive are these assumptions, and how sound is the evidence? It is here that certain separate but related issues must be borne in mind:

(1) The nature of the evidence – how reliable is it, and is there adequate and persuasive contra-evidence?

(2) The theories to account for the evidence – and are there equally convincing alternative theories?

(3) The conclusions which are held to derive from the evidence – and the question of whether quite different conclusions could be drawn from the same data.

(4) And lastly, can we construe that these have any moral dimensions?

It seems to be beyond contention that in certain areas of attitude and practice there have been quite notable changes. For instance, it now seems hard to believe that advocates of contraception were liable to prosecution in the last century. The widespread use of contraceptive devices and techniques, the general availability of sterilisation and the guarded approach to legalised abortion, all highlight the main trends. This increasing *practice* has, in turn, modified attitudes; a new ethos of acceptance and acceptability pervades modern society.

Similarly, attitudes towards more specifically sexual practices have undergone frank reappraisal. Homosexuality would be a case in point. It is not only among the sexual *avant-garde* that homosexuals no longer count as deviants. Gone are the days when after-shave lotions were only used in private by consenting adults. Even the *term* 'deviant' is no longer fashionable, it has now given way to 'variant', a form which has more neutral connotations. This euphemism can effectively cover a whole gamut of practices ranging from transvestism to paedophilia. The boundaries are becoming increasingly blurred, the old standards are going. For some it is apparently now but a short step to full sexual enlightenment, an age of tolerance which promises both sexual and social emancipation. The general public does not seem to be fully aware of this as yet, but we are assured that it is all just a matter of time. At the moment, we are simply witnessing the 'signs of the times'. The new values are implicit in the media; nudity, adultery, etc., no longer excite serious comment. Resentment has been neutralised by rehearsal, and sensitivities have been conditioned by experience. The sexual millennium is almost here. It is the task of believers to perceive the trends and hasten the day of liberation.

Evidence of change can be found in a host of studies of sexuality in a number of societies. These present us with the same main issues: what exactly is the nature of these changes and how are they caused? And, more importantly, are the underlying values changing, or simply their social expressions? One view is that it is not sexuality which is changing society – as the moralists maintain – but society which is changing sexuality. This argument insists that sexuality is a psychodynamic process which complements the biological programme, and that gender roles and gender identity may *not* be congruent with chromosomal and anatomical assignments. For sexual maturation all movement must be away from the Unthinkable towards the Desirable and Essential if real progress is to be made. 'Healthy sexuality' must be discriminating and 'non-pathological'; it must reject the Unthinkable-Permissible orientations of the pre-liberated ethic and be motivated by love – not guilt, anxiety and compulsion. Such ideas, anticipated by Freud and popularised by Wilhelm Reich and many psychotherapists, have come in for closer scrutiny (Szasz, 1981).

The emphasis here is unashamedly experiential and seems to be an attempt to throw off the shackles of biological determinism. It is worth noting how many of its conclusions are based on the premises of the erotic experience and not on the nature or source of the stimuli. In fact, sexual maturity tends to be equated with the capacity to savour and enjoy the erotic as though there were no other dimensions to sexuality. Even 'straight' intercourse need no longer be regarded as the seal of a relationship but simply a quick way of getting to know someone. There is at least the implication that within reason it is really a matter of 'whatever turns you on' providing it is not inordinately exploitative and is predictably free from guilt. This is a much reiterated theme in the current literature. Sex is something to be responsibly enjoyed; the *experience* is paramount – morality can be adjusted where necessary to accommodate its many and varied expressions.

There is a wealth of published material advocating the autonomy-of-sensuality thesis. For some time it has been argued that sexual behaviour has been freed from the 'tutelage of religion and society', and that this is the 'greatest revolution' of our time (R. & D. Roy, 1976). Proponents actively support the cause of liberation, and want to see sex released from the influence of value-creating and value-defining agencies so that there can be an 'expansion of the erotic community'. This movement towards 'meaningful' and 'relational' sex is seen in near Utopian terms, as the dawn of an era of universal sexual (sensual) affluence of the masses. A kind of closer proximity to the means of *re*-production – although the intentions are avowedly recreational rather than procreational.

Sensual sex is regarded as ethically neutral, like enjoying any other aesthetic pleasure such as music. Between significant others, it may have the same sensation but it has a different significance. Such acts cannot, it is argued, be right or wrong in themselves if there is no 'personality' contact. But exactly how this is applied in actual circumstances is not clear. Can sensual experiences remain completely without 'personality contact'? And what can this term possibly mean? Is it simply that any casual sexual encounter which does not have any 'felt' relational dimension is, *ipso facto*, free from 'personality contact' complications? If so, the general thesis is so fraught with contradictions that one is left wondering if there is any *one* thesis. Can sex be concerned with the mutual exploration of personalities, a kind of getting-to-know-you-better operation, which some advocates seem to suggest, and – at the same time – be the mere sensation-seeking enterprise which casual sex implies? Indeed, it could be argued that real personality exploration is only possible where sexual expression is contained. Furthermore, if the relationships which are established are necessarily 'open' to other extra-relational sexual encounters which – as we have seen – is also *de rigueur* for advanced practitioners, how can we be sure that the mutual possession implied by love is not seriously affected by these other-directed intimacies? Obviously there are no guarantees, but it is assumed that new dispositions will develop, and that tolerance and understanding will follow in the wake of the liberated mentality – a kind of realised eschatology.

Changes, then, are obviously taking place in our society. There does seem to be an increase in pre-marital and extra-marital intercourse, and there is certainly a great deal more *discussion* to this effect. But perhaps what we are witnessing is not a sexual revolution but sexual *evolution*. This is particularly marked in the attitudes of women. Much has changed since the days when Kinsey could report that by the age of 17, some 62% of males but only 20% of females had had sexual intercourse. This seems to suggest that a disproportionate number of women were having a rather good time. In fact, Kinsey found a high proportion of these were prostitutes (Kinsey, 1948), a conclusion much revised since by Simon and Gagnon whose research in the USA 25 years later indicated that male attention had been largely transferred to non-professionals. Apparently, only about 2%-5% of adolescent males now frequent prostitutes, a trend which has been especially noted among college males. This development has been – perhaps justly – attributed to the greater availability of college girls. Inadvertently, these girls bear a heavy responsibility. Because of this predilection of researchers for campus studies of sexual behaviour there now seems to be some distortion in the findings for the population as a whole. Of course, it is very understandable that investigators should fasten on to accessible female respondents who appear to cooperate with willing abandon, but this does tend to bias the general conclusions about adolescent sexuality. Campus life is usually free and untrammelled, and encourages certain kinds of community interaction; for these reasons, students must constitute an atypical population.

What precisely does all this tell us? There is no evidence, as yet, that teenage girls are now suffering the pangs of genital deprivation. Admittedly, there is an ethos of increased sexual expectation, fostered largely by the media, but we cannot assume that there is a huge reservoir of unsatisfied female demand. In fact, if magazine advice columns are anything to go by, the opposite is the case. A large proportion of the letters still suggest that girls want to be able to say 'no' without alienating their boyfriends. They want to be both desired and desirable but they are not screaming for coitus – a fact borne out impressionistically by the large amount of cheap romantic fiction which is still sold to teenage girls.

The recent nationwide survey of 'Sexual Attitudes and Lifestyles' in which something in the order of 19,000 people were questioned, actually seems to suggest that the sexual revolution is somewhat past its peak. Admittedly one has to be just a little reserved about surveys concerning sex. Not everyone welcomes a dispassionate probing of the pituitary by some earnest researcher, and not every researcher knows what to make of the responses, which can range from purported ignorance to impossible virility. But if we take this survey at something like its face value, its findings indicate that those over 45 who grew up in a less permissive age certainly have fewer partners than those between 25 and 44 or those for whom sexual activities began in the so-called 'swinging sixties'. Those in the post-AIDS generation appear to be more cautious than one would suppose; in fact, 1 in 5 between 16 and 24 claimed still to be virgins. Some

80% of the males and 75% of the females in this group had only one partner or none at all in the past year, and over 50% claimed to have had only one partner in the last five years. However, those in the middle age groups who were in the more professional classes seem to have had twice as many partners and to have married later than those in the 'lower orders', perhaps because of a happy combination of affluence and increased mobility. Dr Glenn Wilson, a London University psychologist, maintains that much of the new morality can be ascribed to the threat of AIDS: 'now women have a good rationale for avoiding casual sex which many of them never really wanted anyway, it wasn't something many women naturally desire although they have been under pressure to think in a feminist way, seize their new freedom and behave like men' (reported in *Daily Mail*, 4 December 1992).

So there is some doubt as to exactly how the evidence should be interpreted. As we have seen, there appears to be evidence of two quite different trends: on the one hand, there is the movement towards responsible sex, and on the other, to increasingly casual sex. The problem for the observer is to know whether these are, *in fact*, different trends, or whether they are different interpretations of the same trend, and this all becomes further confused by those who attempt a reconcilation in terms of sex as 'personal exploration'. In this there is an ostensible de-emphasis on coitus as the only goal of sexual activity, and the elevation of other forms of sexual play as a means of getting to know 'the whole person'. This, of course, opens the door for homosexuals and others who want to enjoy 'multi-sexual alternatives' and suggests that casual encounters are simply preparatory ways to responsible sex. By a process of experimentation and – presumably – selection, people are said to facilitate their own sexual maturation. And this despite the increase in certain sexually transmitted diseases, especially HIV infection which is widespread among intravenous drug-users and male homosexuals, but still relatively rare among heterosexuals except in parts of Africa – although there are still some uncertainties about the projections of HIV/AIDS (see 'Don't believe the Hype', *Sunday Times*, 1 March 1992).

All social practices are conditioned by their context, but this may be less true of sex than other social phenomena. Its bio-social nature renders it both less and more susceptible to extraneous influences. The appetitional factor, the biological necessity of reproduction, gives it a certain imperviousness even to political and economic restraints. People still mate and reproduce in the most unconducive circumstances. In a sense, the physical basis of love is also its weakness. In these days of genetic hormonal engineering and advanced surgical techniques, both the appetite and its expressions can be manipulated if not actually controlled. It is still a matter of conjecture whether science has had an irreversible effect on marital and family structures; and even on the sex roles themselves. Certainly procreation can now be separated from recreation. With decreasing anxieties, people can command their own fertility, and, with serious qualifications, even decide their own gender. Although feasibility need not imply desirability, modern technology has brought us to the point where not only population numbers but also population types can be theoretically determined.

Sexual practice has therefore been increasingly 'refined' in our more accepting society, but has it actually changed? Nothing we are witnessing today can, in any *essential* sense, be regarded as 'original'. To this extent, the sexual revolution thesis lacks conviction. After all, sexual behaviour is older than man, and the variety of its expressions is certainly not peculiar to man. It follows, therefore, that in human sexual behaviour, the permutations are necessarily limited. Whatever the sexual practice in question, we can be sure that it has been done before at some other time in some other place. Relaxed censorship, nudity, institutionalised sexual deviationism, even contraception and abortion, can all be found in other earlier societies. So what *is* new about the modern sexual scene? Is there anything really distinctive about sexual attitudes and practices today or are we simply in a passing phase? What has changed other than the technology? If we think of our situation against a broad historical background, the great debate is little more than a transient murmur in the long conversation of mankind.

Social work: a re-evaluation

In the recent past, an article appeared in the press which asked the question, why do some people choose to do social work? (*Observer*, 12 May 1991). It pointed to the impressionistic, but unsubstantiated 'fact' that social work – and especially social workers – enjoyed very little support from the general public. Yet courses are full and new ones – sometimes under faintly misleading titles such as 'Applied Social Studies' – are still being launched, mainly as practically-oriented appendages to courses in Sociology and/or Social Policy departments. As Tony Hall, director of the Central Council for Education and Training in Social Work, put it, 'for years social workers have been subject to vilification, yet applications for training have remained buoyant [though] in the last two years there have been some signs of a downturn' (*Observer*, ibid.). This is probably due, in part, to the adverse publicity occasioned by some of the more sensational cases of apparent social work failure. Each year a steady number leave the work; some to look after their own families (two-thirds of social workers are women), but some – almost certainly – from disillusionment and 'burn-out'. Each year, on the other hand, some 4,300 newly qualified social workers are produced by the universities, though this is thought to be 700 too few to meet the needs of the increasing number of clients. Most of the new applicants, graduates and non-graduates, will take the new diploma course which has replaced the old one-year certificate course that many regarded as too shallow in its treatment of the relevant themes. The new course will obviously allow more time for students to gain placement experience, and to appreciate the new challenges (and problems) initiated by the Children Act which came into force in 1991.

All disciplines and professions should be reflective about their own policies and practices, and be prepared to question the fundamentals of their own systems, perhaps to refine them or even to discard them if necessary. So the first question we must ask is *whether social work is worth doing*. Indeed, it could be reasonably hypothesised that social problems tend to increase in direct proportion to the number of social workers available to deal with them. In other words, would a reduction in the number of social workers lead to an ethos – and even the practice – of more self-reliance? (It's a little like the argument that all the time abortion is available, contraceptive techniques, i.e. preventative measures/self-help, may be ignored.) Is social work, after all, just a kind of first-aid expedient – a temporary palliative? Is the first priority some form of effective social (including health) and moral education beginning in the primary schools and reinforced at the secondary level where it is now often regarded as an undemanding makeweight in the school curriculum?

If we are going to get down to really basic issues, we might well question *whether social work is a profession* at all. Is social work really something that *anyone* can do? Can social workers by virtue of their 'training and expertise' be set alongside other acknowledged professionals such as doctors, lawyers, accountants etc.? This naturally calls for some analysis of what is meant by a professional, a term which – in the modern world – connotes someone engaged in certain accepted forms of highly skilled and esteemed work or study that entails some kind of financial remuneration.

What are the main criteria whereby we can assess what is and what is not a professional? With reasonable confidence we can say (1) that a professional is a qualified person by virtue of a specialised course of training. The social worker – certainly in the past – may be a graduate or a non-graduate in a relevant discipline; may have undergone a two-year course, a one-year course, or no particular course at all. Can this be fairly set alongside, say, the training of a doctor or a dentist? In future, if it becomes an all-graduate occupation, it may compare with that of a teacher, or, in some ways, that of a nurse, but are the skills involved really comparable? (I have taught as a guest on social work courses which were designated post-graduate, but the sociology and psychology required was really only sub-degree level.) Such considerations involve (2) the question of knowledge and authority which bring respect. It is a little invidious to speak of 'higher' and 'lower' professionals, but there is certainly a disparity in both the remuneration and esteem that are given to the professions. How much respect is accorded social workers? One suspects not very much, something which may be partly related to the interventionist nature of their work which often generates resentment. A rule-of-thumb measure might be obtained by applying the Reversal Test. How easy is it for a layman to pose as a professional? Could the untrained person satisfactorily 'imitate' a surgeon, architect or barrister? How long would it be before they were rumbled as bogus and incapable? And is this true of the social worker? Isn't social work regarded as a kind of non-task? And is the social worker really any more than a facilitator?

A professional is also usually thought of as someone who observes accepted standards and the requisite professional etiquette which, in turn, necessitates loyalty to peers and to the profession concerned. In some instances – perhaps too many instances in social work – this can mean the closing of ranks in order to thwart the allegations of the critics. Professions normally formulate codes of ethics which they expect their members to observe. The problem for social workers particularly is how to distinguish professional and personal codes of conduct. There are all sorts of circumstances in which the social worker's non-professional commitments can be endangered, such as the young woman who had just completed her training but felt that she was spending too little time at home, and just couldn't tell her husband that she had a case-load of 160. Or the similar case of the more seasoned social worker whose daughter on her 16th birthday left her a simple note saying 'Goodbye Mother'. Complementarily, there are conflicts between professional and personal obligations when the social worker is seen as an exemplar, a referent for other people's behaviour. Can social workers afford to have 'flexible' marital arrangements, entertain promiscuity, divorce, paraphilia and the like, when they are trying to give relevant advice to others? Can they sneak into the corridor for a hasty 'drag' or afford to smell of drink at afternoon sessions when they are trying to counsel youngsters about glue-sniffing or alcohol abuse?

If social work is in doubt as a profession, can we go further and *ask if it is even a skill?* There's no doubt that the term 'skill' has become rather debased in modern society. There is a world of difference between the skill of, say, a craftsman or an artisan, and the cultivation of so-called 'life-skills' – writing letters and answering the telephone. Similarly, it is impossible to class the skill of, say, a good tennis player in the same category as the prized 'listening skills' of the social worker. To speak of skill in this latter way is surely to trivialise – even demean – the true meaning of the word.

Such considerations raise the kindred question of what can and cannot be taught. The political philosopher Michael Oakeshott was keen to point to the difference in what he called *technical* (theoretical) knowledge and *traditional* or practical knowledge (Oakeshott, 1962). He argued that technical knowledge is book knowledge. It can be precisely formulated as rules and instructions; it can thus be learned by rote. It can expound method and elaborate standards. It appears to be complete, yet, in some ways, is obviously lacking. Traditional knowledge seems unimpressive by comparison. It derives from experience, though it may be acquired from someone who is already versed in the skill. *But it cannot be taught.* It is like learning to drive a car – something which probably most of us have already done. We can read any number of manuals, listen to any amount of instruction, but we will never drive a car until we drive a car. No amount of teaching is going to give us the necessary ease with the controls, the capacity to read the road, or to develop that acute sense of distance and anticipation. We only get this through practice, by experience. This also applies to many other areas of life. Can people be taught to teach? Arguably the most important feature of any training course is the placement experience. The theoretical instruction on what to do and what *not* to do in the classroom can really be given in no time at all. What matters is actually doing the work. You can only do it when you do it. The same lesson is relevant to so many things, from sex to sport, and possibly also to casework. There are serious limits to how much we can learn about dealing with people. It is only practice that makes perfect.

Despite its flaws and inadequacies, some will argue that social work still ought to be done. But are social workers the best people to do it? Traditionally, there have been other groups in society, trained professionals, who have acted as reservoirs of expertise in care and counselling. The clergy are a good example of this – true, they too have their faults as individuals and as a profession or vocation. But when all this is taken into consideration, the clergy have an enormous amount of experience in dealing with people's problems and have considerable confidence in helping individuals to cope with life's crises, especially illness, death and bereavement. Did social work develop partly as the result of ministerial failure, or are the perceived insular attitudes of some ministers at all attributable to the near usurpation of many of their tasks by the growing army of social workers? Some clergy have substituted a pre-occupation with ritualistic activities for effective social concern. A new balance of duties might afford them time for both. They certainly have the premises where clients could be seen in confidence and comfort, but, at present, their reputation is such that their members and their status are decreasing in the modern world. Their experience is now not *that* different from that of many social workers whose role is similarly ill-defined. People know what doctors do, what nurses do, but exactly what do ministers and social workers do? Neither inspire much confidence at the ameliorative level.

The teaching profession too might help, although its role is almost too well defined, and most teachers are now overburdened with administrative work in addition to their teaching. There are staff in many schools who are deputised to look after pastoral matters, though it might be better for children to approach respected teachers instead of full-time specialist counsellors. Perhaps a better resource would be the profession of Health Visitors. As trained nurses they would probably be more welcome in the homes of clients, and if they had a somewhat longer, 'broader' training covering certain legal aspects of the work they would seem to be ideal for the task. Their numbers would have to be increased, but then there are many qualified nurses out of work who, in theory at least, could be available for extra training.

If, however, social work is to continue in much the same way, are there some basic changes that should be made to the system? Take the matter of recruitment. Do young social workers lack credibility among older clients? In the words of one teacher, who had been having particular problems with young social workers who presumed to know more about the children than she did, 'All social workers ought to be over forty.' We might think of the not untypical case of the Forces family with a brutal father, an intimidated mother and problem children of low ability where it was all too late to do very much. They were sent a young man on his *first* case. The training, *per se*, does not always enable young aspirants to *recognise* the signs. It might help them to know when, say, a psychiatrist is needed or when the police should be involved. But can they tell when children are manipulating their parents, or both are manipulating the social worker? The tricks of the trade have got to be learned somehow, but there is little doubt that inexperience can be genuinely dangerous in certain cases.

Are the powers that social workers have too great or too small? One suspects they are both, depending on the situation. Perhaps they ought to have more legal sanctions in certain circumstances, for example, the ability to insist on entry without a Court Order in cases of suspected child abuse. Lives might have been saved this way. And what about their specialist functions? Should the generic approach be abandoned? Should social workers return to a concentration on quite specific tasks such as the care of children *or* the aged *or* the handicapped, and 'outlaw' many of their current preoccupations with the feckless, the incorrigible, etc.? Poverty in the West is always a problem, but it is rarely tragic. There is no comparison with Third World standards. Most people have the desired amenities, TV, fridges, etc., and we mustn't close our eyes to the fact that there are such things as incompetent budgeting and ill-considered loans – in short, ignorance and inefficiency. Perhaps all except the aged and incapable should *have* to work for their state benefits, except that the benefits would be enhanced in line with reasonable rates for part-time work. After all, there is much that needs to be done in society that some of those with difficulties arising from poverty could reasonably do.

We should question too the ideology of social work. Essentially, we need to think again about the client-centred emphasis, and the important dichotomy of orientation between the *permissive* and the *prescriptive* approach. Do clients really come just to talk and thereby work out their own problems? Surely there are times when the answers have to be *given* if it is felt to be right, whether the client likes it or not. Liberal policies and practices have often been taken to ridiculous lengths in some special schools and centres for the maladjusted which may be little more than institutional manifestations (errors?) of the 'sin-bin' strategy. Here the clients are sometimes treated as though they were deeply repressed and seriously misunderstood victims of society. Popularly used terms such as 'maladjusted', 'deprived', 'underprivileged', etc., all have exculpatory implications. They are determinist in that they suggest that people can do precious little to help themselves, which is obviously not always the case. Should people be allowed to enjoy their delinquency in a relatively relaxed environment as guests of the State?

A more prescriptive approach is not to everyone's liking, but some clients are not in a position intelligently to appraise their own situations. Prescription may appear to be an infringement of individual liberty, but this may be necessary to protect the liberty of others. Permissive attitudes have their dangers. Some Humanistic psychologists would have us believe that the acceptance of others is the key to understanding and happiness, although it could be argued that it is *non*-acceptance that can alone prove to be ultimately beneficial. Perhaps we should never accept either others or ourselves *as we are*, because it is only non-acceptance (i.e. *dis*satisfaction) that leads to scientific and behavioural progress.

Any consideration of the ideology of social work must include some reference to the encroachments of so-called 'political correctness' (PC). This has permeated the social services to such an extent that practitioners are having to be careful what they say and how they say it. For example, it is apparently no longer acceptable even to hint that love between the sexes is normal or natural behaviour. According to the National Association of Probation Officers, anyone who suggests that boy-meets-girl is in any way better than boy-meets-boy is guilty of 'hetero-sexism' and should be suitably reprimanded. At their 1991 conference they actually had anti-discrimination monitors on duty to try to ensure that no unwanted 'isms' of any kind crept into the debates – such is the zeal of the PC devotees (see *Sunday Express*, 20 October 1991).

Political correctness is really an attempt to eradicate all written or verbal references to those 'sensitive' areas of experience such as sex, race, low IQ, physical deformity, etc. Laudable as this may seem, it is now leading to semantic confusion and downright ridicule. The language we employ has been made to look foolish. Fat people are now 'gravitationally challenged', short people are 'vertically challenged'; presumably prostitutes will be euphemistically embraced with the alternative 'horizontally challenged'? The real 'ism' of which these people should be most aware is extremism. (I was recently told by a social work lecturer that I shouldn't use the term 'girl' about a young female as it 'infantalises' women, yet men are often goodnaturedly referred to as 'lads'. When I remonstrated that *female* and *women* were surely even more suspect terms from a PC point of view I was confidently informed that 'women' had now been changed to 'wimmin' for PC purposes – I wondered how the Examiners would mark that.)

In some institutions of Higher Education, picketing and demands for resignation are sometimes made where a tutor, perhaps in a vain attempt to be humorous, inadvertently or otherwise breaches the 'code'. All this wouldn't be so bad if it were not for the complicity of the faculties themselves (the University of Connecticut, for example, has outlawed 'inappropriately directed laughter'). Sixteen major American universities have replaced many traditional teaching courses with 'social justice' courses, and the University of Missouri has published a *Dictionary of Cautionary Words and Phrases* compiled by its Multicultural Management Programme fellows (Campus Newspeak, *Sunday Times*, 16 June 1991). Academics have been fined, forced to resign and actually dismissed for infringement of the PC code. In England, the same sort of thing is happening, though as yet on a smaller scale. John Casey, an Oxford English don, has been hounded for some unfortunate remarks he made several years ago and has since repudiated, but what can be done in a seat of learning where the Student Union has urged its members to boycott certain lectures and attend instead alternative programmes laid on by such austere bodies as the Radical Philosophy Collective? (*Sunday Times*, 1 December 1991).

Lastly, I think we should query some of the training methods used by social workers and their tutors. Some of the most serious doubts centre on role-playing and group therapy. The great fallacy of role-playing is that everyone knows that it is a purely simulated exercise and therefore cannot be taken completely seriously. This is well brought out by Pitirim Sorokin in his appraisal of OSS training exercises during World War II (Sorokin, 1954). He shows how many who were training as espionage agents and saboteurs often did well in the exercises but rather badly in the field. Why? What was wrong with the training methods? The answer should have surprised no one. It was simply that these exercises were not the real thing, and everyone was aware of this. A similar sort of problem is posed by the use of Interaction Laboratories where two-way mirrors are used to study students acting out their parts in another room. It doesn't take students long to realise what is going on. They are quick to learn the procedures and – consciously or unconsciously – they shape their conduct (performance?) accordingly, especially if they suspect that it is on videotape. So if they know, how valid is the exercise? And as for social workers crawling on the floor among children as if *they too* were children, this fools no one – least of all the children.

Group therapy which is held to 'work' on a cathartic basis is not used by all social workers or social work lecturers, but it does have a strong appeal for a certain type of counsellor. It can include deliberately, often mutually, induced outbursts of temper, inner 'revelations' and, not uncommonly, verbal abuse. It can also involve mawkishness, maudlin confessions and downright exhibitionism. It frequently generates rather than dissipates anger and resentment. It sometimes increases inhibitions rather than banishing them, and evokes negative reactions instead of the positive responses that it is supposed to promote. As part of the vaunted Minnesota Method, it has had some success, but in the hands of some self-appointed experts its antics can sometimes be little short of ludicrous. It gives the impression that some aspects of casework are just a form of poor man's psychiatry. Someone has to care for the needy in our society, but whether it should be social workers must be open to question – certainly given the way social work is presently conceived. Social work, properly conducted, requires specialists of different kinds, and perhaps the work should be divided between different agencies that are there – dare one say it? – to improve, remedy and reform. It could possibly be left to more extensively trained health specialists or to the clergy; or perhaps certain aspects could become the special province of a suitably trained branch of the police. True, the police are not always seen in the best light, but they do, by their very nature, have an authority – one might almost say a presence – that social workers lack. It is often perception that matters most. When it comes to who will and who won't be admitted to a house where there are suspicions of child abuse, or who can 'command' some response to searching questions, the police certainly have the edge over most other agencies.

A key problem in our society is that we want to promote well-being more than anything else; in education, for example, it is often 'happiness' not excellence that is regarded as the end product. Of course, it is nice to be happy and to feel that all is well with the world, and to make others feel it too. But the truth is that life isn't like that, and is never likely to be, and that perhaps we have no right to complacency and self-satisfaction in such circumstances. Yet, having said that, we have to go on trying if we are going to produce – as moralists from Plato onwards have insisted we should – an increase in 'good' responsible behaviour. But this is not going to be done by a strident emphasis on oppression and empowerment – two favourite themes of social work practitioners. These imply that the 'service users' are invariably the victims of the system, society's unfortunates who find themselves in dire straits through no fault of their own. While there is some truth in this, it is by no means always the case. And it may be that if instead of regarding social problems as difficulties that arise from some dark, deep-seated conspiracy against the working-classes (to be defined), minorities, women, or whoever – as the term 'oppression' suggests – we conceded that exploitation was a human failing rather than a class vice, we might begin to move towards a healthier and more rational society.

Consumption and the consumer society

In their writings about capitalism, Marxists often refer to commodity-forms and commodity-fetishism although Marx himself – perhaps understandably – did not anticipate that consumption would one day become as important as production and that it would largely compensate the worker for alienated labour and exploitation. The concept of commodity-fetishism is open to certain objections, especially the assumption that the production and exchange of goods expresses a certain kind of relationship between producers (Abercrombie et al., 1980), but it highlights the fact that, in various ways, consumerism does tie the worker into the satisfaction of capitalist interests. Consumption, then, is about *needs*. It is something in which we are all necessarily engaged, whereas consumerism is said to be an attitude and/or behaviour which expresses a pre-occupation with *false needs*. Virtually anything can be commodified. In modern advertising there is probably no better example than sex, which is used to sell anything from chocolate to car hoods (heavily breasted girls asking if you are 'looking for soft tops?'). Sex can attract attention whether it's booze or bath gels ('things happen after a Badedas bath').

The critical theorist Herbert Marcuse (1987a) sees advanced capitalism as involving commodities and consumption in a process which has changed the connotations of needs and values. He argues that consumerism is a false ideology which promotes false needs. He points out, among other things, that in the USA one has the choice of 89 types of toothpaste, and asks if this is not a highly trivialised waste of resources. This false ideology is said to be fostered by advertising which is seen as an essentially parasitic industry. The problem, of course, is in deciding which are the needs and which are the false needs. What criteria do we use? Sometimes the line is rather hard to draw. If we take the example of diets and slimming, on which there is seemingly insatiable curiosity as well as an unfulfilled need, women particularly are avid for advice, and one suspects that the countless magazines and books which dispense this knowledge are trying to hit upon the least painless method of producing the 'correct' figure. (How many want to believe that what was once called fat is really 'cellulite', for which special, expensive clinical treatment is required?) How do we, then, distinguish between slimming for health, involving diets, doubtful drugs and exercise, and slimming for appearance? Is it really all about body-image, and is this pre-occupation just one step removed from face-lifts and breast implants? Is the craze to be slim 'natural' or is it manipulated? Is it something which for all sorts of reasons is legitimately desirable but which has now been exploited for commercial gain?

Critical theorists would also argue that product promotion gives rise to *false expectations*, and that these rising expectations – which cannot ultimately be met – consequently lead to discontent, and even social agitation. Such ideas are reminiscent of the old unobtainable carrot theory of delinquency which suggested that those who could not achieve suitable satisfactions legitimately sometimes resorted to petty crime as a short-cut to wealth. One feels instinctively that there is something in these ideas when every day in the media, we are bombarded with appeals to buy, own and possess things which many cannot afford. We live in an increasingly home-centred society which is fostered by widespread advertising for such luxuries as double-glazing, fitted kitchens and bedrooms etc., and assurances that it's time we changed our suites, our wallpaper, our carpeting, our 'home entertainment' systems, and took on a mass of other electrical gadgetry (note the rise and fall of the personal computer – once an indispensable adjunct to any self-respecting home). Where do we stop? Until now, civilisation has managed quite well without the electric toothbrush or the digital toaster, yet in the case of the larger household items, people are being asked to part with their savings or take out substantial loans to pay for them. Home improvement may be the thing, but it can cost many thousands of pounds to maintain this new and acceptable standard of living.

It is worth noting that consumer debt has now reached incredible proportions. The amount currently owed in the UK is over £300 billion, some 50 billion of which is accounted for by personal, i.e. non-mortgage, loans. This works out at about £6,000 for every man, woman and child in the country (*Guardian*, 3 December 1991). Credit is still readily available, and stores that are prepared to advance 'immediate credit of £1,000' and more in a feverish attempt to move their merchandise do nothing to ease the burden. What is not always clear to would-be customers – often, admittedly, because of their own ignorance – is the very high cost of borrowing. Access and Visa run at about 27%, and some store cards as high as 40% (1992), and private, unlicensed money-lenders deal in interest rates for short-term loans which go right off the charts.

People recognise themselves in their commodities. Indeed, as Marcuse and others have argued, social control is anchored in these new needs that have been generated and popularised. They are now so much part of our society that it is difficult for us to stand back and view society and its 'needs' dispassionately. Some time ago, I remember a garage proprietor saying, quite uncharacteristically, 'I sometimes wonder what the internal combustion engine has really done for the world.' Obviously it has brought enormous pleasure and benefits to people, especially enthusiastic car-owners like myself, but – in one way and another – it has also brought immeasurable harm. Can we assess in Utilitarian terms which outweighs which?

Consumerism in all its forms is aided and abetted by its indispensable ally, the advertising industry. The system could hardly begin to work without it. The particular issue of false expectations is well illustrated by the promotional activities of the multi-billion pound cosmetics industry which consistently makes spurious and unprovable claims about its products. Sex and status are used extensively as marketing ploys, as is also the very basic promise of youthfulness. Hormone creams, deep cleansers and soaps that can make purchasers 'look younger', deodorants that will disguise every offensive odour and – most notoriously of all – perfumes that hold out the prospect of exciting experiences to come: '*Eau d'Aviance* – the cool way to raise his temperature', and '*Amazone* – bold, fresh, French ...

assertive and asking for trouble' or, for a really sure thing, 'Men can't help acting on *Impulse*' (Coleman, 1981, p. 21).

Much of the time advertising deals in pecuniary pseudo-truths, false statements made to sound as if they were true, and perhaps not intended literally to be believed. No proof is usually offered for these statements, and perhaps none is expected. The 'proof' is simply that the product sells. The task of the marketing agencies is to keep the product name before the public. Advertising, particularly on television, often takes the form of direct, unabashed and unsubtle repetition, but, as we all know, it can also be insidiously indirect in its presentation. If we switch from product promotion to life-style promotion we can see this especially in the pages of the glossy monthlies and their down-market cousins, the cheaper weeklies. Studies of women's magazines show how this is done. Arguably the primary function of these publications is to entertain and only secondarily to inform. The orientation is largely towards escape and fantasy, and the attractive illustrations tend to obviate the need for any close scrutiny of the text. Some, e.g. *Cosmopolitan* and *Options*, are obviously aimed at the career-woman market with an emphasis on independent, 'liberated' decision-making. The dominant themes of leisure, home and so forth are enhanced by calculated representations of consumption that are designed to make the maximum visual and verbal impact. The ideology of consumption is reinforced by images of pleasure-giving commodities (food, clothes, etc.) with a stress on liberated choices and instant satisfactions. They usually exhibit a pervasive optimism about how women can achieve, succeed, and generally do better, whether in business or in bed. And this typically involves some fantasy of displacement and a trans-valuation of interests involving a realignment of focus to such things as more youthful body images, more conducive surroundings (new home, furnishings, etc.) and more congenial company through leisure and holidays. This transposition of values acts as compensation for the would-be aspirant to the more fulfilled life. As a kind of footnote, we must be a little wary of this 'other side' of the sex and repression critique especially as so many feminists have a left-wing orientation. The increased power of capitalist society has – for various reasons – been coincidental with greater sexual freedom, including more egalitarian attitudes towards women. But it could be argued that this too has been commodified via the media. Women may now regard themselves as liberated, but are they liberated from consumerism? Indeed, it is possible to interpret feminism not so much as a movement but as an uncoordinated aspiration which has been promoted and sustained in order to cultivate new, distinctive and lucrative markets for the consumer industry.

Does consumerism, then, really indicate greater freedom in society? Does the extension of choice in consumer goods, something unknown to our forebears, really signal true emancipation? It could be argued that the introduction of machine technology has led to some levelling down in society; at least there is the semblance of greater equality in that more people share the benefits of more consumer goods. In this sense, the masses express their autonomy in consumption. Yet the more this autonomy is exercised, the more both people and producers are tied to the treadmill of the production process, and – in a sense – the *less* emancipated they really are. This is particularly exemplified by the tariff war which is developing between Japan and the USA. Once importees/consumers have become accustomed to the greater variety (and quality?) of overseas goods, e.g. Japanese cars, cameras, electrical goods, etc., the less they wish to give them up. Complementarily, once the exporters/producers become used to manufacturing goods for a particular market, the less likely is it that they will want to relinquish this profitable trade. Consumption interests and industries create dependency needs for producers and consumers *alike*.

Some sociologists adopt a position similar to that of Sir Isaiah Berlin, who holds the view that there are two concepts of liberty: *negative liberty* involving the absence of restraints, and *positive liberty* which necessitates active intervention in Education, Health, etc., by Government. They argue that in capitalist society we are experiencing the *illusion of freedom*. They speak of pseudo-freedom and pseudo-individualism. Real economic freedom, they insist, is freedom *from* economic restraints, and that political freedom is freedom *from* political restrictions; i.e. freedom from economic and political factors. Yet – as we have seen – consumerism imposes *new constraints* to own, to possess and to display. Are cunningly constructed marketing techniques therefore designed to appeal to base instincts and motives, or does advertising actually break down social inequalities by promoting common consumption patterns? (Note the Coca Cola advertisement, 'I'd like to teach the world to sing in perfect harmony'; it is 'visibly' classless and culture-free, and ostensibly addressed to all races and creeds in the interests of equality.) Or is the consumer industry really engaged in subtle forms of manipulation and reproduction? Take the example of another popular soft drink, 7up, which has been recently 're-launched' at the cost of £7 million, much of which was actually spent on marketing research and development. Teenagers, the main target population, have been presented with the image of Fido Dido, the stick figure who is regarded as 'streetwise, cool, clever and culty' (*Guardian*, 26 July 1991), someone who is humorously representative of modern youth. Do such gimmicks really work? And, if so, is there any sense in which the young are being conned, in this and other fashion areas, by the ingenuity of the promotional experts? Many will naturally insist that they are not, and that they actually have a contempt for the consumer culture. But it is interesting to note that in the 1960s, the hey-day of counter-cultural fervour, the 'rebels' were really emphasising the same basic values as the 'straight' culture, namely, pleasure and hedonism, but they divorced these values from commodities and consumerism. The so-called 'freedom revolution' was really an *extension* rather than a reaction against dominant ideological forms.

Consumerism, then, is inextricably bound up with the mass media. Ostensibly, the media exist to provide information, education and entertainment (diversion). They therefore require complex organisation and huge resources (five publishing companies, for example, control 86% of the market); large public audiences with heterogeneous interests, a factor which must affect the levels of presentation; and modern technology which – arguably – only serves to enhance the measure of control that the companies enjoy. They are also one-way systems of communication which act as vehicles for the transmission and reproduction of certain cultural values. As such they

(1) *Can be selective* in their material: a process that is determined by the criteria of acceptability and popularity. It is thus no accident that the 'soaps' command by far the largest viewing audiences for TV, and that in the UK the mass dailies, especially the *Sun* and the *Mirror*, outstrip the other newspapers. The success of the tabloids is also reflected in the Sunday press figures, though, interestingly, even they are not enjoying the circulation they had 20 years ago.

(2) *Are often inventive*: it is not unusual for the media to fabricate or to be economical with the truth, or even to 'enrich' the truth as is known to have happened, for instance, in the engineered protests in Northern Ireland. But then it may be that the people don't want their gossip spoiled by facts. It is certainly difficult to find complete impartiality, especially on political issues, even in the quality press. Neither is it easy to find consistency; it is not unusual to find a newspaper inveighing against some social evil, say, tobacco, and at the same time carrying advertisements for this very commodity. TV is similarly guilty – though indirectly – through its support of sponsorship of sport: motor racing, snooker, etc.

(3) *Frequently sensationalise*: a point that hardly needs elaboration. Some newspapers seem to work on the assumption that most of us need something particularly titillating to brighten our drab lives. And the policy undoubtedly pays. There have even been instances of social scientists who have been investigating some particularly sensitive area of human behaviour being offered 'big money' by the tabloid press if they would reveal the names of their respondents, something which any self-respecting researcher would never do.

(4) *May be guilty of trivialisation*: even important issues can be reduced to human interest proportions. (I confess to some naïveté here. In preparing a book on male sexual dysfunction – a quite widespread and often tragic condition – I was interviewed by a reporter from the *Daily Mirror*. We had quite a serious discussion lasting several hours, but any resemblance between this and the article which appeared a few days later was purely accidental. Predictably, the regional newspapers – the jackals of the trade

– then pawed over the carcass until the material became almost unrecognisable.)

(5) *Can be invasive and manipulative*: cheque-book journalism is now taken pretty much for granted and the TV interviewer's inane how-do-you-feel? to a family – invariably found crowded on a settee – that has just been sadly bereaved, goes without mention.

(6) *May shape attitudes, values and tastes*: this is perhaps best seen in the reporting (dignifying?) of pop culture. Do the media reflect popular taste or determine it? Or is there a subtle interaction between the two? This is evident in general in terms of fashion, life-style and pre-packaged opinions. And it can also be seen more specifically in the growing practice in film and TV of product placing, technically forbidden by the ITC's code of sponsorship, which maintains that it is out of order to include or make a reference to 'a product or service within a programme in return for payment or other valuable consideration' (*Observer*, 5 May 1991). But with the trend towards greater realism, and with budgets becoming tighter, the code is repeatedly infringed as companies act as brokers between manufacturers and the programme-makers. It's a question of sales by association. Advertising may be a parasitic industry, but at around £5 billion a year in the UK the big bucks flourished by the moguls can effectively blinker the opposition.

(7) *May well represent political control*: it is worth asking if the media tell us what they 'need' to hear? It is always instructive to see how material is prioritised, and how articles and programmes are trimmed and edited for public consumption. We all need information, and much media material is truly exemplary, but it is not uncommon to find that even this contains *mis*information (error) and even *dis*information (deliberate falsehood).

In trying to relate ethical theory to consumption and consumerism, so much turns on the kind of analysis that is applied. As an example of this we could look at the alcohol issue. Between 1905 and 1935 in the UK, there was a significant *decrease* (75%) in alcohol-related offences. There was also a comparable decrease in alcohol-related diseases: cirrhosis of the liver, intestinal cancer, etc. Between 1910 and 1916 there was a notable reduction presumably because during World War I there was growing pressure for overall efficiency, greater outputs in production and, of course, military effort. On a Marxist analysis this worked in the interests of the dominant class. Greater efficiency meant greater profits for the industrialists, thus prohibition and temperance movements could be seen to encourage a reduction of consumption in order to facilitate higher industrial production. This approach to the issue tends to overlook the indisputable social benefits that a decrease in alcohol consumption can bring. In the UK it is interesting to see how closely demand is related to price. From 1955 to 1985, alcohol consumption doubled while the 'real' price halved, and there was a radical increase in both diseases and offences. Of course, all sorts of other factors affect the statistics, but the trend is obvious. It is estimated that now one in five beds in NHS hospitals are occupied by people with either drink-related diseases or drink-related problems.

At the political level, it could be argued that there should be government interference to counter the overwhelming superiority of alcohol-promotion advertising, although on balance most MPs are against such a move – 88% at the last count, but then the brewers contribute handsomely to party funds, giving £3/4 million to the Conservatives in 1987. The public response to a possible ban is similar, approximately 70% against in the 15-35 age group (*Observer*, 16 August 1991). The Government via the Health Education Council spends about £1 million a year warning people about the possible harmful effects of drink, while the alcohol industry spends around £300 million trying to persuade us of its irresistible delights. Is the situation really dominated by the profit motive? The figures show that certain fiscal measures could noticeably affect consumption patterns. So should it be just a matter of private concern, or should there be official intervention? And if so, what form should it take? (Note that the post-World War I prohibition movement in the USA, which was a political and cultural failure, was not a *health* failure.) Should people be free to effect their own destruction if they so wish, and should the brewing industry be allowed free rein in the interests of the liberty of the individual?

In thinking about these matters in terms of values, it is perhaps significant that in recent years there has been a movement away from alcohol consumption as something that is morally reprehensible to one of qualified acceptability. There has been a de-emphasis on alcohol as the cause of various social ills, and a greater concentration on alcohol as a socially respectable relaxant which is simply abused by certain weak individuals who are biologically predisposed to over-indulgence. Alcoholism itself is seen as a 'disease' like any other disease, even though there is no evidence for such a diagnosis. This has supplanted the view that alcohol is a drug, even – as for the old Temperance Societies – as an evil, which becomes disease-*like* in its effects because the body develops a biological and psychological 'need' for more of the same. Even the Health Education Council – perhaps out of what they feel to be expedient realism – emphasise 'sensible' drinking. 'Learning to drink' has now taken the place of abstinence as a virtue – something akin to the general trend towards the *control* of drug dependency rather than a categorical and absolute denunciation of drug indulgence. It sounds like a counsel of despair; the UK may yet have to pay the price for the capitulation that we have already seen in other societies which are seriously thinking of legalising hard drugs because they feel that they have lost the battle.

Bibliography

Abercrombie, N., Hill, S. & Turner, B. (1980) *The Dominant Ideology Thesis* (London: Allen & Unwin)

Acton, H.B. (1970) *Kant's Moral Philosophy* (London: Macmillan)

Adie, K. (1988) 'Misunderstanding TV Violence', *Listener*, 18 February 1988

Aiken, H. (1957) *Age of Ideology* (New York: Mentor)

Alavi, H. & Shanin, T. (1982) *An Introduction to the Sociology of 'Developing Societies'* (London: Macmillan)

Almond, B. & Hill, D. (1991) *Applied Philosophy* (London: Routledge)

Althusser, L. (1969) *For Marx* (Harmondsworth: Allan Lane)

Altman, D. (1973) *Homosexual: Oppression and Liberation* (New York: Avon)

Andreski, S. (1968) *Military Organisation and Society* (London: RKP)

Ashby, R. (1972) *The Guidebook for the Study of Psychical Research* (London: Rider Books)

Ashley, P. (1983) *The Money Problems of the Poor* (London: Gower)

Atkinson, R. (1978) *Knowledge and Explanation in History* (London: Macmillan)

Ayer, A. (1946) *Language, Truth and Logic* (Harmondsworth: Penguin)

Ayer, A. (1976) *The Central Questions of Philosophy* (Harmondsworth: Pelican)

Baggaley, J. & Duck, S. (1976) *The Dynamics of Television* (London: Gower)

Baker, D. (ed.) (1975) *The Politics of Race* (London: Gower)

Banton, M. (1988) *Racial Consciousness* (London: Longman)

Barbour, I. (1974) *Myths, Models and Paradigms* (London: SCM)

Barnes, B. (1982) *T.S. Kuhn and Social Science* (London: Macmillan)

Barnett, C. (1990) *Hitler's Generals* (London: Weidenfeld & Nicolson)

Baron, R. (1977) *Human Aggression* (New York: Plenum Press)

Barrow, P. (1991) *Utilitarianism* (Aldershot: Elgar)

Beck, R. & Orr, J. (1970) *Ethical Choice: a case study approach* (London: Free Press/Collier-Macmillan

Behr, E. (1961) *The Algerian Problem* (Harmondsworth: Penguin)

Beloff, J. (1977) 'Historical Review' in B. Wolman (ed.) *Handbook of Parapsychology* (New York: Van Nostrand Reinhold)

Benn, S. & Peters, A. (1958) *Social Principles of the Democratic State* (London: Allen & Unwin)

Berger, P. (1966) *Invitation to Sociology* (Harmondsworth: Pelican)

Berger, P. (1967) *The Social Reality of Religion* (London: Faber)

Berger, P. (1970) *A Rumour of Angels* (Harmondsworth: Penguin)

Berger, P. & Kellner, H. (1981) *Sociology Re-interpreted* (Harmondsworth: Pelican)

Berger, P. & Luckmann, T. (1967) *The Social Construction of Reality* (Harmondsworth: Penguin)

Berkowitz, L. (1962) *Aggression: a socio-psychological analysis* (New York: McGraw-Hill

Bierstedt, R. (1959) 'Sociology and History', *BJS*, June
Billington, R. (1988) *Living Philosophy* (London: Routledge)
Birren, J. & Schale, K. (eds) (1977) *Handbook of the Psychology of Ageing* (New York: Van Nostrand Reinhold)
Blackham, H.J. (1965) *Six Existentialist Thinkers* (London: RKP)
Boardman, J. & LaRocca, E. (1978) *Eros in Greece* (London: John Murray)
Bottomore, T. (1976) 'Structure and History' in P. Blau (ed.) *Approaches to the Study of Social Structure* (London: Open Books)
Box, S. (1981) *Deviance, Reality and Society* (Eastbourne: Holt-Saunders)
Brewster-Smith, M. (1991) *Values, Self and Society* (Plymouth: Transaction)
Broad, C.D. (1962) *Five Types of Ethical Theory* (London: RKP)
Broadbent, D. (1974) *In Defence of Empirical Psychology* (London: Methuen)
Brown, A. (1984) *Consultation: an aid to successful social work* (London: Gower)
Brubaker, S. (1972) *To Live on Earth* (New York: Mentor)
Bullough, V. (1976) *Sexual Variance in Society and in History* (Chicago: University of Chicago Press)
Burgess, R. (ed.) (1986) *Key Variables in Social Investigation* (London: RKP)
Butrym, Z. (1976) *The Nature of Social Work* (London: Macmillan)
Carlton, E. (1977) *Ideology and Social Order* (London: RKP)
Carlton, E. (1980) *Sexual Anxiety* (Oxford: Martin Robertson)
Carlton, E. (1982) 'The Autonomy of Values Problem', *International Journal of Sociology and Social Policy*, Spring
Carlton, E. (1990) *War and Ideology* (London: Routledge)
Carlton, E. (1992) *Occupation: the policies and practices of military conquerors* (London: Routledge)
Carlton, E. (1994) *Massacres: an historical perspective* (Aldershot: Scolar)
Carr, E.H. (1965) *What is History?* (Harmondsworth: Penguin)
Centre for Health Economics, *Research Training Bulletins* (University of York)
Centre for Professional Development (1986) *Unemployment: a challenge to public health*, Occasional Papers No. 10, Unemployment and Health Study Group, Department of Community Medicine (University of Manchester)
Coleman, V. (1981) *Face Values* (London: Pan Books)
Coleman, V. (1989) *Drugs: the argument for decriminalisation* (Committee for a Free Britain)
Collins, H. & Pinch, T. (1982) *Frames of Meaning: the social construction of extraordinary science* (London: RKP)
Collins, J.C.M. (1981) *Achieving Change in Social Work* (London: Gower)
Connerton, P. (ed.) (1976) *Critical Sociology* (Harmondsworth: Penguin)
Connor, S. (1989) *Postmodernist Culture* (Oxford: Blackwell)
Conquest, R. (1990) *The Great Terror* (2nd ed.) (London: Hutchinson)
Cook, D. (1988) *The Moral Image* (London: SPCK)
Cook, J. & Lewington, M. (eds) (1979) *Images of Alcoholism* (London: British Film Institute)
Cook, M. (1992) *Levels of Personality* (London: Cassell)
Coon, C. (1962) *The History of Man* (Harmondsworth: Penguin)
Cooper, J. & Palmer, J. (eds) (1991) *The Environment in Question* (London: Routledge)
Copp, D. & Wendall, S. (1986) *Pornography and Censorship* (Prometheus)
Crick, B. (1973) 'Of Molecules and Men', *Real Time* (London: Picador), pp. 232-3
Cullingford, C. (1982) *Children and Television* (London: Gower)
Darlington, C. (1969) *The Evolution of Man* (London: Allen & Unwin)
Davidoff, L. (1980) *Introduction to Psychology* (2nd ed.) (New York: McGraw-Hill)

Davies, C. (1975) *Permissive Britain* (London: Pitman)

Deaux, K. & Wrightsman, L. (1984) *Social Psychology in the 80s* (Monterey: Brooks/Cole)

de Grazia, A. (1978) 'The Scientific Reception System' in A. de Grazia (ed.) *The Velikovsky Affair* (London: Abacus)

de Jouvenel, B. (1967) *The Art of Conjecture* (London: Weidenfeld & Nicolson)

Department of Health (1991) *The Health of the Nation* (London: HMSO)

DHSS (1985) *On the State of Public Health* (London: HMSO)

Diodorus Siculus (1933) *History* (ed. W. Oldfather) (London: Heinemann)

Docherty, D. & Morrison, D. (1988) 'Censorship is a turn-off for most viewers', *Listener*, 11 February

Doyal, L. & Harris, R. (1986) *Empiricism, Explanation and Rationality* (London: Routledge)

Durkheim, E. (1964) *Rules of Sociological Method* (London: Free Press)

Durkheim, E. (1968) *Elementary Forms of Religious Life* (London: Allen and Unwin)

Dworkin, A. (1981) *Pornography* (London: Women's Press)

Dworkin, G. (ed.) (1970) *Determinism, Free-will and Moral Responsibility* (Englewood Cliffs: Prentice-Hall)

Edwards, R. (1972) *Reason and Religion* (New York: Harcourt Brace)

Ekins, P. (1992) *A New World Order* (London: Routledge)

Eliade, M. (1960) *Myths, Dreams and Mysteries* (Harvill Press)

Elias, N. (1977) *The Civilising Process* (Oxford: Blackwell)

Emmett, D. (1966) *Rules, Roles and Relations* (London: Macmillan)

Engelsman, E. (1989) 'Dutch Policy on the Management of Drug-related Problems', *B.J. Addiction* 84(2), pp. 211-18

Evans, H. (1982) *Intrusions – Society and the Paranormal* (London: RKP)

Evans, H. (1984) *Visions, Apparitions: alien visitors* (Wellingborough: Thorsen)

Ewing, A. (1957) *Ethics* (London: London Universities Press)

Eysenck, H.J. (1979) *The Psychology of Sex* (London: Nelson)

Eysenck, H.J. (1981) *Intelligence* (London: Macmillan)

Eysenck, H.J. & Nias, D. (1980) *Sex, Violence and the Media* (London: Paladin)

Fagan, B. (1981) *The Aztecs* (New York: Freeman)

Feldman, P. (1987) *Sex and Sexuality* (London: Longman)

Feldman, S. & Feldman, F. (1967) 'Transition of Sex Differences in Cheating' in G. LeFrancois, *Psychology* (London: Wadsworth), p. 351

Ferguson, H. (1991) *Religious Transformation in Western Society* (London: Routledge)

Festinger, L. (1962) 'Cognitive Dissonance', *Scientific American* 207, pp. 93-100

Finley, M.I. (1962) *The World of Odysseus* (Harmondsworth: Pelican)

Finley, M.I. (1964) *Slavery in Classical Antiquity* (Cambridge: Heffer)

Finley, M.I. (1983) *Ancient Slavery and Modern Ideology* (Harmondsworth: Pelican)

Fisher, J. (1972) Foreword to Brubaker, *To Live On Earth* (New York: Mentor)

Ford, B. (1979) *Patterns of Sex* (London: Macdonald & James)

Ford, K. & Jones, A. (1985) *Student Supervision in Social Work* (London: Macmillan)

Fowler, B. (1979) ' "True to me Always": An Analysis of Women's Magazine Fiction', *BJS*, vol. 30, no. 1, March

Fox, A. (ed.) (1987) *Inequalities of Health within Europe* (Aldershot: Gower)

Fox, A. (1991) *Encounter with Anthropology* (Plymouth: Transaction)

Francis, L. (1982) *Experience of Adulthood* (London: Gower)

Frankena, W. (1963) *Ethics* (Englewood Cliffs: Prentice-Hall)

Freud, S. (1953) 'Civilization and its Discontents' in the *Complete Psychological Works of Sigmund Freud* (London: Hogarth Press)

Freud, S. (1963) *Introductory Lectures on Psychoanalysis* (London: Hogarth Press)

Gambrill, E. & Pruger, R. (1982) *Controversial Issues in Social Work* (Hemel Hempstead: Allyn & Bacon)

Gardiner, P. (ed.) (1959) *Theories of History* (New York: Free Press)

Gardiner, P. (1961) *The Nature of Historical Explanation* (London: OUP)

Garlan, Y. (1975) *War in the Ancient World* (London: Chatto & Windus)

Gaute, J. & Odell, R. (1979) *The Murderers' Who's Who* (London: Pan)

Geen, R. & Donnerstein, E. (eds) (1982) *Aggression: theoretical and empirical views* (New York: Academic Press)

Gellner, E. (1959) *Words and Things* (Harmondsworth: Penguin)

Gellner, E. (1963) *Thought and Change* (London: Weidenfeld & Nicolson)

Gellner, E. (1979) *Legitimation and Belief* (Cambridge: CUP)

Gellner, E. (1985) *Relativism and the Social Sciences* (Cambridge: CUP)

George, S. (1988) *A Fate Worse than Debt* (Harmondsworth: Penguin)

Giddens, A. (1976) *New Rules of Sociological Method* (London: Hutchinson)

Gillan, R. (1976) *Sex Therapy Today* (London: Open Books)

Ginsberg, M. (1956) *On the Diversity of Morals* (London: Heinemann)

Ginsberg, M. (1965) *On Justice in Society* (Harmondsworth: Penguin)

Glazer, N. & Young, K. (eds) (1983) *Ethnic Pluralism and Public Policy* (London: Gower)

Glock, C. & Stark, R. (1965) *Religion and Society in Tension* (New York: Rand McNally)

Gordon, S. (1991) *The History and Philosophy of Science* (London: Routledge)

Gordon, S. & Libby, G. (eds) (1976) *Sexuality Today and Tomorrow*, The Harvard Studies of Professor Kohlberg (New York: Duxbury Press)

Gouldner, A. (1971) *The Coming Crisis in Western Sociology* (London: Heinemann)

Grant, M. (1952) *Ancient History* (London: Methuen)

Gratten-Guinness, J. (1985) His review of James McClennon, 'Deviant Sciences: the case of Parapsychology', *JSPR*, vol. 53, no. 800

Greenleaf, W. (1962) *Oakeshott's Philosophical Politics* (London: Longman)

Gregory, A. (1983) Unpublished letter to *Nature*, 30 January 1983 (SPR Archives: Gregory Papers)

Gregory, A. (1985) *The Strange Case of Rudi Schneider* (New Jersey: Scarecrow Press)

Griffin, S. (1981) *Pornography and Silence* (London: Women's Press)

Griffith, G. (1948) *Makers of Modern Thought* (London: Lutterworth)

Guerra, F. (1971) *The Pre-Columbian Mind* (London: Seminar Press)

Haas, J. (ed.) (1990) *The Anthropology of War* (Cambridge: CUP)

Habermas, J. (1974) *Theory and Practice* (London: Heinemann)

Habermas, J. (1990) *Moral Consciousness and Communicative Action* (Oxford: Polity Press)

Hacker, P. (1991) *Appearance and Reality* (Oxford: Blackwell)

Hall, S. (1977) *On Ideology* (London: Hutchinson)

Hare, J. & Joynt, C. (1982) *Ethics and International Affairs* (New York: Plenum)

Hare, R.M. (1964) *The Language of Morals* (London: OUP)

Harris, J. (1989) *The Value of Life* (London: Routledge)

Harvey, P. (1989) *Health Psychology* (London: Longman)

Hawking, S. (1988) *A Short History of the Universe* (London: Bantam)

Heather, N. (1976) *Radical Perspectives in Psychology* (London: Methuen)

Held, D. (1980) *Introduction to Critical Theory* (London: Hutchinson)

Henderson, N. (1982) 'Human Behaviour Genetics', *Annual Review of Psychology* 33, 403-40

Hobhouse, L., Ginsberg, M. & Wheeler (1915) *The Material Culture and Social Institutions of Simpler Peoples* (London: Chapman)

Hobhouse, L. (1951) *Morals in Evolution* (1st ed. 1906) (London: Chapman & Hall)

Hollis, M. (1986) *Invitation to Philosophy* (Oxford: Blackwell)

Homan, R. (1991) *Ethics of Social Research* (London: Longman)

Hopkins, K. (1978) *Conquerors and Slaves* (Cambridge: CUP)

Hopkins, K. (1983) *Death and Renewal* (Cambridge: CUP)

Hospers, J. (1961) *Human Conduct* (New York: Harcourt, Brace & World)

Howitt, D. (1982) *Mass Media and Social Problems* (Oxford: Pergamon)

Hoyle, F. (1983) *The Intelligent Universe* (London: Michael Joseph)

Hoyle, R.L. (1965) *Checan: essay on erotic elements in Peruvian art* (Geneva: Nagel)

Huby, P. (1967) *Greek Ethics* (London: Macmillan)

Huxley, A. (1955) *Brave New World* (Harmondsworth: Penguin)

Illich, J. (1991) *In the Mirror of the Past* (London: Marion Boyars)

Irving, D. (1983) *Hitler's War* (2 vols) (London: Macmillan)

Jensen, A. (1968) 'Social Class, Race & Genetics: Implications for Education', *American Educational Research Journal* 5, 1-42

Joad, C.E.M. (1942) *Guide to Modern Thought* (London: Faber)

Joad, C.E.M. (1960) *Philosophy* (London: English University Press)

Jones, K. & Simmons, K. (1990) *The Retail Environment* (London: Routledge)

Joynson, R. (1974) *Psychology and Common Sense* (London: RKP)

Kamenka, E. (1969) *Marxism and Ethics* (London: Macmillan)

Kaufmann, W. (1958) *Critique of Religion and Philosophy* (London: Faber)

Kemp, B. (1989) *Ancient Egypt* (London: Routledge)

Kemp, J. (1964) *Reason, Reaction and Morality* (London: RKP)

Kilner, J. (1990) *Who Lives? Who Dies?* (London: Yale)

Kinsey, A. (1948) *The Sexual Behaviour of the Human Male* (New York: Saunders)

Koestler, A. (1956) *Reflections on Hanging* (London: Gollancz)

Koestler, A. (1959) *The Sleepwalkers* (London: Hutchinson)

Koestler, A. & Smythies, J. (eds) (1970) *Beyond Reductionism: new perspectives in the life sciences* (London: Macmillan)

Korner, S. (1964) *Kant* (Harmondsworth: Penguin)

Kovel, J. (1970) *White Racism* (New York: Pantheon)

Kuper, L. (1975) *Race, Science and Society* (London: Allen & Unwin)

Larrain, J. (1979) *The Concept of Ideology* (London: Hutchinson)

Layton-Henry, Z. & Rich, P. (eds) *Race, Government and Politics in Britain* (London: Macmillan)

Leach, E. (1970) *Lévi-Strauss* (London: Fontana)

Le Francois, G. (1983) *Psychology* (2nd ed.) (Belmont: Wadsworth)

Lessnoff, M. (1974) *The Structure of Social Science* (London: Allen & Unwin)

Levack, B. (1987) *The Witch-Hunt in Early Modern Europe* (London: Longman)

Lévi-Strauss, C. (1952) 'Social Structure', A.L. Kroeber (ed), *Anthropology Today* (Chicago: University of Chicago Press), pp. 321-90

Lewis, C.S. (1960) *Miracles* (London: Collins)

Lewis, J. (1974) *History of Philosophy* (3rd imp.) (London: English University Press)

Lickona, T. (1976) *Moral Development and Behaviour* (New York: Holt, Rinehart & Winston)

Lipset, S. (1976) 'Social Structure and Social Change' in P. Blau (ed.) *Approaches to the Study of Social Structure* (Wells, Somerset: Open Books)

Lorenz, K. (1966) *On Aggression* (London: Methuen)

Louch, A. (1966) *Explanation and Human Action* (Oxford: Blackwell)

Luckmann, T. (1971) 'The Notion of Belief' in R. Carporale & A. Grimaldi (eds) *The Culture of Unbelief* (University of California Press), p. 210
Lyons, J. (1970) *Chomsky* (London: Fontana)
Mabbott, J. (1966) *An Introduction to Ethics* (London: Hutchinson)
McClean, S. & Mather, G. (1983) *Medicine, Morals and the Law* (London: Gower)
McConnell, R. (1983) *An Introduction to Parapsychology in the Context of Science* (Pittsburgh: University of Pittsburgh Press)
MacIntyre, A. (1967) *A Short History of Ethics* (London: Routledge)
MacIntyre, A. (1970) *Herbert Marcuse* (London: Fontana)
McKeown, T. (1991) *The Origins of Human Disease* (Oxford: Blackwell)
Mackie, J. (1990) *Ethics: Inventing Right and Wrong* (Harmondsworth: Penguin)
Macl.Currie, H. (1986) 'Review of Michel Foucault, *Histoire de la Sexualité* vols. II & III', *Theory, Culture and Society*, no. 3, vol. III
McNaught, A. (1985) 'Race and Health Care in the UK', Occasional Paper No. 2 (London: HEC)
MacNiven (ed.) (1989) *Moral Expertise* (London: Routledge)
Maconohay, J. & Hough, J. (1976) 'Symbolic Racism', *Journal of Social Issues* 32
Magee, B. (1973) *Popper* (London: Fontana)
Maguire, D. (1984) *The Moral Choice* (Holt, Rinehart & Winston/Cassell)
Mair, L. (1984) *Anthropology and Development* (London: Macmillan)
Malinowski, B. (1922) *Argonauts of the Western Pacific* (London: RKP)
Malinowski, B. (1932) *The Sexual Life of Savages* (London: RKP)
Manning, D. & Robinson, T. (1985) *The Place of Ideology in Political Life* (Croom Helm)
Mantegazza, P. (1935) *The Sexual Relations of Mankind* (New York: Eugenics Publishing Co.)
Marcuse, H. (1987a) *One Dimensional Man* (2nd ed.) (London: Routledge)
Marcuse, H. (1987b) *Eros and Civilization* (London: Routledge)
Marks, I. (1978) *Living with Fear* (New York: McGraw-Hill)
Maslow, A. (1970) *Motivation and Personality* (New York: Harper Row)
Mathews, F. (1991) *The Ecological Self* (London: Routledge)
Matlin, M. (1988) *Sensation and Perception* (New York: Allyn & Bacon)
Mauskopf, S. & McVaugh, M. (1980) *The Elusive Sciences: origins of experimental psychical research* (Johns Hopkins University Press)
Maxwell, S. (ed.) (1991) *To Cure all Hunger: food security and food policy* (London: JT Publications)
Mead, G.H. (1934) *Mind, Self and Society* (Chicago: University of Chicago Press)
Medawar, P. (1960) *The Future of Man* (London: Methuen)
Mennell, S. (1974) *Sociological Theory: its uses and unities* (London: Nelson)
Meyerhoff, H. (1963) 'Freud and the Ambiguity of Culture' in B. Mazlish (ed.) *Psychoanalysis and History* (London: Spectrum Books)
Michael, R. (ed.) (1968) *Endrocrinology and Human Behaviour* (London: OUP)
Mills, C.W. (1967) *The Sociological Imagination* (Oxford: OUP)
Mischel, W. (1973) 'Toward a Cognitive Social Learning Reconceptualization of Personality', *Psychological Review* 80 (4), pp. 252-83
Montagu, A. (1979) *Nature of Human Aggression* (Oxford: OUP)
Moore, G. (1947) *Ethics* (Oxford: OUP)
Morris, J. (1986) 'Inequality, Poverty and Health', *Lancet* ii, 662
Morton, A. (1990) *Disasters and Dilemmas* (Oxford: Blackwell)
Moser, K. et al. (1987) 'Unemployment and Mortality', *BMJ* 294, pp. 86-90
Murphy, J. (1970) *Kant: the philosophy of right* (London: Macmillan)

Nadel, S. (1953) *Anthropology and Modern Life,* Inaugural Lecture (Australian National University), p. 17

Nagel, E. (1960) 'Determinism in History', *Philosophy and Phenomenological Research* XX, no. 3, March, pp. 291-317

Nagel, T. (1974) *War and Moral Responsibility* (Princeton: University of Princeton)

Nagel, T. (1991) *Mortal Questions* (Cambridge: CUP)

Nelkin, D. (ed.) (1991) *A Disease of Society* (Cambrige: CUP)

Neppe, V. (1984) 'Extrasensory Perception: an Anachronism and Anathema', *JSPR,* vol. 52, no. 798, October 1984

Norris, C. (1992) *Uncritical Theory* (London: Lawrence & Wishart)

Nowell-Smith, P. (1964) *Ethics* (Harmondsworth: Pelican)

Nuttall, J. (1993) *Moral Questions* (Cambridge: Polity Press)

Oakeshott, M. (1962) *Rationalism in Politics and other essays* (London: Methuen)

Oakley, J. (1991) *Morality and the Emotions* (London: Routledge)

O'Dea, T. (1970) *Sociology and the Study of Religion* (New York: Basic Books)

Olivova, A. (1984) *Sports and Games in the Ancient World* (London: Orbis Books)

Olson, A. (ed.) (1980) *Myth, Symbol and Reality* (London: University of Notre Dame Press)

O'Toole, R. (1985) *Religion: classic sociological approaches* (New York: McGraw-Hill Ryerson)

Palmer, M. (1988) *Genesis or Nemesis* (London: Dryad)

Parrish, R. (1991) 'Policy or Public Procrastination?', *Health Education Journal*, vol. 50, no. 3 (London: HEA), pp. 138-45

Parsons, T. (1937) *The Structure of Social Action* (New York: McGraw-Hill)

Parsons, T. (1957) 'Religion as a Source of Creative Innovation' in M.Y. Yinger (ed.) *Religion, Society and the Individual* (New York: Macmillan)

Parsons, T. (1961a) *Theories of Society* (New York: Free Press)

Parsons, T. (1961b) 'An Approach to the Sociology of Knowledge' in *Transactions of the 4th World Congress of Sociology,* vol. 4 (International Sociological Assocation), p. 25

Parsons, T. (1966) *Societies: evolutionary and comparative perspectives* (New Jersey: Prentice-Hall)

Parsons, T. (1968) 'On the Concept of Value-Commitments', *Sociological Inquiry,* vol. XXXVIII, no. 2, Spring 1968

Piaget, J. & Inhelder, B. (1968) *The Pyschology of the Child* (New York: Basic Books)

Piaget, J. (1970) *Structuralism* (New York: Basic Books)

Piliavin, J. et al. (1981) *Emergency Intervention* (London: Academic Press)

Pipes, M. (1986) *Understanding Abortion* (London: Women's Press)

Plamenatz, J. (1958) *The English Utilitarians* (2nd rev. ed.) (Oxford: Blackwell)

Plamenatz, J. (1963) *Man and Society* (London: Longman)

Plato (1981) *The Republic* (trans. G. Grube) (London: Pan Books)

Platts, M. (1991) *Moral Realities* (London: Routledge)

Ploss, H. & Bartels, M. & P. (1967) *Woman in the Sexual Relation* (New York: Tower Books)

Popper, K. (1963) *The Poverty of Historicism* (London: RKP)

Popper, K. (1966) *The Open Society and its Enemies* (London: RKP)

Poretsky, E. (1963) *Our Own People: a memoir of Ignace Reiss and his friends* (Ann Arbor: University of Michigan Press)

Porritt, J. (1990) *Where on Earth are we Going?* (London: Guild Books)

Prior, W. (1990) *Virtue and Knowledge* (London: Routledge)

Rajchman, J. (1991) *Truth and Eros* (London: Routledge)

Reiss, I. (ed.) (1972) *Readings in the Family System: Pre-Marital Sexuality: Past, Present and Future* (New York: Holt, Rinehart & Winston)

Rex, J. & Mason, D. (1988) *Theories of Race and Ethnic Relations* (Cambridge: CUP)

Ribbens, G. (1979) *Patterns of Behaviour* (London: Arnold)

Rieber, R. (ed.) (1991) *The Psychology of War and Peace* (London: Plenum)

Rieff, P. (1965) *Freud: the mind of a moralist* (London: Methuen)

Roberts, R. (1977) *The Zulu Kings* (London: Sphere)

Robertson, J. (1989) *Future Wealth* (London: Cassell)

Robertson, R. (1970) *The Sociological Interpretation of Religion* (Oxford: Blackwell)

Rocher, G. (1974) *Talcott Parsons and American Sociology* (London: Nelson)

Roderick, R. (1985) *Habermas and Critical Theory* (London: Macmillan)

Roy, R. & D. (1976) 'The Autonomy of Sexuality' in S. Gordon & G. Libby (eds), *Sexuality Today and Tomorrow* (New York: Duxbury Press)

Russell, B. (1948) *A History of Western Philosophy* (London: Allen & Unwin)

Rutherford, D. (1988) *A Lot of Bottle* (London: Institute of Alcohol Studies)

Samborn, S. (1971) 'Means and Ends: Moral Development and Moral Education', *Harvard Graduate School of Education Bulletin*, Fall 1971, Cambridge, Massachusetts

Sargant, W. (1959) *Battle for the Mind* (London: Pan)

Sartre. J.-P. (1957) *Being and Nothingness* (tr. H. Barnes) (London: Methuen)

Scarr, J. & Weinberg, R. (1976) 'IQ test performance of black children adopted by white families', *American Psychologist* 31 (10), pp. 726-39

Schwartz, G. (1977) 'Psychosomatic Disorders and Biofeedback' in J. Maser and M. Seligman (eds) *Psychopathology: experimental models* (San Francisco: Freeman)

Schwarz, B. (ed.) (1978) *On Ideology* (Harmondsworth: Penguin)

Schillit, R. & Gomberg, E. (1991) *Drugs and Behaviour* (London: Sage)

Seabrook, R. (1988) *The Race for Riches* (London: Greenprint)

Seidel, G. (1987) *The Holocaust Denial* (Leeds: Beyond the Pale Collective)

Seidler, V. (1989) *Kant, Respect and Injustice* (London: Routledge)

Sellars, W. & Hospers, J. (1953) *Readings in Ethical Theory* (New York: Appleton-Century-Crofts)

Service, E. (1978) *Profiles in Ethnology* (New York: Harper Row)

Sheldon, W. & Stevens, S. (1942) *The Variety of Temperament: a psychology of constitutional differences* (New York: Harper Row)

Simon, W. & Gagnon, J. (1948) *Sexual Conduct: the social sources of human sexuality* (New York: Aldine)

Simon, W. & Gagnon, J. (eds) (1973) *The Sexual Scene* (Brunswick, N.J.: Transaction Books)

Sjoberg, G. (1965) *The Pre-Industrial City* (New York: Free Press)

Skellington, R. & Morris, P. (1991) *Race in Britain Today* (London: Sage)

Smith, G. & Kellner, P. (1980) 'The Good, the Bad, and the British', MORI Poll, *Sunday Times*, 2 March 1980

Snare, F. (1991) *The Nature of Moral Thinking* (London: Routledge)

Snowden, F. (1983) *Before Colour Prejudice* (Cambridge, Massachusetts: Harvard University Press)

Sorokin, P. (1954) *Fads and Foibles of Sociology* (New York: Regnery)

Spaeman, R. (1989) *Basic Moral Concepts* (London: Routledge)

Sprigge, T. (1990) *The Rational Foundations of Ethics* (London: Routledge)

Stafford-Clark, D. (1965) *What Freud Really Said* (Harmondsworth: Pelican)

Stanesby, B. (1988) *Science, Reason and Religion* (London: Routledge)

Staub, E. (1990) *The Roots of Evil* (Cambridge: CUP)

Steinberg, D. (1992) *All or Nothing: the Axis and the Holocaust* (London: Routledge)

Sternberg, R. (1990) *Metaphors of Mind* (Cambridge: CUP)

Storr, A. (1991) *Human Destructiveness* (London: Routledge)

Sutherland, D.M. (1985) *France 1789-1815: revolution and counter-revolution* (London: Fontana)

Szasz, T. (1981) *Sex: facts, frauds and follies* (Oxford: Blackwell)

Taylor, C. (1992) *The Ethics of Authenticity* (Harvard University Press)

Teff, H. (1975) *Drugs, Society and the Law* (London: Gower)

Thorpe, G. & Olsen, S. (1990) *Behaviour Therapy* (New York: Allyn & Bacon)

Tiger, L. & Fox, R. (1974) *The Imperial Animal* (St Albans: Paladin)

Toates, F. (1990) *Obsessional Thoughts and Behaviour: help for an obsessive compulsive disorder* (Wellingborough: Thorsens)

Tomlinson, S. (1983) *Ethnic Minorities in British Schools* (London: Gower)

Toulmin, S.E. (1986) *The Place of Reason in Ethics* (Chicago: University of Chicago Press)

Tucker, R. (1964) *Philosophy and Myth in Karl Marx* (London: CUP)

Turner, C. et al. (1976) 'Dimensions of Racial Ideology', *Journal of Social Issues* 32

Underhill, R. (1971) *Red Man's America* (Chicago: University of Chicago Press)

Vallee, J. (1974) *Anatomy of a Phenomenon: UFOs in space* (London: Tandem)

Van Gulik, R.H. (1961) *Sexual Life in Ancient China* (Leiden: Brill)

Varnis, S. (1990) *Reluctant Aid* (Plymouth: Transaction)

Walgate, R. (1990) *Miracle or Menace: biotechnology in the Third World* (London: Panos)

Wallis, R. & Bruce, S. (1986) *Sociological Theory, Religion and Collective Action* (Belfast: Queen's University Press)

Walsh, M. (1971) *War and the Human Race* (Barking: Elsevier)

Warmington, B.H. (1960) *Carthage* (Harmondsworth: Pelican)

Warnock, M. (1963) *Ethics since 1900* (London: OUP)

Warnock, M. (1967) *Existentialist Ethics* (London: Macmillan)

Warnock, M. (1985) *A Question of Life* (London: OUP)

Wasserstrom, R. (1970) *War and Morality* (Belmont: Wadsworth)

Weatherford, R. (1991) *The Implications of Determinism* (London: Routledge)

Weber, M. (1949) *The Methodology of the Social Sciences* (New York: Free Press)

Weeks, J. (1989) *Sex, Politics and Society* (London: Longman)

Wegner, D. (1989) 'White Bears and Other Unwanted Thoughts', *Psychology Today* (New York), June

Wells, A. (1970) *Social Institutions* (London: Heinemann)

West, D. (1982) *Delinquency* (London: Gower)

Westergaard, T. & Schrodder, K. (1985) *The Language of Advertising* (Oxford: Blackwell)

Whitehead, M. (ed.) *The Health Divide* (London: HEA)

Wiggins, D. (1991) *Needs, Values, Truth* (Oxford: Blackwell)

Wilkinson, R. (ed.) (1986) *Class and Health* (London: Tavistock)

Williams, R. (1985) *Ethics and the Limits of Philosophy* (London: Fontana)

Wilson, B. (ed.) (1970) *Rationality* (Oxford: Blackwell)

Wilson, J. (1961) *Reason and Morals* (Cambridge: CUP)

Wilson, J. (1990) *A New Introduction to Moral Education* (London: Cassell)

Wolf, R. (1971) *Philosophy: a modern encounter* (Englewood Cliffs: Prentice-Hall)

Wolff, L. (1958) *In Flanders Fields* (London: Longmans, Green)

Wren, T. (1991) *Caring about Morality* (London: Routledge)

Yinger, J.M. (1946) *Religion in the Struggle for Power* (North Carolina: Duke University Press)

Zanders, J. (1972) *American Minority Relations: the sociology of racial and ethnic groups* (Oxford: Ronald)

Zillman, D. (1978) *Hostility and Aggression* (Hillsdale, N.J.: H. Eribaum)

Index